The Fierce Embrace

The Fierce Embrace .
A Study of Contemporary American Poetry

Charles Molesworth

University of Missouri Press
Columbia & London, 1979

Copyright © 1979 by the
Curators of the University of Missouri
Library of Congress Catalog Card Number 79-1561
Printed and bound in the United States of America
University of Missouri Press, Columbia, Missouri 65211

LIBRARY OF CONGRESS CATALOGING IN PUBLICATION DATA

Molesworth, Charles.
The fierce embrace.

Includes index.
1. American poetry—20th century—
History and criticism.   I. Title.
PS323.5.M55   811'.5'409   79-1561
ISBN 0-8262-0278-0
ISBN 0-8262-0283-7 pbk.

For permissions, see pp. 213-14

For Carol, with love and pleasure

Contents

Preface

I have borrowed the title of this book from the opening of Blake's visionary poem "America." There the poet imagines Orc, the spirit of Revolution, as possessing a "fierce embrace," and this incendiary gesture is both furious and salvational. This book's main assumption (it is less than a detailed thesis but more than a mood) holds that American poetry since the Second World War has grown increasingly immersive in its strategy, abandoning the defensive irony that was largely prevalent in the wake of the modernist era. This shift to a poetry of immersion—a rhetorical strategy, an aesthetic disposition, and an emotional need—entails an embrace not only of the raw and chaotic energies of contemporary life, but also of the interior life of individual subjects, the singular voices that are very much a part of our literature.

Such a shift in our poetry is not, of course, the whole story. Many poets of considerable talent are not discussed here; furthermore, the book treats primarily those poets born after the First World War and before 1930. There is now a generation (possibly two) born since 1930 that is continuing, but also diversifying and challenging, the work of the poets discussed here. This newer group of poets resembles its predecessor in at least one significant way: it is extremely diverse in its interests and its poetic languages, although it has a more coherent "period style" than it likes to admit. Such diversity and such coherence make the criticism of contemporary poetry especially hazardous. The superficial resemblance can be instructive or deluding, just as the apparent heterodoxy can be considered healthy or merely confusing.

My plan in this book is to identify such coherence as seems to me instructive, but also to acknowledge and criticize singularity. The book treats about a dozen poets at length. But it also groups writers on generally accepted grounds (the confessional poets), links others not usually associated or assumed to be similar (Lowell and Ginsberg), and separately discusses some who are often taken together (O'Hara and Ashbery). It also treats, albeit briefly, contemporary poetics and examines some of the "working conditions" of poets (the use of small magazines and the sense of generational identity). Such a seemingly arbitrary congeries of approaches struck me as the best way to deal with very diverse phenomena. Obviously, in time, more order will be apparent, and whatever clarity I have discovered here may turn out to be an imposition.

Another word about the approach of this book: its fundamental method is close reading, although it often borrows from psychology, as well as from sociology. The criticism of poetry demands, I believe, close reading in order to justify itself as an intellectual discipline. But it need not—it should not—restrict itself to close reading. Explication is an indispensable part of the critical act, so this book assumes, for only then can we test the critic's "testing"; but explication by itself ends in formalism, or what is worse, a kind of scholiastic piling up of interpretations that are often little more than subjective exercises in appreciation. As Geoffrey Hartman has argued, the critic must use formalism to go beyond formalism. He must add historical, psychological, and social awareness to his concern with the resonance of single words, the complexities of tone, and the integral beauty of significant form. All poems, at least all good poems, invite us to ask questions *about* them, questions of description, analysis, interpretation. But they also invite us to ask questions *of* them, questions that address the problems of authority, value, and human concern.

During the writing of this book many people have been supportive of my efforts. This support I appreciate and wish to acknowledge, with the usual disclaimer that these people are in no way responsible for the book's errors and shortcomings. But I also wish to add a special testimony here, for more than once I almost decided to leave the book unfinished or unpublished. Those who supported me, with criticism and encouragement, often did so out of a desire to see contemporary poetry discussed in some other context than that of the ephemeral review, rather than out of a specific agreement with my argument. There are people, not themselves poets, who care, intelligently and insistently, about the part poetry plays in our cultural life, and I hope this book will add something positive to that concern.

The criticism of Charles Altieri has been of great help to me. His is, in my opinion, the finest theoretical criticism of contemporary poetry by far; as a practical critic he has few peers. Other people read all or part of the book in manuscript and made many valuable suggestions, and I gratefully single them out: Joseph McElroy, Charles Martin, Tom Frosch, Morris Dickstein, and especially George Held. Certain editors of magazines were also supportive and allowed me to use the pages of their journals to test my ideas: Stanley Lindberg, Wayne Dodd, John Moore, and most important, Robert Boyers, whose help was invaluable in many ways.

I also wish to thank the staff of the library in the George Pompidou Center for National Culture in Paris, where the final pages of this book were written. And I wish to thank the staff of the Boothbay Harbor Library in Maine, where the idea for this book was first conceived.

C. M., 30 March 1979

"We Have Come This Far"
Audience and Form in Contemporary Poetry

Perhaps the easiest, and certainly the safest, way to characterize the idiom of contemporary American poetry is to call it various. Poets born in the second and third decades of this century generally arrived at maturity during either the Second World War or the Korean War; the profound disillusion that followed the First World War had already been assimilated or repressed. Yet most people in 1941 knew they were repeating something so horrendous that it should never again have occurred. It remains of great importance that this later war was fought against an ideology that reveled in its own extremes, extremes of rhetoric but also of actions that defied comprehension. This peculiar situation, then, of having to repeat the horrendous in order to eradicate the incomprehensible extreme made up one of the major controlling forces of the idiom of postwar American poetry. "He and the world had winked" says Karl Shapiro in his first book, called *V-Letter and Other Poems*. The line refers to a midwesterner who views soldiering in the war as the great adventure of his life but whose sense of victory remains circumscribed by his own resources. But it could equally well stand for the poet who wrote it, and for all his contemporaries, for it reflects the half-cynical knowingness, the almost exhausted irony prevailing in the poetic idiom until, roughly, 1960. But this very prevalent idiom was realized through a variety of means. Each poet's exhaustion had an individualized flair, and this individualism often stood as the last scant barrier against total failure. Write from your *own* experience, this generation of poets was to repeat endlessly in the writing seminars that often formed their only audiences. What resulted was a poetry of limitations, a modest poetry speaking of nearly unspeakable pain and embarrassment among a small circle of similar, and hence sympathetic, near-victims. Cynicism, as Raymond Williams has observed, is opposition unwilling to surrender its privileges. Many American poets, however their wry self-depreciation might shield the fact, enjoyed a fairly privileged situation in the fifteen years after the Second World War. Universities in increasing numbers made places for writers, paying them as little as possible but cushioning their trade with the title *poet in residence*. The overstuffed comfort implicit in that phrase can

only be appreciated with detaching irony, and everywhere this generation proved equal to the task.

And so "academic poetry" was born. The phrase *academic poetry* was
a descriptive one, thrown down in halfhearted scorn and more often
apologized for than taken up in pride. Like a classically compulsive
form of behavior, this poetry was overdetermined, formed by literary
precedents, intellectual structures, and social forces much vaster than
the scope of their product. Take the umbrella of Eliot and Pound, for
instance; here was an accomplishment freighted with conflicting values, still in need of defense and certainly of explanation, born of the
bleakest despair and the most overweening confidence. Many so-
called academic poets, often in the university through the auspices of
the GI bill—adult education for survivors—and possessed of experienced horrors, could only view this work with a numbed shudder.
Pound's emphasis on the image, on the notion of craft as the measure
of sincerity, and Eliot's narcotizing sense of the impulsive will as the
source of all moral disruption and confusion, struck the riveting blows.
But in choosing such work and such men as their models, the academic
poets were destined to draw up templates over which all enthusiasm
was forbidden. One can hardly "beat the drum" for a poem like *The
Waste Land*. The Southern Agrarians, led by Tate and Ransom, read the
poem as a condemnation of modernism and liberalism; urban poets
could only nod silently at the sense of alienation it so conclusively
encapsulated. In the controversy over awarding the Bollingen Prize to
Pound in 1949, the main furor was over a principle, not an individual,
and not, for long, a particular poem or book of poems. The furor
essentially involved an antienthusiastic stance: one must never be
moved by *what* is said and thus fail to pay full attention to *how* it is said.
Subject matter must be bracketed because pluralism, individualism,
and aesthetic liberty demand it. We all have axes to grind, the
Bollingen panel seemed to say, and some may be neurotic or even
repulsive, but the distancing mechanism of the poem and the control of
ironic displacement will protect us until our examination is complete.
In a way, a poem becomes like an academic thesis because it seeks not
what must or should be attested, but what might be convincingly said
to a disinterested audience.[1]

The literary "moment" of the immediate postwar years was a peculiar one and bore odd fruit, none more so, perhaps, than the Bollingen
controversy itself. Great as the modernist experiment was, in American poetry it was concentrated on a special form of failure: the failure of
moral energy, as in Prufrock, or the larger failed energies of the culture,
against which some of the early *Cantos* railed. There was little point for
a poet in 1950 to add to the list of enervated figures; neither was there

much for him to praise. He had heard "the dogs of Europe bark," and now he had to consider such animal blindness in the possession of atomic weapons. All around him the postwar economic recovery was producing an American form of capitalism based on unlimited credit, trust in unlimited resources, and the drive toward unfettered consumption. Official morality was content to reassert the vindication of its system of individual enterprise over the mass hysteria of Nazism and to promise that the same system would prevail against the equally collectivistic evil of communism. The American eighth of the species was well on its way to using four-fifths of the globe's supplies. Art and poetry had no chance of prevailing against such an ethos, as the earlier eras of Dreiser and Henry Adams had made clear. Failure would continue to be the subject matter of poetry, but it would be a second-generation failure, without the lingering pathos of Prufrockian twilight. The audience, on the other hand, would no longer be assumed to be the philistines or even the nouveaux riches, for that would be a hopeless whistling in the wind. Instead, poets began to speak to each other almost exclusively. Irony, aesthetic in Pound, or corrosive in Eliot, appeared in a lower register, as poets began to speak of "flat defeats in a flat voice," to quote James Wright. More often and more directly, the focus for poetry became poetry itself, not as in the heroic self-mythologizing of Yeats, but as in the quotidian tones of people talking shop. This strain culminated in John Berryman's *Dream Songs*, which when read in sequence slowly exclude all concerns but their own completion. Berryman finishes them partly as a challenge to his fellow poets, a mocking taunt he thoroughly enjoys, and partly to establish conclusively that this is one project he will not fail.

One way for academic poetry to avoid total enervation is by directing its ironic beams in every possible direction. Since the audience is often tacitly assumed to be other poets, the test of a good poem will be how many various contexts, how many qualified, partial truths can be woven together without becoming a mere miscellany. Another way of putting this is to ask how often can the mind subdivide its own trust in itself before it gives over to confusion and chaos? Like the surrealists' attempt to level all values, this procedure entails a cancelling out; unlike their French antecedents in search of the antirational, these American poets desperately want some unequivocal term upon which to rest their final saying. Berryman, in his *Dream Songs*, mocks himself and his audience and their shared cultural milieu by envisioning the assistant professor who makes it to associate professorhood through writing a thesis on the *Dream Songs*. Nowhere, however, does Berryman mention the fact that he was a full professor in a literature department and achieved such position partly because of his reputation as a poet. Beneath all the ironic distrust of false values, this sort of poetry still conveys a belief in "Love and Fame," to use two of Berryman's terms. It is as if irony can assimilate any position, since it works by pitting one stance against another, asking its audience to hear every echo and halftone, even though the ironic mode cannot relinquish its own detachment.[2] Mistrustful of all beliefs as the incipient forms of extremism, the ironic poet sustains himself by trusting in the autonomy of art, where the only danger is a puerile, degraded form of romanticism. Though "poetry makes nothing happen," as the master ironist put it, it still "survives in the valley of its saying," and the topography of that land is often studded with ivory towers and ivied walls. As mistrustful as it is of all false security, this poetry can occasionally reveal a certain smugness, its ironic defenses drawn so close that its only illumination is a fading inner light.

Much good analysis has been expended on the relationship between this dominant mode of poetry and "New Criticism," from Karl Shapiro's polemics to Walter Ong's reasoned dissection in "The Genie in the Well Wrought Urn."[3] Together the poetry and the criticism formed a literary orthodoxy, ascendant, if not rampant, in American universities from the early forties until the early sixties. Gradually, under pressures as various as undergraduate interest in certain "cult" figures and plain boredom with the methodology of explication, the academy has begun to include other figures in the curriculum. These newly sanctioned poets, long at work developing their own distinctive and various styles, are often in revolt against academic poetry. The anthology "wars" of the late fifties and early sixties were an attempt to clarify the battle lines between academic and beat, raw and cooked, establishment and outsider schools of poetry. But this proliferation of labels and anthologies, as many were quick to note even at the time, gave birth to many straw men of literary argumentation. Poets such as Charles Olson, once referred to contemptuously as an "aging beatnik," wrote a language dense with expert knowledge, much of it often abstruse. Olson's early essay "Projective Verse" formulated the polarities of open and closed verse and urged "composition by field," which was the antithesis of a highly structured, tensely argued academic poetry. Olson's argument produced much theorizing in its wake, and it clarified the incipient practices of a number of poets, many of whom were liberated in diverse ways by the habits of thought it exhibited. But American poets have a Gallophobic mistrust of manifestos and movements, and a great many men and women spent their time explaining that they weren't exactly in either camp, closed or open.

It might be worthwhile for a moment to stop and ask an off-center question: what, if anything, did the academic poet and the projective, or any antiacademic, poet have in common? One tentative answer suggests itself. The contemporary American poet works with an atomized consciousness. The differences between the two types of poets result from their methods of attempting to organize that particular kind of fragmentation, through ironic tension or through a yielding immersion. Whether the speaker sounds like the one in Olson's *Maximus* or the uncertain, overwrought one in Robert Creeley's lyrics, like the exacerbated, neurotic worrier in Lowell's *Notebook* or the lamenting quester of Adrienne Rich's *Diving into the Wreck*, we are met with a problematic disjunction between fact and value. Such a disjunction made several traditional poetic responses unavailable to the majority of contemporary poets. No one was able to deal straightforwardly with narrative; few could avoid a harsh, scraping irony; no one could build up or work out of a clear set of intellectual formulations; few could move beyond what was finally a singular, often narrow range of subject matter. By almost any standards, a superficial comparison with romantic or Augustan or Victorian poetry pointed to a barrenness in American poetry. It was almost mandatory to establish a highly individual, stylized language and set of concerns, to find "one's voice," as the critical cliché has it.[4] Thus, the typical American poet exhibits a self eager for an Emersonian dissolution into all the crazed and jarring surfaces of mundane reality, while at the same time—and here Berryman's *Dream Songs* provides an extreme, almost farcical example—he wants to establish an authoritative, transcendent ego beyond all strictures of community and limitations of view. Consider the difficulties inherent in accepting Rimbaud's mandate to be absolutely modern yet knowing that the mode of irony has exhausted itself and is no longer able to contain any but the more aestheticized portions of your experience. Meanwhile, the notion of an epic vision or a mythical resonance has proved to be an insolvable problem in literary history. And, all the time, like the contemporary painter, you are composing with the breath of the curator on your neck. Style thus becomes a commodity, its exchange value, its attractiveness outstripping its use value, its felt needs. Everywhere the play of mind predominates, and nowhere is there an audience to appreciate your anguish, unless you count those waiting for you to finish so they can have their turn.

Though there are over seven hundred manuscripts submitted each year to the Yale Younger Poet competition, scarcely any first book by an American poet will sell that many copies. A small magazine of modest reputation, *Poetry Northwest*, considers forty thousand poems a year, though the magazine has fewer than one thousand subscribers. Grim quip that it is, it is true: more people write poetry than read it. As I have been suggesting, one of the corollaries of this is that the people who do attend to poetry are extremely "critical," both in the sense of being finely discriminating and in the sense of being at least marginally querulous. For a variety of reasons, most poets still manage to avoid extreme forms of aestheticism or inbred alexandrinism. But what results from this situation resembles a grotesque parody of what the large majority of these poets would be united in despising, the notion of the automobile manufacturers' "model year" change of style. For, once the orthodoxy of academic poetry was shattered in the late fifties and early sixties, a proliferation of styles, voices, schools, and camps followed. For a while most of these "dissenting styles" stayed fairly close to one another in spirit at least, but eventually—almost inevitably—the "styles" began to subdivide. Donald Allen's highly influential anthology, *The New American Poetry*, contained at least three such divisions: the projectivists; the New York school, headed by O'Hara, Koch, and Ashbery; and the San Francisco, or beat group, including Ginsberg, Snyder, Spicer, and others. There was of course some overlapping; for example, Robert Duncan was clearly a projectivist, but having lived many years in San Francisco he had ties with such poets as Spicer. Likewise, Snyder began in a circle dominated by Ginsberg, went on to be influenced by Olson, and was eventually close in spirit to poets like Bly and Kinnell. But the groups were there, held together like many groupings in America by the thin threads of geography, personal temperament, and underlying, often intangible commitments. Younger poets often, willingly or unwillingly, merge with one of these groupings, study in their seminars, publish in their magazines, and develop with or against the grain of the group. Many other young poets avoid such identification, and some have even published magazines of their own that seek to include representative poets from across the spectrum—magazines such as *Ironwood* and *Lillabulero*. Often, however, the talk and attention of these younger poets, and of many of the critics and reviewers as well, are concerned with matters of style and allegiance, rather than with subject matter or visionary excellence.

What emerged as the most praised poetic values in the early 1950s were those of Pound and Eliot, though by then these men had in effect completed their poetic careers. It was this set of values—concision; wit; irony; imagistic density; and tight, even if playful, argumentation—that the poets in Allen's anthology challenged. But more than literary issues were at stake, of course; and the argument centered on what in the sixties were to be called "life-styles." One can easily blur the distinctions by pointing out that many of those poets generally considered beat or projective attached themselves to universities. But a strongly felt distinction operated, for the projective poets did include among themselves art curators, stevedores, bohemians, archeologists, and other assorted laborers, skilled and unskilled. University life represented a rejection of American values, but only in their grossest forms; and the campus rebellions of the sixties partially clarified the relation between university faculties and the power elite. That relation is complex and problematic; what is more, it is dialectical, and no chaotic, disorganized set of protests can conclusively demonstrate its fundamental lineaments. But poetry in universities in the postwar years was at best a weak and easily co-opted source of countervalues. What the antiacademic poets offered by way of values or value systems was hardly sufficient to counter the dominant morality either. But we hear, in Ginsberg's "America," for instance, a different quality of discourse, an irony that doesn't act defensively to protect the harbor of cynicism often found in academic poetry. Ginsberg often unfurls an imagistic density, modeled in part on Pound's dictum that "the natural object is always the adequate symbol," but he rejects the concise argumentation of academic poetry. What we find in "America" is an embracing, almost a surrendering, irony in which the contradictory and destructive values of the supercapitalistic state are mockingly celebrated. A greater, more inclusive sense of what it is like to live in America comes about in this poem, I would argue, because Ginsberg addresses some other audience than his fellow poets.

Some might argue that in addressing the abstraction of geopolitical phenomena we call America, Ginsberg simply resorts to a crude rhetorical device more appropriate to propaganda than poetry. But Ginsberg follows the lead of Pound in making dense the surface of the poem with historical and social objects; at the same time, he avoids the enervation that results from the type of irony we hear in the early Pound, an irony similar to that of Laforgue and Gautier. Ginsberg almost succeeds in recapturing Whitman's innocence along with a Whitmanesque sweep, but of course too much has intervened for that to happen totally. But the sweep, even for those who insist on seeing it as a putative sweep, a histrionic gesture, erupts from a stance that is intended to do more than protect the speaker. One can hear in this poem something of the same plaintive, almost self-pitying persona who chops his way through Berryman's *Dream Songs* and Lowell's *Notebook*. Complex, erratic, strident, turning over the charred remains of his desire with exquisitely inflationary self-interest, this speaker takes on a subject in Ginsberg's work that he approaches only through exempla in Lowell's and with limiting disdain in Berryman's. The subject is the very audience he is addressing. Each of these poets makes use, on other occasions, of an interlocutor: for Ginsberg it is often the ghost of his paranoid mother; for Lowell, his illustrious ancestors or his ineffectual parents; and for Berryman, some *poète maudit* or his father, who committed suicide. Again and again in American poetry the speaker will summon up some single figure to address, and my intuitive sense is that this occurs at least as often as the persona being allowed to speak on his or her own terms. This fretful struggle *just to be heard* dominates much of contemporary poetry and thereby shapes its idiom.

Karl Shapiro once told of how, when he attended *Poetry* magazine's annual dinner in 1963 and heard his fellow poets on the dais address the guests in rhyme, he felt like crawling under the table. Lowell, of course, has spoken of how, although many of the poems in *Life Studies* were first written in rhyming couplets, he decided to break up the rhymed units, though the vestiges of couplets can still be found in those poems. Lowell may well have made his decision for purely aesthetic reasons, feeling that the subject matter, intimate as it was, could hardly be well served by strictly punctuated measures. But Shapiro's reaction took in a larger, more extensive purview. The language we call *American* is marked by a wide range of regional and individual differences, as every linguist is quick to point out, and its variability arises from each speaker's need "to say his say," as Paul Goodman has argued.[5] This antinomian streak in the national character mitigates against rhyme, as, obviously, does modernism, with its primitivistic strain. But equally effective in diminishing the status of rhyme, and the status of other regularizing prosodic devices as well, is this tendency toward a private language in America. By and large, the public language of America continues to be outstandingly vapid and evasive when heard in political discourse. The Nixon administration, for example, could not bring itself to name its action of revising the international exchange rates *devaluation*, though when it was forced to revise the rates again, within thirteen months of what the president called the "greatest monetary agreement in the history of the world," the word crept into official news releases. Advertising, on the other hand, which might be regarded as the "other" public language in this country, works largely with phrases, often themselves developed from popular slang or vaguely imitating it, and so makes a mockery out of the discursive possibilities of language and reduces the responses of its audience to a collection of emotional stabs of acquisitiveness. What is left over from these two modes of language pollution is a weakly cohesive amalgam of not-quite-dialects that reduce the general level of *shared* literacy to an alarmingly low point. Most contemporary poets have no audience not because they fail to raise issues of interest and concern, but because in making full use of the affective and articulative reaches of their language, they inevitably decrease the size of their potential audience. This in turn has caused many poets to roughen their language, to seek a *lingua franca*, to challenge, as it were, the very impermeability of the consumer-oriented fabric of social intercourse. Often we are offered words, as well as merchandise, "wholesale," with no special frills, no markup. To extend the analogy another step, each speaker regards himself as a totally free agent, unfettered by the forces of the market, unbound by the shared conditions of like users of the material.

The variety of poetic styles in America has several causes, among them the obvious social heterogeneity—a heterogeneity often experienced as a lack of social forms rather than as an abundance of possibilities—which has increased since the end of the Second World War in geometrical, almost exponential, measure. To this we should add at least two other causes: the monetization of relationships and the uprooting of language by the media. Immemorial uses of language in the marketplace or in places of worship or in political assemblies count for very little in American life. Many people feel that the less said in a supermarket the better; the language of transcendence often occurs only in a satirical context; politicians are perceived as people who "must" say what they say, and as a result they are scarcely attended to outside of their demagogic roles. Public language, as a way of addressing objective reality in the context of shared values in order to initiate and correct communal enterprises, has only minimal vitality in this country. Apart from neighborhood identification, most urban Americans use the expressive values of language only to describe the most subjective, least articulated feelings. The language of the media, especially that of television, possesses a superfluous status at worst and a superannuated one at best, for on television the words seem "added on," and in newspaper editorials they seem either to echo a nineteenth-century moral bombast or to follow lamely in the wake of local and ephemeral crises. Again, the place where the monetization of relationships and the placeless language of the media converge is in advertising. Many wags in the fifties went so far as to suggest that admen, or copywriters for advertising companies at any rate, were the modern poets par excellence, the troubadours who simultaneously expressed our longings and sublimated them into socially acceptable form by making them over into acquirable objects.

About five years ago Allen Tate, himself the author of several rather inflated jacket blurbs, excoriated Robert Bly for his "self-advertising through his own journal, *The Sixties*, his publicity-seeking at sit-ins on the Vietnam war, his general insensitivity and boorish public manners." More than a difference in aesthetic outlook or life-style lies behind this sort of attack, and behind similar attacks mounted by Bly against other poets. What the attack manifests is the virtual impossibility of using any public discourse in poetry. This impossibility, often explained as a legacy of "New Criticism" or of autotelic theories of art, is rather the damaged fruit of a different planting. Poetic language can only be as rich as the common language to which it is grafted, and no Mallarmean impulse to purify the language of the tribe can fundamentally alter that cultural truism. Poetry in America has been farmed out to private and subjective areas not out of a sense that there it will best flourish, but out of the recognition of a simple necessity: public language in America is intended to deceive, to foster a false consensus, or to lubricate the gears that mesh induced appetites and shabby products. Who, we might ask Mr. Tate, can possibly address a large audience through poetry in any forum without opening himself to the spurious charge of self-advertising and publicity seeking? The problem compounds itself when we try to ascertain just how spurious the charge is. Can Mr. Tate not accept Mr. Bly's convictions in the political sphere simply because Tate mistrusts anything that can be called "publicity"? To be public in America is almost by definition to be self-seeking.

II

Yet, for the beginning of the period we are considering, various forms of self-removal were the norm in American poetry. And where to place the self in the confines of the poem—centrally, invisibly, histrionically, or marginally—was often the implicit point of contention among the differing camps of poetic theory. Where a poet placed the self often signalled the poet's sense of his or her audience as well. This is Elizabeth Bishop's "Cirque D'Hiver":[6]

Across the floor flits the mechanical toy,
fit for a king of several centuries back.
A little circus horse with real white hair.
His eyes are glossy black.
He bears a little dancer on his back.

She stands upon her toes and turns and turns.
A slanting spray of artificial roses
is stitched across her skirt and tinsel bodice.
Above her head she poses
another spray of artificial roses.

His mane and tail are straight from Chirico.
He has a formal, melancholy soul.
He feels her pink toes dangle towards his back

along the little pole
that pierces both her body and her soul

and goes through his, and reappears below,
under his belly, as a big tin key.
He canters three steps, then he makes a bow,
canters again, bows on one knee,
canters, then clicks and stops, and looks at me.

The dancer, by this time, has turned her back.
He is the more intelligent by far.
Facing each other rather desperately—
his eye is like a star—
we stare and say, "Well, we have come this far."

This poem signals the sensibility that was to be largely dominant in American poetry until at least 1950, and for some years beyond, though in decreasing strength. Forced to a one-word description, an average reader might call it modest, but if he were sensitive he would not mean modest as a form of failure, but rather as a form of achievement. Having chosen an aestheticized subject, the poet goes ahead with humanizing it; restricting herself to low-key description, she lets the incipiently luminous qualities of the object take shape very slowly; by concentrating an almost undue attention on the facts of the object, she reorganizes our value-laden perceptions just enough to question those values. What appears ordinary is never allowed to become ponderous, though our human penchant for ignoring issues of value or, what is the same thing, for having them fall into preset patterns gets indirectly chided. What is accomplishment? What is the distinction, and can it ever be clearly drawn, between mere survival and easy, unassuming triumph? Further in the background are other questions about man's need to replicate the world in forms at once mechanical, charming, and controlled. But the effect of modesty prevails.

This is due chiefly, of course, to Bishop's knowing that she can rely on her restricted audience to be willing, if not eager, to use aesthetic exempla as occasions for reflection on larger moral issues. Likewise, her reticence in forming an argument through implicit connections rather than asserting the connections and challenging her reader to accept or reject them utterly, fulfills her end of the author–reader contract. The poet's feelings, her affective energies, are sublimated and suffused throughout the texture of the poem.

In the triangular relation of speaker–object–hearer, the line from object to hearer vibrates faintly as a consequence of the speaker–object relation being so nearly invisible. This dampening of any explicitly affective or hortatory language in the poem necessitates, for its ultimately successful force, an almost total identification between speaker and hearer. But unlike the relation between speaker and hearer in propagandistic discourse, which might be thought of as the opposite extreme, this identification rests on no common experience or willingness to act in concert. Rather, it implies what we call an *understanding*, as that word is used to mean a sharing of attitudes despite the presence of opposing points of view, an agreement not so much to disagree, but an agreement that brackets the normal connection between opinion and action. The same understanding achieved between speaker and "horse" in the poem obtains between the author and reader in this kind of poetry.

In one of Bishop's most famous poems, "The Fish," the speaker, after long struggle and rapt reflection, releases her catch. Everywhere a source of beauty and dazzlement, the world of nature (and of art as well, since the fish is also clearly aestheticized in the poem) is made for looking at and wondering at, but not for possession. Or to put it differently, our most valuable possessions are mental ones, knowledge turning into wisdom rather than, say, experience turning into knowledge. In what is perhaps her finest poem, "At the Fishhouses," she says that knowledge comes to us, "flowing" like the sea, "dark, salt, clear, moving, utterly free." "Flowing" completes a crucial movement in this melody of qualities because it demonstrates how concerned the American poet is never to conclude in the realm of fixity. Even the most reflective, structured, and intuitive achievement must send us back into a world of flux and process. Bishop's poetry provides us with the best view of how the great innovative art of the early modernist era, the poetic strengths of Marianne Moore and William Carlos Williams, has been transferred to the next generation. The demanding precision of Marianne Moore and that part of Williams's work (especially characterized by his short lyrics) most concerned with recording the morphology of perceptual energy are brought together by Bishop and serve as one of the true high-water marks of a branch of American poetry.

Another, rather different sensibility entered at midcentury. It continued to use much of the same sort of ironic detachment we find in Bishop's work, but some of the postwar shock started to abate, and an undercurrent of new anxiety began to build. The early modernist masters were completing their careers or, like Auden, experiencing a reaction against any program that relied excessively on innovation. In a sense the battle *épater les bourgeois* faded, or simply took the form of cosmopolitan critics countering the scoffs of provincial readers with temperate explanations. Shapiro could still begin a poem on "The Fly" with an invocation to the "Hideous little bat, the size of snot," but the

Rimbaudian frisson was lacking. Still, a quality of intense concern, a voice of something like a domestic panic developed, and it was different from that concern sounded by Williams, Pound, or even Eliot. Though these three poets have done more than seemed necessary to broaden the range of subjects that could be poetically approached in the modern, urbanized world of mass man, none has turned a coldly analytic eye on the horrors of everyday life. Here is the beginning of Karl Shapiro's "Auto Wreck":

> Its quick soft silver bell beating, beating,
> And down the dark one ruby flare
> Pulsing out red light like an artery,
> The ambulance at top speed floating down
> Past beacons and illuminated clocks

The designedly ironic bell of the first line isn't much different from the "big, tin key" of Bishop's poem, and the illuminated clocks reflect the same deprecatory placing of the surrounding environment in a mock-tragic context. But what does set the poem off is its third line; it has the grim wit of Donne and the visual acuity of an imagist poem. More importantly, it has assimilated a modern device from the realm of ordinary, workaday reality and broken open its poetic possibilities. It may seem a small enough accomplishment from our present vantage point, but compared with Bishop's allusion to the paintings of de Chirico, it seems a measurable advance. Here is how the poem ends, after the ambulance has driven the injured from the scene:

> Our throats were tight as tourniquets,
> Our feet were bound with splints, but now
> Like convalescents intimate and gauche,
> We speak through sickly smiles and warn
> With the stubborn saw of common sense,
> The grim joke and the banal resolution.
> The traffic moves around with care,
> But we remain, touching a wound
> That opens to our richest horror.
> Already old, the question Who shall die?
> Becomes unspoken Who is innocent?
> For death in war is done by hands;
> Suicide has cause; and stillbirth, logic.
> But this invites the occult mind,
> Cancels our physics with a sneer,
> And spatters all we know of denouement
> Across the wicked and expedient stones.

We can see rather clearly now how Eliot's importation of Donne's style has borne an overdeveloped fruit. Tying the seams of its argument a bit too neatly to its basic body of imagery, this poem almost explicates itself. The individual auto accident, in becoming the vehicle for reflections on the dark unknowability of fate, strikes us as a bit too "thesis ridden," as if the poet had been reading critical theory on the notion of the concrete universal and its aesthetic uses. But just as the poem is about to crumble under its own intellection, it comes back to the level of dense imagery and in so doing resolves its musings by placing the moral disvalue it has cumbrously raised back onto the street itself. "The wicked and expedient stones" rings out as a sure stroke of poetic resolution, insightfully grim and rhetorically chilling. It says much more than "We have come this far," but the poem's understanding reflects an equal amount of passivity, as does that in Bishop's poem; this is due in part to what the ending of the poem replaces or turns away from: "a wound/that opens to our richest horror."

But we should also consider for a moment the two different scopes encompassed by the first-person plural in the endings of the poems. Bishop's "we" includes, at the most literal level, the speaker and the horse, but clearly it implies the speaker and reader as well. By extension, it includes any thoughtful observer and his or her attentive listener, as long as they accept the traditional requirements of the poetic discourse. In the Shapiro poem, however, the "we," though in some ways equally impersonal, is much less disinterested. This "we" includes, virtually, any citizen, any witness to the daily accident. Both poems turn from any conclusive or universal wisdom toward an admitted limitation, but Shapiro's does so in the name of us all, and so ends with a quite extensive consciousness after all. (Just by saying the reflections spatter "all we know," the poet enlarges his putative audience, since everyone's formulation—layman's and expert's—must be remade.) In Shapiro's poem, however, there are more than a few lingering traces of the habit of addressing a self-conscious audience self-consciously. "The stubborn saw of common sense," for example, would have a colloquial vigor or even crudeness that the diction of the poem cannot allow to be quoted directly. Many readers might well go over these lines without seeing what they refer to; that is, the readers would not formulate to their own hearing the actual language used on this occasion. Although the poet may be attempting to speak to a wider audience, he allows the propriety of diction to direct the thrust of the poem so that it speaks *about* a general audience rather than *to* one. Interestingly enough, the lines about the saw, the joke, and the resolution are themselves among the less ironically complicated, at least in their surface texture (compare, for example, "Cancels our physics with a sneer" and its use of the archaic meaning of physic to achieve a pun), and this suggests that Shapiro was trying to address some other audience than his fellow poets. Moreover, Shapiro has more obviously employed an affectively charged vocabulary and thus has avoided Bishop's remoteness from her subject without losing her observational accuracy. Though the two poets have much in common and clearly share many assumptions—about the need to tie fact and value together with scrupulous, almost conservative care, for instance—they yet can serve as counters for two separate moments in the course of contemporary poetry.[7]

The use of an interlocutor can serve merely rhetorical ends; but such usage in an idiom dominated by impersonal constructions signals a different intent. In Ginsberg's "Sunflower Sutra," a poem contemporary with those of Bishop and Shapiro, the audience included in the poem shifts and enlarges through the course of the experience recounted. Beginning with a standard opening familiar to readers of romantic quest poetry, Ginsberg quickly adds a companion (and addresses this interlocutor) in what we expected might be a solitary, visionary exploration. Just as the poem locates its visionary intensity in the setting of an industrial wasteland, it mixes the solitary plaintiveness of the quest poem with tones reminiscent of an informal verse letter. In a sense this interlocutor, Jack Kerouac, bears an analogous resemblance to the sunflower Ginsberg finds amid the debris, for Kerouac is the soul's companion that one finds at the end of night, the lover amid the alienation. Ginsberg's autobiographical directness distinguishes his poetry from that of his contemporaries, especially that written in the 1950s. But this directness is more than an unbridled exhibitionism, for it clearly marks out the possibility of new development in American poetry, though at the time of its appearance it was viewed as a cheap, dead-end aberration. What hindsight now allows us comfortably to see is Ginsberg's use of romantic motifs and strategies, which had been largely expelled from American poetry through the hegemony of the Pound–Eliot poetics with its emphasis on rational, almost scientistic structures. The voices of Blake and Shelley obviously echo throughout Ginsberg's early poetry, sometimes even drowning out the strain of Christopher Smart and Rimbaud. The beatific childishness of Ginsberg's vision in "Sunflower Sutra" was nonetheless self-conscious enough to protect itself, not, however, with the self-cancelling irony of Shapiro or Bishop, but by tenderly encircling itself with a tentatively infinite audience.

> You were never no locomotive, Sunflower, you were a sunflower!
> And you Locomotive, you are a locomotive, forget me not!
> So I grabbed up the skeleton thick sunflower and stuck it at
>   my side like a scepter,
> and deliver my sermon to my soul, and Jack's soul too, and

anyone who'll listen,
—We're not our skin of grime, we're not our dread black
dusty imageless locomotive, we're all beautiful golden
sunflowers inside, we're blessed by our own seed and
golden hairy naked accomplishment—bodies growing into
mad black formal sunflowers in the sunset, spied on by
our eyes under the shadow of the mad locomotive river-
bank sunset Frisco hilly tincan evening sitdown vision.

The quest ends in a vision, self-consciously called a sermon as if more
than a little trace of diffidence and embarrassment underlay the climactic moment. But this passage, brief as it is, contains several indicators of
Ginsberg's ties with a long tradition as well as of his virtually prophetic
sense of new developments in thought and feeling. We can almost hear
echoes of Tennyson's "I feed the yew tree," as our bodies grow into
"black formal sunflowers in the sunset," which suggests that the
flowers are funereal as well as ecstatic counters for the poet. The
movement toward sunset and death has an accepting bias, anticipating
people like Norman O. Brown. But the seriousness of this poetry
continued to be obscured for several years as the tone of chanting
subliteracy evident in phrases like "were never no locomotive" and the
insouciant mugging of "you are a locomotive, forget me not!" made up
the most obvious features of Ginsberg's public identity.

What we can also see in this passage is Ginsberg's use of a paratactical structure, a placing of sensations side by side without the hierarchi-
cal imputation of value and disvalue. The last ten words make a long
noun clause with nine equal modifiers all abjuring any adjectival
supremacy yet all clearing the way for the last word, the noun *vision*,
with a daffy particularity that finally comes lyrical in its spontaneous
inclusiveness. This paratactic strategy clearly resembles that technique
urged by poets such as Charles Olson and Robert Duncan in their
theories based on a "composition by field." Equally important for other
poets is Ginsberg's body-centered mysticism, for Robert Bly emphati-
cally argued for a return to such a consciousness in his theories of the
"deep image." But the sunflower-turned-scepter allows Ginsberg to
imagine an audience at once particular, in the person of Jack Kerouac,
and putatively universal, so that the "we" of his "sermon" is simultaneously editorial, royal (though with some obvious irony in this
context), and American, looking as it does to a definite sociohistorical
moment. Kerouac's role as silent interlocutor enables this audience to
have its multiple possibilities without a hectoring or grandiose cast.

As Ginsberg begins his "sermon" in "Sunflower Sutra" he shifts to
the present tense ("deliver"). This emphasis on the phenomenal present in contemporary poetry increased considerably between 1950 and

1970. And to no other poet is such emphasis of more central importance than it is to Frank O'Hara. O'Hara was the crown prince of
simultaneity, an archimprovisor who more than anyone else rejected
the sense of the poem as a "well wrought urn," as a static construct
deliberately placed outside the ravages of time and the flow of mundane events. O'Hara's sensibility reflects many of the same assumptions as Ginsberg's, for both poets refuse to separate the mundane
from the transcendent as they search for an immanent spirituality in
and through a kind of Bergsonian flux: the flow *is* the bridge to the
other world. But instead of the chanted, accumulating energy of
Ginsberg, O'Hara offers an offhandedness, a serendipitous sense of
structure that alternates between cockiness and self-effacement. Beneath this attitude, however, there persists an anxiety, what Richard
Howard sees as a dread of mortality.[8] This anxiety leads O'Hara to
create for himself an audience of initiates, a close circle of friends,
people "in the know," who can serve as comfort and barrier in a world
of madcap surreality. This can be seen in one of his best poems, "The
Day Lady Died":

> I go on to the bank
> and Miss Stillwagon (first name Linda I once heard)
> doesn't even look up my balance for once in her life
> and in the GOLDEN GRIFFIN I get a little Verlaine
> for Patsy with drawings by Bonnard although I do
> think of Hesiod, trans. Richmond Lattimore or
> Brendan Behan's new play or *Le Balcon* or *Les Nègres*
> of Genet, but I don't, I stick with Verlaine
> after practically going to sleep with quandariness
>
> and for Mike I just stroll into the PARK LANE
> Liquor Store and ask for a bottle of Strega and
> then I go back where I came from to 6th Avenue
> and the tobacconist in the Ziegfeld Theatre and
> casually ask for a carton of Gauloises and a carton
> of Picayunes, and a NEW YORK POST with her face on it
>
> and I am sweating a lot by now and thinking of
> leaning on the john door in the FIVE SPOT
> while she whispered a song along the keyboard
> to Mal Waldron and everyone and I stopped breathing

The alienation and confusion of urban life, especially at the street level,
come into disorienting focus with the news of the death of Billie
Holiday, the jazz singer whose self-destructiveness ("Heroin kills you
the slow way") clearly mesmerizes O'Hara when it is transformed into
a lyrical whisper. The poem, for all its looseness, tries to mimic that
improvisational quality, as O'Hara's own self-destructiveness (the

Gauloises and Picayunes) shifts uneasily beneath a cover of stylish gesture ("casually ask"). Unlike the Ginsberg "Sutra," this phenomenal present intersects a transcendent moment with evanescent ease. The ease, however, belies the anxiety ("I am sweating a lot by now") that O'Hara attempts to conceal in a supernaturalistic journalism (the poem opens by telling us it is July 17th and O'Hara's sweating can obviously be "explained" by the summer heat of New York).

The sense of audience in O'Hara's poem challenges easy definition. In one sense the poem is clearly demotic; its diction and ordinariness invite the most inclusive set of readers, as if the audience were to be congruent with that of the *New York Post*. But about halfway through (about where the above quote begins) the selectivity of the speaker and his highbrow cultural concerns quiver ironically against the foreground of the casual "everyday" shopper. O'Hara's audience apparently narrows to practically the same people we described as the audience of Bishop's "Cirque D'Hiver." But "culture" in O'Hara's world is more widely defined than we might expect in an academic poet. For no sooner does he leave the Golden Griffin than O'Hara returns to a New York scene that millions of people (literally) would recognize and presents us with a "typical" urban experience by having the newspaper headline, with its announcement of some tragic "event," serve as a sudden, crude displacement of our reverie. Obviously, more people in America could recognize and empathize with the structuring *event* in O'Hara's poem than with the equivalent moment in Bishop or Ginsberg. But then, of course, O'Hara takes us from the universally available front page of the *New York Post* to a moment from the past open only to the cognoscenti. As O'Hara presents the moment, he seems to have a double sense of his audience: for those who recognize Mal Waldron as Billie Holiday's accompanist there is a shock of recognition, and the moment's uniqueness is heightened, its transitoriness made more vulnerable, more precious. On the other hand, the word *everyone* in the last line refers to the audience that particular night, the people who admire Billie Holiday's genius (regardless of whether they've heard her in a "live" performance), and finally all the urban throng, who by their momentarily caught breaths signal their admiration for the marvellous and for their own mortality. In many ways this poem elegizes with traditional devices, praising the dead artist as somehow the "carrier" of our universal mortality and through the artist's heightened sensitivity creating a special occasion for intense reflection.

O'Hara's poetry, even as early as the first years of the 1950s, operated with split awareness, and split intentions. Clearly resembling Whitman in his democratizing impulses, his attempt to devalue "poetic" language and replace it with a demotic, spontaneous language, O'Hara also operates in the tradition of French surrealism, especially as that tradition was transmitted to this country through painters such as those in the New York school. This tradition contains elitist elements; in it the artist is presented as a priest figure, though his liturgy is intensely individualistic and his altar is his own studio. Because of this joining of impulses, O'Hara's poetry was little appreciated by either academics, who found it too unfinished, or the larger audience of general readers, who found it too hermetic. Such a split in audience results from trying to join potentially conflicting artistic aims, and it continues to plague American poetry. Most poets are unwilling to accept the minority status of poetry, or at least to use the inevitable smallness of its audience to justify continued use of self-protective irony. What O'Hara never openly addressed, because of his own temperament and his sense of poetic ends, was just this split impulse in American poetry: to speak openly to all, and to whisper only to other like souls. But then most poets today are more the victims of the split than its open challengers.

It might also serve us well to be a bit more schematic for a moment. Imagine the following four poems placed along a spectrum: Bishop's "Cirque D'Hiver," Shapiro's "Auto Wreck," Ginsberg's "Sunflower Sutra," and O'Hara's "The Day Lady Died." Obviously, as we move on this spectrum from Bishop to O'Hara, we are increasingly submerged in the mundane details of unrelieved dailiness, and any preset aestheticized framework fades away. (In O'Hara's poem there are aesthetic objects, such as books of poems, but they are clearly equated with Gaulois cigarettes and the *New York Post* in the realm of mere commodities.) Also, the same movement along this spectrum takes us away from the personal, disinterested stance of Bishop toward the intimate and self-revealing speaker in Ginsberg's poem. But then, and this is important for our argument, as we reach O'Hara the immersion in the mundane is checked to a certain extent by a dulling of the tones of intimacy. Now it is true that O'Hara's voice in his poem reflects the numbing grief and quieting nostalgia that he feels suddenly overwhelm him at the end of the poem. But the felt weight and presence of the objects O'Hara details in the poem flatten and almost oppress anyone who looks to them for significance; the objects are clearly in the poem as an antipoetic weight. "I want the poem to be the subject, and not about it," O'Hara said, and in this poem he comes close to realizing that aesthetic. As the speaker in Ginsberg's poem erects his mystical awareness, he "descends" to objects below the level of mundane commerce and surrounds himself with the *disjecta membra* of industrialized, urbanized man. There, as if by a kind of willed reversal, transcendence appears in this unpromising context. In O'Hara's world, the context is one of sufficient objects; and the transcendence, such as it is, evanescently captures the subject, but hardly transforms him. What happens on the spectrum instructs us in what happened to an important segment of American poetry in the late fifties and early sixties, for I would argue that in a key sense the spectrum folds back on itself, if we consider the detached, suspended sensibility of the speakers. Instead of what we find in Bishop, a world of aesthetic objects considered with fond irony, we discover in O'Hara's poem a gathering of mundane objects fondled by an aestheticizing irony. (It may also be instructive to notice that in both poems the speaker gradually moves his or her own affective response to the foreground as the poem ends.) But the two attitudes are similar in their gesture of holding up an object taken from its context, "lifted" in the several meanings of that word, and using that object as a kind of cathexis for otherwise unformulable recognitions. This pattern is one of the traditional forms of lyric poetry, to be sure, but here it enables us to focus on how American lyric poets want to approach the world of objects but often do so by falling back on traditional methods.

The most important exemplar for such lifting of objects in American poetry remains, of course, William Carlos Williams.[9] It should be remembered that Bishop's work contains instances different from the one we've cited, as does O'Hara's, but it bears notice that we can trace the influence of Williams in two poems that are typical of Bishop's and O'Hara's work and that show their abilities very favorably. What was most remarkable about Williams's innovation was his ability to at once set and transform an object in a field that felt richly experiential since it partook of the structures of perception in an unobtrusive way. Williams did not abandon affect, nor did he fail to see that affect had an important cognitive function, but in his greatest poems, like "Desert Music" and "Asphodel, That Greeny Flower," the affective and descriptive elements are nearly equivalent and are joined in such a way as to send the reader on, through their transparencies, to a world of objects. But the objects, thus transparently viewed, reflect our attention back to the deceptively simple process that so presented them. In the poetry of Bishop and O'Hara we sense their desire for a sort of anonymity, their trust that in the object itself we will find all the ideational content we need. But the longer we dwell on their poems the more we feel their attitudes at work, and while part of the energies of the poems coalesces on things, another and almost equal part expresses an air of suffocation in the face of objects, a feeling that things made and used and sold are somehow fallen and lessened and entrapping.

"Things are in the saddle, and they ride mankind," comes that ancient and sagacious voice, and no poet wants to be a beast of burden.

No simple scheme, even one that tries to graph both audience and the status accorded the world of objects in the poem, can fully convey the variety of voices and the complexity of desire in contemporary poetry since 1950. What we can see, however, is an emerging tradition of catholicity among our poets, a willingness to remain open not only to experience, long an American poetic dream, but also to one another, now a possibility more proximate. The anthology "wars" of the late fifties and early sixties were clearly a manifestation of a narrowness, a sense that there weren't enough spoils to go around, as well as a revelation of imminent changes in poetic modes. Now that these changes have become manifest, it only remains for contemporary poetry to find the audience it so deeply, though often confusingly, desires. Whitman's shopworn adjuration that only great audiences can make great poetry possible has lost none of its weight or edge. As Gary Snyder argued a few years ago, "It is a mistake to think that we are searching, now, for 'new forms'. What is needed is a totally new approach to the very idea of form." It might be that a new awareness of whom to address and what to lift to consciousness will be an important force in shaping the new ideas of form.

2

"Songs of a Happy Man"
The Poetry of Theodore Roethke

Though it is plainly heterodox in beliefs and forms, American poetry gathers much of its strength and interest from a recurrent concern: the individuation of the poet. This individuation mediates between the burdens and the possibilities of selfhood, since the American poet is clearly postromantic and sees himself (we might even say *sings* himself) free of the circumstances of continuity. As an individual, the poet insists on shaping himself; on the other hand, the song he gathers begins its pulse in a given world, and nothing short of the *compass* of this world can measure the song's totality. Emily Dickinson says her business is circumference. Emerson, in "Circles," claims, "Permanence is a word of degrees. Everything is medial. Moons are no more bounds to spiritual power than bat-balls." The very sufficiencies of a centering self, its limitations in time, thrust against its insistent growth; its memory-haunted thrownness is obliterated by its indefatigable autonomy: these are the songs our poets bring forth, partly as curses, partly as interdictions, and partly as celebrations. Theodore Roethke's poetry participates in this "medial" tradition, and broadens its range as well, for Roethke was above all a poet of selfhood, or more exactly, a poet of the self-as-problematic. Therefore, he was a poet of growth, a singer who needed to gather up his origins as he moved further and further toward the completion of his entelechy. He needed, in other words, to encircle himself while he was desperately bursting all containment.

The concern with origins in Roethke's poetry is transformed into a fascination with metamorphoses and gestures. The original template might never be recoverable, but at each stage of growth both the seed and the wet sheath it has sprouted forth can claim new origins. The procedure, however, is crucial, for Roethke was to realize that the poem can easily become "loosely oracular" and that real recovery can be obfuscated by the too-ready dazzle of feigned madness. The poet must be somewhere between Ophelia and Lear, partly lyrical and partly accursed in his meanderings. This is why the innovative language of "The Lost Son," for example, is by turns catechetical and tentative and passes through several other shades of firmness in between. The sequence's mélange of rhetorical modes confesses Roethke's uncertainty at the same time that it claims his authority; the poet becomes both self-effacing initiate and self-taught master. Like Pound in *Pisan Cantos*, Roethke must confess his crimes and reveal his strengths; but unlike the mastery of Pound's allusiveness and historical placements, Roethke's *periploi* describe a voyage more inward and less specifically located. The surface of Pound's text is almost archeologically horizontal, whereas Roethke's text forms like a crystal, its overall shape often distorted by accretions of insolvent matter. Pound's criticism renders sensory data accurate to the point of photographic clarity; Roethke's images of natural phenomena are more ecstatically presented. Pound wants to illustrate, Roethke to celebrate.

The title sequence from *The Lost Son* exemplifies a surrealist texture and structure that has since become commonplace in American poetry. In some senses, to the reader of the seventies this sequence might seem contemporary; though it would surely stand out among its later epigones, its true inventiveness might be obscured. But a few reminders will partially reset the context of Roethke's innovation. When "The Lost Son" appeared, "Notes Toward a Supreme Fiction" was only a few years old; *The Pisan Cantos* had just come out; and Eliot had not yet completed all of *The Four Quartets*. In other words, the "masters" of modernism were producing the capstones of their careers, and the next generation had just begun to find its voice; Lowell's *Land of Unlikeness* was contemporary with Roethke's *Lost Son*, for example, though the distinctive mode Lowell was to develop was not securely in hand until *Lord Weary's Castle*, two years later. So when we read in Roethke's essay "How to Write Like Somebody Else" that "one dares to stand up to a great style," we know he is not just reiterating apothegms or offering a concealed defense of his own imitativeness. "The Lost Son," whatever it produced in his later style, however it shaped the course of his self-definition, was surely a daring exploration. Rather than simply continue in the mode he had already brought to such high polish in his first book, *Open House*, Roethke took a much-heralded plunge into his own psyche. The heralding came later, to be sure, though Roethke himself, as he shows in the "Open Letter" discussing the "sources" of his procedure, thought of the plunge as a recovery rather than a discovery, as a reclamation by the ego of those marshy, imbedded roots of feeling and association. It is as if Roethke discovered the seeds of several modes that were later to dominate contemporary poetry: confessionalism, neosurrealism, deep images. In speaking of looking for "some clue to existence from the sub-human," Roethke describes the poet as one who looks from an angle of vision ordinarily closed to public or discursive language. "He sees," Roethke says, trying to formulate an approach rather than a definition, "and yet does not see:

they are almost tail-flicks, from another world, seen out of the corner of
the eye." These "clues" are just that, traces of a previous or incipient
existence or presence, something not yet, or just under or beyond.
"The experience. . .is at once literal and symbolical," and its medial
frames of reference, the epistemological status of its observations, keep
shifting, now certain, now whimsical, part revelation, part willed
invention. In this sense Roethke may also be recognized as one precur-
sor of "composition by field," or "projective verse" as Charles Olson
called it, whereby the poet situates himself in an attitude toward his
or her consciousness and, mixing attentiveness and abandonment,
strives to create the *feel* of thought in all its multifariousness and
interconnectedness.

> By snails, by leaps of frog, I came here, spirit.
> Tell me, body without skin, does a fish sweat?
> I can't crawl back through these veins,
> I ache for another choice.
> The cliffs! The cliffs! They fling me back.
> Eternity howls in the last crags,
> The field is no longer simple:
> It's a soul's crossing time.
> The dead speak noise.

The journeying here starts from impulses evolutionary and mystical,
and the senses are both the means to and the impediments of new
knowledge. The progress of the sequence is often humorous and is not
above a certain self-deprecatory undercutting of its own vatic yearning, as the second line here shows. In any more or less typical stretch of
"The Lost Son," the mode of discourse may shift often and abruptly.
We can move from a rhetorical question, to what seems a scrap from a
nursery rhyme, to a quick axiomatic stab. In each case the language will
be dominated by simple, often one syllable nouns, there will be a
relative absence of adjectives, at least of a sophisticated or precise sort,
and the verbs will frequently be of simple physical scope: crawling,
whispering, or sleeping. One line of bare description will spark
another that is apparently symbolic, the spark jumping across a
"mythical" association, or a pun; as soon as a discursive context is
generated by some clause of subordination or apposition, it is suddenly abandoned for a string of three or four sentences randomly
connected. Clearly the total effect of this must be cumulative, for while
the sense and feel of the poem's central thrust (or of that of one of its
sections) may be forceful, the precise shape and texture of the poem's
argument become most distinct after several readings, and Roethke's
insistence on the necessity of reading the poem aloud makes sense
when we realize the nature of the poem's affective structure. It is made

of language that is at once obsessive and anonymous; its shifting gestures become the poet's inchoate attempt to make up, and make up *for*, his unacknowledged fears. The poem's theme, if it can be formulated succinctly, might be called the struggle of the self to circumscribe itself, fighting off the equally tempting but equally fallacious notions of solipsism and determinism. By turns the "I" in the poem fears and flaunts its own self-generation and its own hereditary "tunnel"; "I've seen my father's face before/Deep in the belly of a thing to be," says Roethke, making the father something realizable instead of given, a future to be grown toward rather than a past to be fled. Later he says, "A son has many fathers," as if a mediating refuge might be found in emotional polytheism.

Roetheke included in *The Lost Son* volume, besides the long title sequence, three other sections. The middle sections of the book contain several lyrics written in the mode of his first book, *Open House*: imagistically straightforward, fairly tightly argued, and conventionally rhymed and metered. Some few of these, such as "Dolor" with its "duplicate grey standard faces" from the world of bureaucratic clerical employees, introduce a more mundane and less pastoral subject matter into Roethke's work, but the overall effect here is of an unsuccessful attempt to revitalize a past mode. However, the opening section of *The Lost Son and Other Poems* exhibits Roethke's sensibility in one of its most distinctive modes, as beautiful and as challenging in many ways as the surreality of "The Lost Son" sequence. The subject in these poems is the greenhouse environment of his childhood, the root cellar, the steam pipes, the rich loam and dank air of horticultural activity. This is Roethke's world of "underness," as Frederick Hoffman calls it,[1] a world of slow movement below the surfaces of vision, a world highly tactile and olfactory in its moist complexity. Everything becomes instinct, pushing upward toward light; all the processes of change are as determinedly gradual as they are invisible. Virtually every poem here ends with a gesture on or toward the borders of transformation. Roethke uses the carefully modulated personification and allegorization we can see in an early poem like "Night Journey"; the "merely" human order of consciousness is never triumphant over the vegetable existence it nurtures but whose subhuman mysteries it only fitfully comprehends.

> I can hear, underground, that sucking and sobbing,
> In my veins, in my bones I feel it,
> The small waters seeping upward,
> The tight grains parting at last.
> When sprouts break out,
> Slippery as fish,

I quail, lean to beginnings, sheath-wet.

The present participles here shade into a present tense that seems almost optative rather than declarative, as the wish for participation *becomes* the main source of awareness and intention. In "Moss-Gathering," his version of Wordsworth's "Nutting," he says, "But something always went out of me when I dug loose those carpets/Of green. . . ." Taken all together, the poems are a loose system of conduits; they are poems not of origins, but of mediations and thresholds. The sequence might recall Wordsworth's Lucy poems, not in its subject or manner to be sure, but in the special revelations it provides about its author. We see and hear in these lyrics part of a peculiar psychological configuration that resists explication yet must be taken into account in any overall "portrait" of the author. "Even the dirt kept breathing a small breath," Roethke says, and we realize that our sense of scale must be adjusted. In the poetry of natural history, the reader must often reconstruct the sequence of biologic events with a metaphoric bridge, since the poet, in his efforts not to betray the otherness of the observed world into blurring sentimentality, has had to guard himself against a reductive taxonomy. (Emerson complains of the young men who go into the fields with their Latin nomenclature and remain blind.) And if the natural world is appropriated simply to illustrate some initially subjective crisis, the system of naming will be equally benighted. The pressure of mind Roethke uses in these poems prepares us in a way for "The Lost Son," with its anonymous yet intimate revelations, for these poems are also spoken from a self-concealing premise—they are constantly pointing out *there*—yet their hushed, almost reverent testimony stands out as clearly personal. They form a key part of Roethke's work; by blending almost seamlessly with other parts of his sensibility, the sources of his awareness in these poems were to nourish the final success of the "North American Sequence."

Roethke's poetry rests on a body of sentiment rather than an articulated network of ideas; but in two of his major sequences, "The Dying Man" and "Meditations of An Old Woman," we can glimpse through his poetic formulations some of the philosophical elements of existentialism. Both of these sequences concentrate on process, and they view the self as problematic, as a construct that constantly gives itself over to other forces; and, in its attempts to mediate between the inner and outer reality it faces, this self is sustained more by a trust in its faculties than by any lasting pride in its accomplishments. "I am that final thing/A man learning to sing," as the dying man says, so finality appears as a formative process, and reality is a form of instruction rather than a lesson to be mastered. And the old woman, near the end of her meditations, says:

> To try to become like God
> Is far from becoming God.
> O! but I seek and care!
> I rock in my own dark,
> Thinking, God has need of me.
> The dead love the unborn.

If these sequences test the assumptions of existentialism about the primacy of existence over essence, of process over product, they also explore the sense existentialism fostered that only through and in death are our values truly revealed. Ordinary waking consciousness structures itself through the aid of several convenient deceptions: truth will make itself clear; the universe is consistent and explorable by rational methods; we know our own minds. But death, especially in the form of the mortality of the individual, threatens these deceptions with an unsettling redefinition. Instead of the testing growth of metamorphosis, death's transformation redefines the whole series of changes; the truth of process, once a comfort and a potentially heroizing struggle, threatens to become a final, inert product. "The dead love the unborn," perhaps because the ongoingness of the species makes death less terminal, more explicable. The lines also suggest that the dead God of existentialism mockingly loves the shapeless humanity it has deserted. But the sequence "The Dying Man" ends with these lines, probably the bleakest Roethke ever wrote:

> The edges of the summit still appal
> When we brood on the dead or the beloved;
> Nor can imagination do it all
> In this last place of light: he dares to live
> Who stops being a bird, yet beats his wings
> Against the immense immeasurable emptiness of things.

Poetry will not avail; the bird of romantic transcendence, whether Shelley's skylark or Yeats's bird made of "gold and gold enameling," deceives us. Death and love, those enchanting, twin nightmares, still present a summit, however; we must stop being a bird, but we must not cease the birdlike action of "beating against," for only in critical struggle is the sleight of hand we call reality checked and illuminated.

In these sequences, the dying man and the old woman both seek a place for themselves, a place that will itself be the culmination and the vindication of their experience. But this place becomes only as revealing as the light that floods it. In these sequences, Roethke comes closest to a tragic vision of life, and he does so in the images of light. Vision—the natural light and mystical illumination beyond the borders of the physically seen—centers all of Roethke's major poetry; it is for him what memory is for Wordsworth, the occasion and the result of his deepest love, his strongest affective energies. "Who would know the dawn/When there's a dazzling dark behind the sun?" The "would" here can mean either that no one would choose to know the dawn, or else that no one would be able to see the order of a diurnal world once they had glimpsed a transsolar perspective. The dying man, whether he chooses to pass beyond his boundaries or has them shattered, can imagine only a "dazzling" dark, for even nonexistence must have a visually energized aspect. The visual field becomes for Roethke almost equivalent to the self; or rather, as the visual faculty takes shape, has appetites, and is challenged by both outer and inner disequilibriums, so also does the self.

> Though it reject dry borders of the seen,
> What sensual eye can keep an image pure,
> Leaning across a sill to greet the dawn?
> A slow growth is a hard thing to endure.
> When figures out of obscure shadow rave,
> All sensual love's but dancing on the grave.

Again, "the visible obscures," as the eye wants to see *into* things, not just their surfaces; likewise, the self wants possession of the world, not just contact with it. Both eye and self want the "not yet," the transference into a new order; at the same time, they both know that the unseen, the unformed confront them with a threat to order that can only be relieved by defiantly excessive sensual indulgence, "dancing on the grave." "I want more than the world,/Or after-image of the inner thing," cries the dying man, who, though he realizes "all exultation is a dangerous thing," nevertheless knows,

> What's seen recedes; Forever's what we know!—
> Eternity defined, and strewn with straw,
> The fury of the slug beneath the stone.
> The vision moves, and yet remains the same.
> In heaven's praise, I dread the thing I am.

Dissatisfaction with the self, if not indeed self-loathing, becomes the origin of the transcendent; the crawling, sluglike self is furious in the presence of stonelike necessity, and that fury *is* eternity. As Camus's Sisyphus comes to love his rock, so the underness of Roethke's world flowers at the borders of the visible.

The structure of "Meditations of an Old Woman" makes use of the associative movement Roethke discovered in "The Lost Son." While "The Dying Man" uses the traditional verse forms and tightly ironic sentences that were such a dominant part of the prevailing idiom in American poetry in the 1950s, Roethke's "other" confrontation with death looks forward to a freer, less rational language. The first two poems in the "Meditations" sequence are fairly traditional, and they use the motif of the journey to picture the reminiscences and reverie of the old woman. But with the third of the five meditations, the structure changes and becomes more associative—or perhaps, more dissociated, since Roethke is clearly trying to suggest a weakening of the old woman's faculties as she approaches death. But here the ambiguity of structure parallels the ambiguity of "meaning," since the closer the woman comes to death the clearer her "vision" becomes.

> In the long fields, I leave my father's eye;
> And shake the secrets from my deepest bones;
> My spirit rises with the rising wind;
> I'm thick with leaves and tender as a dove,
> I take the liberties a short life permits—
> I seek my own meekness;
> I recover my tenderness by long looking.
> By midnight I love everything alive.
> Who took the darkness from the air?
> I'm wet with another life.
> Yea, I have gone and stayed.

This resembles the language of "testifying," that public proclamation of newfound evangelical fervor. (The speaker, like the woman in Stevens's "Sunday Morning," is clearly haunted by the "encroach-ment of that old catastrophe.") Earlier in the sequence Roethke had begun to rely on rhetorical questions and self-questionings to propel the poem forward. This reversion to the mode of surreal catechesis, used so frequently in "The Lost Son," doesn't untrack the poem, however. In fact, the last two meditations have a gentle, formulative quality about their statements; they seem less driven, less haunted, as if the woman knows ahead of time the false dawns that will break to confuse and mislead her. The poem's magnificence comes in large measure from this sense of full struggle with a never-ending, and never-changing, problem:

> Beginner,
> Perpetual beginner,
> The soul knows not what to believe,
> In its small folds, stirring sluggishly,
> In the least place of its life,
> A pulse beyond nothingness,
> A fearful ignorance.

and a few lines later:

> O my bones,
> Beware those perpetual beginnings,
> Thinning the soul's substance;

The old woman's acceptance of the need for "beginning" results in no easy comfort, yet the temptation toward surcease never triumphs: "I live in light's extreme; I stretch in all directions;/Sometimes I think I'm several."

The self imagined as several offers a riveting image for the language that Roethke was to develop in his poetry and that was to become so severely important to later poets. Roethke's work is permeated by a consciousness of being body-centered. Yet the poet's body, gestural, supple, organic, and instinctual as it is, never rests in oneness. For Roethke, it is always searching for the other in order to achieve its own completion. This "other" can be a place, or a time, or a stage of growth, as well as an-other body. Indeed, the body, because of its very resiliency, needs a multiplicity of "others" in order to complete itself. Roethke's body-centered mysticism is echoed in the poetry of Robert Bly and Galway Kinnell. His confessionalism, his offering of his body as the irreducible evidence of his scarred world, has its analogues in the work of Berryman, Lowell, and even Diane Wakoski. As Roethke's body bears metaphorically the traces of its own seeds, as it is linked through the species to that "other" time of myth, his poetry suggests later developments in poets as diverse as W. S. Merwin and Gary Snyder. In each of his long sequences, from "The Lost Son" to "North American Sequence," Roethke achieves a fullness of voice that derives in part from a fondling irony, a playing with appearances and stances that avoids dogma and ideology, but also in part from an "openness to experience," a testing of consciousness in both its circular and threshold configurations, which allows him to celebrate his gatherings and test his limitations with equal force. The structuring of these sequences relies on several obvious devices—such as the persona, or imagistic clustering, or mythical reverberations—but on no single aesthetic program. Because of their pluralism, the sequences, seen as a group, are the perfect embodiment of the poet's bodily growth and psychical sinuosities, since the thematic coherence we experience behind them never becomes dry or forced; they sacrifice neither their wisdom for experimentation nor their daring for mere consolation.

The language of the "North American Sequence" gathers up the exfoliating parts of Roethke's sensibility; and, while this integral speech is something new and distinctive in Roethke's work (as well as in contemporary American poetry), its roots are many and traditional. Biblical rhythms, the long line and catalogue of Whitman, the ecstatic litany of Smart, the meditative energy of Stevens, and the commonplace grandeur of Eliot's *Four Quartets*: all these elements grace the sequence, though none dominates it. Roethke is here both litanist and botanist, to use terms Karl Shapiro once employed to distinguish the symbolist aesthetic of Poe from the native strain of Whitman. Roethke's work doesn't fit into any neat categorization of contemporary poetry, in part because he wasn't interested in theory and hence took little concern with groups or schools of poets, but also because he drew widely and unabashedly on both traditional and innovative currents of poetic energy. Nowhere is this more apparent than in the language of "North American Sequence," yet most appreciative readers of Roethke consider it his "authentic" voice, the fruition of his lifelong attempt to come to terms with his burdens and possibilities.

Not only the language but also the formal structure of this sequence rests on a complexity at once densely affective and semantically straightforward. The central image is that of a journey, both as a movement to a new place and as a change to a new form; the natural cycles and stages of physical growth are gracefully, almost tangentially aligned with emotional growth. Much of the pleasure of reading the sequence comes from the lyric and equitable distribution of its parts into circular meditations and unfolding exultations. Either the circle or the threshold subtends most of the poem's images and thematic developments. Both of these "figures" can be reassuring or threatening in their immediate thrust or their larger implications; for example, the cyclical return of plant life is counterposed by the circular spins of the wheels of an automobile stuck in a snowdrift, return balanced by frustration. Mixing the traditional tropes and arguments of landscape poetry and mystical literature, the sequence draws on a resonant symbolic background, but it never courts obscurantism for its own sake; though it has clear "autobiographical" contexts, it never becomes plangently confessional. But perhaps a brief look at each of its six sections, and their relationships, will show how measured and yet how powerful are Roethke's journeyings.

In the first section, "The Longing," movement is clearly stymied: "On things asleep, no balm." The quiescence doesn't so much threaten as stultify, and this is the only section to use the rhetorical self-questionings that appear in much of Roethke's earlier work. From the questions—"What dream's enough to breathe in? A dark dream."—Roethke moves to the optative mood. "I would with the fish..., I would believe my pain. . . , I long for the imperishable quiet at the heart of form": these faint stirrings of desire occur in the last part of the poem, where the "disorder of this mortal life" is called an "ambush" and a "silence." The poem ends with a mocking reference to Eliot's *Four Quartets* and what we can read as a gentle, self-deprecating use of the rhetorical question:

Old men should be explorers?
I'll be an Indian.

Ogalala?
Iroquois.

The humor here reveals that Roethke's search will, if possible, avoid violence in favor of some medial, settled means of transference. Also, the tone of the affirmation here quivers with reticence, as the poet takes up his "duties" with a diffidence and a shred of "free choice" to conceal his desperation. The next section, "Meditation at Oyster River," turns from the interrogative mood to one of quiet observation. The images are all of faint movements: the turn of the tide, the thawing of a river. The speaker rocks "with the motion of morning," while lamenting, "The self persists like a dying star,/In sleep, afraid," as most forms of life are extinguished before the surfaces record the cessation. But, likewise, the sources of renewal are in motion beneath the frozen face of things:

> The sudden sucking roar as the culvert loosens its debris of
>   branches and sticks,
> Welter of tin cans, pails, old bird nests, a child's shoe
>   riding a log,
> As the piled ice breaks away from the battered spiles,
> And the whole river begins to move forward, its bridges
>   shaking.

"Water's my will, and my way," he sings in the last few lines of the poem, and this will be one of the most recurrent of the sequence's natural images, taking on the force and scope of a mythical symbol, though first introduced at the level of the "naturally commonplace." The tone of this second section retains, however, some of the diffidence of the first: "The flesh takes on the pure poise of the spirit,/ Acquires, *for a time*, the sandpiper's insouciance" (italics added). At this point the journey and the transformation are beyond will, beyond control.

In "Journey to the Interior," the third section of the sequence, Roethke shifts to an automobile journey for his metaphoric base, and the theme of the sequence is expressed in terms of the difficulties of the journey or, to use the terms of the metaphor, in terms of the detours and hazards of the road surface. In the second part of this section, the poet adroitly shifts to natural images as they are seen from the car—"I am not moving but they are." Then in the last part of this poem the voice of testimony enters: "I see the flower of all water, above and below me." This is symbolic of the "soul at a stand-still," for the visionary moment is "the moment of time when the small drop forms, but does not fall." This moment resembles a rehearsal for death, it is terminal but not necessarily transformative. "On one side of silence there is no smile," the poet says, and the images of sound and silence begin to gain dominance as they become a further mediating agency, yet another measure of growth and cessation. "And the dead begin from their dark to sing in my sleep," this section concludes, and the possibilities of integrating the moment of silence into the noise of everyday life remain problematic. The fourth section of the sequence, "The Long Waters," demonstrates a journey to new forms of life, but does so in a specially qualified context, having as its symbolic location a landlocked bay, in which growth and decay seem comfortably self-encircling, yet which is "a vulnerable place." Here the poet "acknowledges his foolishness" and says, "I still delight in my last fall." The phrase *last fall* can portend the end of his mortal life, it can refer simply to the preceding season, or it can suggest that mythical event that produces his alienated but singing consciousness, content at least to know there is no more fall once he accepts his mortality, his humanness. The language in the fourth section is among the most melodic, the most Whitmanesque of the whole sequence. The return from the still moment of silence in the third section is gradually recognized here as a triumph, and the fourth section ends with the strongest affirmation so far:

I, who came back from the depths laughing too loudly,
Become another thing;
My eyes extend beyond the farthest bloom of the waves;
I lose and find myself in the long water;
I am gathered together once more;
I embrace the world.

Both self and world are here encompassed, as circular embrace and linear expansion become congruent. Transformation of the self, occasioned by new sensory powers, a self-surrender that is identical with self-definition, all culminate in an acceptance of reality: the complex of awarenesses and changes we have seen before, but here the almost understated surety of it gives a fresh force to the healing.

Almost as if to avoid the sense that the healing was too easily achieved, Roethke returns in the fifth section, "The Far Field," to images of a stalled journey and to imagery from the preceding four sections in order to test and measure the validity of his "embrace" of the world. "I have come to a still, but not a deep center," he says in this protoclimactic poem, and he dwells on recollections and meditations of how "All finite things reveal infinitude." This section brings to fruition Roethke's interest in edges, in the consciousness of an object or event that is most truly revealed only at the border of its outline or form. "I feel a weightless change" he notes at one point, and the poem has an especially lovely tentativeness, relying in part on present participles and gerunds (there are six in one seven-line stretch) and in part on a tone that hovers between calm acceptance and rapt indifference:

> A man faced with his own immensity
> Wakes all the waves, all their loose wandering fire.
> The murmur of the absolute, the why
> Of being born fails on his naked ears.
> His spirit moves like monumental wind
> That gentles on a sunny blue plateau.
> He is the end of things, the final man.

The last phrase here recalls Stevens's "single man" from "Notes on a Supreme Fiction," but the quietly resolved tension between the implicit agnosticism of "fails on his naked ears" and the firm faith of "monumental wind" remains distinctly Roethke's. "What I love is near at hand,/Always, in earth and air," he tells us, giving to airy nothingness not only a local habitation and a name, but also a place in relation to his own corporal awareness. The old man in this section is pictured in "robes of green, in garments of adieu," and the sense of acceptance becomes more pervasive.

The final, sixth section of the poem, "The Rose," revolves around images of place more than of journeying; but again, as in the "vulnerable place" of the fourth section, the location is one where change and process can be fully revealed. The rose, "flowering out of the dark," is Dante's rose, and Blake's, and Eliot's, but also Roethke's father's:

> And I think of roses, roses,
> White and red, in the wide six-hundred-foot greenhouses,
> And my father standing astride the cement benches,
> Lifting me high over the four-foot stems, the Mrs. Russells,
>   and his own elaborate hybrids,
> And how those flowerheads seemed to flow toward me, to
>   beckon me, only a child, out of myself.

Ecstasy and transcendence have very local origins: "What need for heaven, then,/With that man, and those roses?" he asks, in the highest spirits of the sequence. He calls up an image of a "single sound" when "the mind remembers all," and this sound leads him to recognize his self-sufficiency: "Beautiful my desire, and the place of my desire." The place here, for the son who has at last found himself, is at once geographic, temporal, and cognitive. He sees now where he belongs, where he fits in, and realizes his love has brought his world close at hand.

This last section builds its complexity by resolving the journey motif into images of place, but also by raising the images of sound and silence to a new level of importance. "I think of the rock singing, and light making its own silence," he tells us, as the ordinary sensory order is transposed and the solid, the placed, becomes harmonious while the seen, the visible, becomes hushed. The poem's conclusion reiterates the central theme of self-transformation and self-acceptance:

> Near this rose, in this grove of sun-parched, wind-warped
>   madronas,
> Among the half-dead trees, I came upon the true ease of myself,
> As if another man appeared out of the depths of my being,
> And I stood outside myself,
> Beyond becoming and perishing,
> A something wholly other,
> As if I swayed out of the wildest wave alive,
> And yet was still.
> And I rejoiced in being what I was: . . .

The vision of the poem is created in terms of a locatable place where the movements of the wind are harmonized into a music that alternates with, and thus defines, a totally dazzling stillness:

> And in this rose, this rose in the sea-wind,
> Rooted in stone, keeping the whole of light,
> Gathering to itself sound and silence,
> Mine and the sea-wind's.

At the end the poet's voice achieves a status commensurate with a natural force. It is almost as if Roethke were reversing the story of Orpheus and, instead of leading the rocks and trees, joining *them* and being gathered at last into the first of rhythms, into himself.[2]

And so the rage that warped his clearest cry to witless agony in the opening poem of his total book is here mediated into a different form, a "true ease" of himself, and the search concludes. Roethke's career, by which we mean the intersection of his life and his genius as he is able to record it in his poetry, is as perfect as that of any other modern poet. Its intensity is posited on a search for individuation; though the career is limited by its lack of a sustaining audience and by the concomitant absence of any socially oriented vision, Roethke did all he could to make his vision clear, to publicize, in the good sense of the word, his agony and his ease. It's possible to see him as he saw Stevens, as the father of the next generation of poets. For one can trace and sense in various parts of Roethke's work many of the modes of poetry that were to dominate the 1960s and early 1970s, such modes as deep imagery, confessionalism, neosurrealism, and the return to a kind of pastoral ecstasy, as well as the use of mythical parable. Merwin, Bly, Strand, Kinnell, Levertov, Wakoski, Ashbery, Ammons: the list of his debtors is extensive, and ironic, considering that his reputation was once limited by those who argued he was too derivative. It is difficult to be either traditional *or* as modern as possible, to write either spiritual autobiography in a heroic vein *or* naturalistic lyrics with anonymous ease, without borrowing something from Roethke's poetry. No doubt his place in contemporary poetry will become clearer with time, and we can surmise that this one last transformation would have pleased him, for we have his word for it that "The right thing happens to the happy man."

3

Republican Objects and Utopian Moments

The Poetry of Robert Lowell and Allen Ginsberg

Robert Lowell and Allen Ginsberg, arguably the best poets of their generation, have perhaps succeeded most notably in surviving their own publicity. They have been able to write good poetry for thirty years in part because the publicity that surrounded them was generated by others who were quick to attend not so much to talent as to popularity. Lowell and Ginsberg became well known in different ways, of course, but both ways grew out of their talents for an endless, often *driven* form of speaking that at one and the same time clarified itself and grew more inclusive of the historical complexity it recorded. This speaking—one often thinks of both poets as "commentators"—has a confessional cast to it, and both men have made the private order into public occasion more than once. But their fullest voices were achieved through their ability to make the public events they often deplored into something like private musings. The languages they discovered to enable this transformation are sometimes similar; for all the apparent differences in their sensibilities, it might be interesting to see just what lies behind, and inside, their distinctive modes of speech.

Lowell's poetry, from *Lord Weary's Castle* (1946) to the revised *Notebook* (1970), has evolved into a language dense with phrases and broken sentences, chipped and scarred by a nervous allusiveness, a learned poetry made even more cluttered by diffidence. Lowell's energy often comes from, or results in, the twisting of phrases, the buckling of syntax till it yields the curves, however gnarled, of his sensibility. Though the poetry is often superficially confessional, it heaves toward a release from self, and such release as it does find often takes the form of a gesture. These gestures can be plaintive or absurd, and they often come forth as statements. In *Notebook*, for example, these statements are often the conversational aperçus of friends or the unspoken gaffs of Lowell himself. But the lyric form that preserves such gestures, or is completed by their discovery, often sputters forward; and the gesture, the final saving words, is often an admission of defeat or limitation, the words seem to ask forgiveness for not being, or becoming, the *Word*. Lowell's language rests, of course, on a highly developed historical sense. At its most hopeful, this sense of history is almost republican, in a Roman way, since it centers on secular power justified through time by its civilizing energies and its moral balances. But much more often, of course, the sense of history is rather like a failed republicanism; then history becomes a series of long-distance recriminations, a series of broken promises that one is tempted to "read" as the record of exploding vanity, of power justified only by power. When the latter sense is ascendant, Lowell's pessimism chokes his language even more and the recording, the commentating voice wavers between an accusatory splutter and a self-berating anxiety.

Ginsberg's poetry has developed out of an aesthetic of immediacy and produced a syntax that mediates between a flat, uniform perception and a swirling, flashing registry of states of consciousness in which perceptions are constantly disarranged, even deranged, by fissures or leaps in awareness. Ginsberg's poetry often reads like a conscious mix of newspaper headlines (the ephemeral cast into the forms of "mass production," made at once striking and easily assimilable) and tape recordings (the simultaneous made into circuitry, the moment wrapped into a continuous spool, the mind spun into a paranoid Möbius strip). Such a poetry relies more on paratactical orderings than on anything like a recognizably ordered syntax. This parataxis, this parallel placing of "notations," resembles a litany, of course; and Ginsberg's public reading voice is an extremely pleasurable instrument that at its best seems to partake of the structural complexity of an Eastern raga and the improvisational push of jazz. This language, at its fullest in a poem like "Wichita Vortex Sutra," needs a voice analogous to the field of vision in a hallucinatory state: constantly changing, yet made continuous by a dampening of tone or affect, loosely attentive yet not so alert as to become self-seeking, trusting in the absence of structure in the short run to vindicate a larger, more inclusive ordering. Ginsberg's language always includes, but is seldom conclusive. The end of things, in a temporal or chronological sense, gets indefinitely postponed lest it disrupt or betray the end, the goal, or telos, in the messianic sense. The notion of a sentence as a "complete idea" makes the sentence a foreign substance in Ginsberg's poetry; almost all sentences are made or spoken by the enemy, namely, the government in all its various duplicitous forms. Hallucination and the posthallucinatory moment both share a privileged status, since either can yield a perception just beyond the borders of established or official reality. Ginsberg's lyric shaping often begins with a chanting, meditative flattening out of the daily order, an unwinding of the logical mind's coils of expended pressure. His poems then often end with an anagogic leap, a sudden breakthrough of new awareness; less often, but perhaps more movingly, they end with a breakdown in the sustaining vision of things, a rupture in the cohesive will to love and observe without violence or force. The apocalyptic is clearly as much a source of dread for Ginsberg as it is a point of triumphant release or vindication. The nonordering, nonsubjugating syntax results finally from a deep, underlying sense that the outcome is still in doubt. The victories of order are either false or momentary, and this makes Ginsberg's language kaleidoscopic, fitful, even perfervid, whether it is busily celebrating or warily cautioning. The period is for Ginsberg only a breathing space.

As for the differences in sensibility between Ginsberg and Lowell, they are manifold and come from a variety of sources. For Lowell, the nuclear family, with all its pressures, and the weight of the historical past are clearly more in the nature of handicaps than advantages; but neither the family nor the legacy of a past glory can be ignored, and Lowell's imagination has been shaped, some might even say deformed, by the historicism of the nineteenth century. The feeling, and the insistence, in Freud, Marx, and Darwin that all we might do or fail to do, we do in a historical nexus only partly of our own willed making, flows through Lowell's poetry either as the occasion for immediate rebukes, or as a leaching out of the strength, the resolve of any intelligent person.

> We feel the machine slipping from our hands,
> as if some one else were steering;
> if we see light at the end of the tunnel,
> it's the light of the oncoming train.

These lines are from a poem Lowell published in the 29 May 1975 issue of the *New York Review of Books*, and their savagely ironic completion of a figure of speech once used to describe American military prospects in the Vietnam War has an undercurrent of pity, a note of the "black humor" that is more than an occasional element in Lowell's poetry.

The source of Ginsberg's sensibility, on the other hand, is the affinity group rather than the nuclear family. In contrast to Lowell's historical burdens, Ginsberg's social and political consciousness, and even his conscience, seems looser and yet more extensive. Lowell's political awareness takes shapes in key epochs, or even key moments, that serve as measures of values, tests of true progress, while at the same time hinting that all is devolutionary. Ginsberg's polis is always a future, utopian one; though he shares Lowell's sense of America's massive failure as a political "experiment," that failure has a different texture, a different moral weight in his poetry than it does in Lowell's. Both men seem to realize the sharp limitations of liberal individualism, and both seem stymied by imagining the next great political myth that might replace individualism as the sustaining vision of western European, and even global, history. Ginsberg's much publicized ecological consciousness and his use of Eastern thought, based as it is on control and scarcity rather than on the Western values of growth and consumption, increasingly come to dominate his thought and his poetry in the late sixties and early seventies. Lowell possesses nothing similar, really, and this is perhaps what constitutes the greatest difference in their sensibilities. But lately, in *The Fall of America* (1972) and especially in his acceptance speech at the National Book Award ceremony honoring that book, Ginsberg's outlook has grown as gloomy as Lowell's.[1]

Both Lowell and Ginsberg have shaped their language in such a way as to enable them to include large and often disparate aspects of contemporary reality in their poetry. Many of our novelists, such as Mailer and Baldwin, have resorted to the essay to supplement their fictions in addressing the issues confronted by the artist in America today. Poets have often felt a similar pressure to turn to other media; thus, many contemporary American poets have used criticism, and a few have written fiction. But Lowell and Ginsberg have confined themselves almost solely to poetry; this "confinement," of course, is not felt as such, since their poetic language has moved at times very close to prose and has even taken as its subject matter the aspects of social and historical reality usually reserved for novels. It would be misleading to call either Lowell or Ginsberg a narrative poet, yet both have relied on narrative devices to broaden their lyric ranges. Lowell's *Life Studies*, he tells us, began as an autobiography, and its prose section, "91 Revere Street," besides being extremely effective as prose, serves as an almost radiant piece of gist to illumine Lowell's other writings. Ginsberg, of course, with his extremely free verse, seems to feel few generic restrictions about writing a "prosy" poetry. Indeed, in the *Paris Review* interview of Lowell, we are told,

> The ideal modern form seems to be the novel and certain short stories. Maybe Tolstoi would be the perfect example—his work is imagistic, it deals with all experience, and there seems no conflict of the form and content. So one thing is to get into poetry that kind of human richness in rather simple descriptive language. Then there's another side of poetry: compression, something highly rhythmical and perhaps wrenched into a small space. I've always been fascinated by both these things.

Lowell speaks throughout this interview about novelists and about prose fiction's ability to include a "kind of human richness." We may here be reminded of the passage set in the pub in the second section of Eliot's *The Waste Land* and of Pound's concern to get a kind of novelistic texture into parts of his Mauberly sequence as classic examples of modern poets' attempts to broaden the subject matter of poetry. Though Lowell's early career saw him struggling with a dense, clotting imagery in rhyming verse, both he and Ginsberg have often resorted to using juxtaposition, to relying heavily on "non-poetic" techniques, and to an increasingly free sense of stanzaic or prosodic regularity. The sonnets in Lowell's *Notebook* seem to flaunt their arbitrary form and their lack of rhyme; and one senses that Lowell resorted to the fourteen-line divisions in order to display a need to have some way of moving from point to point and from day to day in the course of his "diary." In fact, in Ginsberg's *The Fall of America*, the journal format, though less structured even than that of Lowell's *Notebook*, shows how inclusiveness rather than compression, a quotidian stock-taking rather than a transtemporal artifice, has become the only form not at odds with the poet's content. Lowell has been reluctant to drop the demands and strictures of conventional verse, but lately the pressure of his historical concerns, his regard for the measures of the past as test of the present's worthiness, has been overridden.

Obviously, for all their differences in sensibility, Lowell and Ginsberg have certain concerns in common, and their solutions are not as different as they might first appear. Both poets have advanced beyond the psychologized mire of "confessionalism" by continuing to enunciate a historical and social dimension in their work. They have been uneasy moral sages, to be sure; but implicit, and occasionally explicit, statements in their poetry have always removed them from the simple or hermetic pleasures of an autotelic art. Both men seem capable of being in the public eye without degenerating into poseurs. The poster of Ginsberg in an Uncle Sam top hat, seeing oneself carried into and then through the domain of public imagemaking, is the sort of thing that would have spelled the end to many a lesser poet's sense of balance; the portrait of Lowell in Norman Mailer's *Armies of the Night* might one day be read with the interest reserved for Hazlitt's portrait of Wordsworth. Ginsberg and Lowell emerged from the tepid, academic poetics of the fifties from different directions; more importantly, their emergence did not necessarily spell the end of their poetic growth. They continued to batter the language, to submit their medium to the fallen and mundane forces that disrupt the worth of language, both its affectiveness and its intelligibility, and by so doing they hoped to buy back some authenticated version of the contemporary conscience. Perhaps equally important, especially with Lowell, has been their refusal to set themselves up as either infallible literary or political sages; their laments almost always imply a sorrow that all public discourse, not just their own, fails to uncover or even generate enough socially purposive meaning to give American society a chance to justify the trust many people have placed in it. Though both are preeminently lyric poets, the range of their interest and the responsiveness of their language have kept them a considerable distance above the level of "mere" song. Read chronologically, their works show a decline of political trust in any solution currently at hand; at the same time, they demonstrate the need to return again and again to a language made inclusively honest by the pressure of mind and the shaping flow of emotion.

We can see this in three poems of Lowell's, taken from three points in his career and each involving a political vision in which large historical forces are "addressed" in terms of a single moment. The single moment pits an expression of hope, or of failed hope, against what are seen as indomitable cruelties. First, the last two stanzas of "Christmas Eve under Hooker's Statue," published in 1946:[2]

> Now storm clouds shelter Christmas, once again
> Mars meets his fruitless star with open arms,
> His heavy saber flashes with the rime,
> The war-god's bronzed and empty forehead forms
> Anonymous machinery from raw men;
> The cannon on the Common cannot stun
> The blundering butcher as he rides on Time—
> The barrel clinks with holly. I am cold:
> I ask for bread, my father gives me mould;
>
> His stocking is full of stones. Santa in red
> Is crowned with wizened berries. Man of war,
> Where is the summer's garden? In its bed
> The ancient speckled serpent will appear,
> And black-eyed susan with her frizzled head.
> When Chancellorsville mowed down the volunteer,
> "All wars are boyish," Herman Melville said;
> But we are old, our fields are running wild:
> Till Christ again turn wanderer and child.

The occasion is wartime, of course (the poem begins, "Tonight a blackout"), and the lines are turned out with ironic twists to heighten every image. The images are indeed so "chosen," so loaded with affective qualifiers ("The war-god's. . . empty forehead," "Santa . . . crowned with wizened berries") that Lowell's imagination seems aggressively Catholic and sacramental, making everything in the material world carry a spiritual significance. The influence of southern poets such as Ransom and Tate stands out clearly as the tight-lipped, almost bizarrely comic irony reminiscent of Ransom ("His stocking is full of stones") alternates with the faded grandeur of Tate's haunted plangency ("The ancient speckled serpent will appear"). But Lowell generates an anxiety absent from the controlled verse of his elders; the last line of the first stanza here, for example, contains a hint of obstreperous desire that flickers in the most intense "cold." Lowell's Catholicism is one of passivity, a religion at bay in a thoroughly secularized world, conscious of an imperial past, now envisioning its savior not as the "King of Kings," but as a wandering child. *Lord Weary's Castle*, from which this poem is taken, is suffused with a Catholic sense of history, or more precisely a modern Catholic sense, relying as it does on an awareness of a *deus absconditus*, of a god hiding from the searching cries of a few believers while the masses succumb to false values and hollow virtues. Resembling somewhat the religious feeling of Wilde or Huysmans, Lowell's sensibility in his early poetry is overlaid, as a more narrowly aesthetic one would not be, with a mixed reaction to the symbols and possibilities of a martial heroism. Lowell's role as a conscientious objector must be remembered clearly; he had earlier tried to enlist but was rejected, and only after the mass Allied bombing of German towns did he refuse induction. Of course, I do not mean to suggest Lowell was a "trimmer": his stand was courageous and highly conscionable, and I'm sure it cost him a great deal to defend. But throughout *Lord Weary's Castle*, and even as late as *Near the Ocean* (1967), Lowell's pacifism is bound up with the wrecked dreams of a global order, a kind of *pax Romanum* he knows can never reoccur (one doubtlessly based on repression and brutality in the first case); but the hope for such an order seems to be the species's badly misunderstood version of its own brotherhood. (Even in *Notebook* Lowell says, "I feel I have failed to avoid the themes and gigantism of the sonnet." Does he have in mind here Milton's political sonnets, themselves the utterances of a putative holy warrior?) Here is another poem, "Inauguration Day: January 1953," from *Life Studies* (1959):

> The snow had buried Stuyvesant.
> The subways drummed the vault. I heard
> the El's green girders charge on Third,
> Manhattan's truss of adamant,
> that groaned on ermine, slummed on want. . . .
> Cyclonic zero of the word,
> God of our armies, who interred
> Cold Harbor's blue immortals, Grant!
> Horseman, your sword is in the groove!
>
> Ice, ice. Our wheels no longer move.
> Look, the fixed stars, all just alike
> as lack-land atoms, split apart,
> and the Republic summons Ike,
> the mausoleum in her heart.

Again, a winter scene seems best for reflecting on the failure of national purpose, though the images of emptiness are here turned into images of furious energy without direction or even movement. The patrician irony of Boston is replaced with the grim metropolitan alienation of New York; instead of a father who gives the speaker mold under Hooker's statue, we have an impersonal means of conveyance built on economic exploitation. The "want" of the fifth line echoes a line from Cole Porter's song "The Lady is a Tramp," but it fails to come into sharp focus. Perhaps Lowell sensed that his irony might not be sufficient to protect him from the full panoply of social decay one used to find beneath the Third Avenue elevated railroad, and of course still finds today, though the rails are underground. But some of Lowell's earlier patrician sentiment survives if we read those fixed stars as the citizens of the modern democratic state, "all just alike," yet "split apart" and reduced to a small, atomic scale, lacking will or intelligence of their own as they course along obedient to laws beyond their grasp. The last line is grammatically ambiguous and can be read either as an adverbial clause, suggesting that the Republic summons its leader under conditions of grave self-doubt and loss of purpose, or as a clause in apposition to "Ike," suggesting that the newly elected leader is in reality the ancestral voice of failure, a figure from a spectral past monumentalized, which is to say in this context frozen into futility, by his funereal emptiness. Both this poem and the one on Hooker's statue take place on a day of communal celebration intended to mark a new beginning, a day set aside to redefine the larger purposes, and both of course curse the lack of historical purpose. The early poem holds out hope, however otherworldly or messianic; the later poem dissolves its particles of hope in a bitter solution of corrosive irony. The vox populi of the later poem seems as dehumanizing, if not more so, than the earlier poem's jingoism hidden beneath the cloak of piety. The crisp articulation of "Christmas Eve," with its subordinate clause, its quick shifts from ironic observation and rhetorical question to prediction and historical citation and then on to a subjunctive qualification of a generalization (all this in the last stanza), indicates an almost Horatian control of tone and balanced assessment of the poem's own vision. "Inauguration Day" jostles flat portentous statement with personal testimony and breaks off with an ellipsis to leap ahead with an ironic vocative. The poem ends with a stanza that sputters fragmentarily, then moves to a first-person plural that both incriminates and excuses its audience as it swings out toward a metaphoric gesture richly, ambiguously studded with a resonant image. Lowell's language has grown, if we use these two poems as a measure, from a controlled, syntactically balanced, stanzaically structured and rhyming verse to a nervous, mercurial, almost self-blocking (and certainly self-shattering) rhetoric, where the rhymes might be separated by a stanza break or

become partial (Stuyvesant/adamant/want/Grant) to the point of bur-
lesque. The statue of Hooker, empty-headed as it is, resounds with
slightly less futility than does the cordial mausoleum.

The third poem, "Munich 1938," comes from Lowell's *Notebook*,
published first in 1969 and in a revised version in 1970. The text of this
poem was unchanged:

> Hitler, Mussolini, Daladier, Chamberlain:
> that historic confrontation of the great—
> firm on one thing, they were against the war;
> each won there, by shoving the war ahead twelve months.
> Is it worse to choke on the vomit of cowardice,
> or blow the world up on a point of honor? . . .
> John Crowe Ransom at Kenyon College, Gambier, Ohio,
> looking at primitive African art on loan:
> gleam-bottomed naked warriors of oiled brown wood,
> makeshift tin straws in their hands for spears;
> far from the bearded, armored, all-profile hoplites
> on the Greek vase; not distant maybe in their gods—
> John saying, "Well, they might not have been good neighbors,
> but they never troubled the rest of the world!"

Lowell dates this poem "August 22, 1968," or in between the Russian
invasion of Czechoslovakia and the riots occasioned by the Democratic
National Convention, as the dates Lowell included in the back of the
book make clear. This poem, even more anxious and pessimistic than
the earlier two, builds to a rhetorical question that tails off into an
ellipsis. Notice, too, that this rhetorical question hardly applies to the
pre–Second World War conference, since *both* the alternatives it
exaggeratedly presents actually occurred. Instead, Lowell no doubt
has in mind the nonreaction of America to the Russian invasion, since
Lowell's politics have never excluded a strong anti-Soviet, anticom-
munist element. (As he said in a recent *New York Review of Books*[3]
"symposium" on the aftermath of America's defeat in Vietnam, "The
black prophet is now drowned by his truth. In our defeat communism
is inevitable and cleansing, though tyrannical forever." Seldom does
Lowell's political vision have such finality.) This sonnet, like the two
earlier poems, catches history at a moment of supposed revelation or
resolution, though again the moment is a false one and the hopes that
might blaze briefly are all the more taken as signs of an ever encroach-
ing doom. This poem's irony goes almost limp, however, as phrases
like "the great" and the sense that each "statesman" got what he
wanted rest not on any struggle of mind against the deceptions of
reality, but instead contentedly assume a shared disillusion with any
larger moral purpose. Ransom's quip recalls the words of Melville in

Lowell's "Christmas Eve" poem, and the statuary of the two earlier poems here becomes small models of preurbanized, non-Western man, as if to say that only wisdom limited in scope and remote from the daily push of politics and "affairs of state" can counterbalance the hollowness of received opinion and mass deception. The loving care with which Lowell "places" Ransom in his academic, small-town abode and the description of the primitive artifacts convey a fated sense of retreat and failure, and we remember that Lowell's 1967 experience of marching on the Pentagon has intervened between "Inauguration Day: January 1953" and this poem. As Lowell says in "The March II," also from *Notebook*:

> I sat in the sunset shade of their Bastille,
> the Pentagon, nursing leg- and arch-cramps,
> my cowardly foolhardy heart . . .

Cowardice and foolhardiness, especially as self-pronounced failures, seem the destiny of the liberal conscience, and even the historical primitivism of the African sculpture and the "timeless" wisdom of Ransom are qualified by the twelfth line of the sonnet: "not distant maybe from their gods." Lowell suggests here that even if the African tribesmen didn't trouble the rest of their world, their martial imagemaking, their warrior deities were probably on a much larger scale than their culture could permit or sustain.

"Munich 1938" opens with the names of the four historical personages, reduced to almost empty counters, like a list of substantives; then slowly the men are humanized by the following three appositive clauses. First, they are described as a "confrontation," then with predicate adjectives ("firm" and "against the war"), and finally with active verbs, though of course their action of "shoving the war ahead twelve months" is the ironic completion of their compulsions and irrationalities. Lowell's syntax reduces history to an object lesson in futility and twisted will; one thinks of Auden's "forgiving all/But will its negative inversion" from "Petition," an ironic masterpiece more camp than what Lowell's sensibility could produce, but sympathetic with his self-effacing, ironic anxiety. With the figures of Ransom and the African sculptures the treatment is just the opposite, as Lowell gives the artifacts a fleshiness, even a mythical imagination, as if they were figures on a Keatsian urn, and Ransom is allowed an almost offhanded observation about them that weighs heavily against the whole historical burden of Munich and the Second World War, as well as against the history that was unfolding in Europe as Lowell wrote. If anything, this sonnet has a reverse Italian form, the six lines at the beginning present a problem, while the concluding "octave" resolves it, though such a six–eight division was probably fortuitous, considering the other unstructured sonnets in *Notebook*. But certainly the "gigantism" of the sonnet is deliberately invoked, even if tenderly qualified by the figure of Ransom.

The admittedly skeletal graph made of these three poems may allow some generalizations. Lowell's need to find a transcendent meaning in history has not abated since the days of his Catholicism, but his faith that any such transcendence is formulable has weakened. With his brief spate of personal activism in the antiwar protests of the late sixties seems to have come a growing sense of individual weightlessness in the balance of historical forces, yet he seems to have little if any supplementary belief in the efficacy or worth of mass action. More and more, since the public poems of *For the Union Dead* and *Near the Ocean*, Lowell's poetry has turned to a language that seems to use a personal context of meaning to contain its historical ironies. This pattern, of continuing to note discrete instances of large but almost random historical ironies inside a lyric structure, has been used by several contemporary poets. With Ginsberg we can see the same tension between a lonely singer and a world insanely awry; but Lowell, unlike Ginsberg, continues to lack even the bare outlines of an alternative order. Lowell's sensibility obviously excludes him from the world history, or at least from an imaginative set of metaphors based on such a view, that Ginsberg has drawn up from his distinctive mélange of Eastern thought and natural or drug-induced ecstasy. Lowell's historical imagination often is most comfortable operating with memorials, with some statuary that fixes and resolves and preserves a historical set of values and events. Like the historicism of domestic life in *Life Studies*, with its photograph albums, Tauchnitz editions, and lawn furniture, Lowell's memorializing impulses are inextricably joined with his thirst for images. As he says in "91 Revere Street":

> Major Mordecai Myers' portrait has been mislaid past finding, but out of my memories I often come on it in the setting of our Revere Street house, a setting now fixed in the mind, where it survives all the distortions of fantasy, all the blank befogging of forgetfulness. There the vast number of remembered *things* remains rocklike. Each is in its place, each has its function, its history, its drama. There all is preserved by that motherly care that one either ignored or resented in his youth. The things and their owners come back urgent with life and meaning—because finished, they are endurable and perfect.

It is easy from this passage to see why Lowell found in southern poets like Tate and Ransom a sympathetic sensibility; I would also urge that this familial, ancestral valuing is what Lowell projects onto his ideal of historical meaning on the social scale. Of course, when it is so projected it is almost bound to lose its force, even if it is briefly allied with a putatively sustaining theology like that of Catholicism with its authoritarian pieties and ancient continuities. Such a sensibility is then registered, or rather its laments are then protected, by the anecdotal style of much of Lowell's poetry, with its frozen gestures, its perfervid images, and its almost telegraphic syntax with appositive clauses jammed against each other, now apologetically, now accusingly. The plays that Lowell wrote in the sixties, as well as his numerous translations, can be seen as attempts to broaden his public voice, to widen the range of his audience by at once theatricalizing and Europeanizing his art. But in his later work he returned to the clotted, image-laden syntax of his earliest poetry; and the impulse he spoke of in his *Paris Review* interview, of loosening his verse in order "to get it over," to reach the audience that attended poetry readings in greater numbers throughout the sixties, seems to have reverted to a patrician impulse simply to "take note of" the confusion and the pain of his individual existence.

II

Both Lowell and Ginsberg, as do almost all contemporary poets, strive for a poetry that can incorporate what might be called the flesh of the world, and this need to have the poem simultaneously an energized construct and a redemption of sensation derives in part from the tradition of symbolist poetics and the theoretic formulations of Ezra Pound in his "imagist" period. Pound's urging that "the natural object is always the adequate symbol," and his sense of the "image" as an emotional and intellectual complex in an instant of time, compelled many who followed him to develop a technique whereby the "objective" world, the things of man's making as well as of the natural order, would aesthetically contain, release, and eventually reorder the world of sensations. Or to put it the other way around, a world of sensation, the only field upon which authenticity could finally be tested, would produce a poetry dense with images, that is, with the verbal representations of sensory experience. Both Lowell and Ginsberg have spoken of their sense of imagery in the poem, and the two following quotes are, I think, striking in their similarity, one might almost say in their desperation in the face of the sensory superficies of the modern world. It is also interesting to note that Ginsberg's ideas were formulated in his *Paris Review* interview of 1965 and refer to his practice in poems written ten years earlier. Lowell's remarks come from the "Afterthought" published in the revised *Notebook* of 1970. First, Lowell:

> I lean heavily to the rational, but am devoted to unrealism. An unrealist must not say, 'The man entered a house,' but, 'The man entered a police-whistle,' or 'Seasick with marital happiness, the wife plunges her eyes in

> her husband swimming like vagueness on the grass.' Or make some bent
> generalization: 'Weak wills command the gods.' Or more subtly, words
> that seem right, though loosely in touch with reason: 'Saved by my anger
> from cruelty.' Unrealism can degenerate into meaningless clinical halluci-
> nations or rhetorical machinery, but the true unreal is about something,
> and eats from the abundance of reality.

Certain of Lowell's early associates might be disturbed by this passage,
which reads like a description of surrealism despite the use of the word
unrealism and despite the lack of such elaborate rhetorical and
methodological machinery as we would expect from Breton or some
other French theorizer. Perhaps those who associate Lowell's early
poetry with an aesthetic conservatism would even read a heavy touch
of irony in his voice here: "must not say" and "degenerate into meaningless. . .rhetorical machinery" are phrases used, with irony and
condescension respectively, by critics very unsympathetic to the surrealist legacy in contemporary poetry. But Lowell is quite serious,
though his examples here are not as good as the "bent generalizations"
one finds frequently in the *Notebook*. But the threat of producing either
meaningless clinical hallucinations or rhetorical machinery must be
ignored at least for the moment, while the search for an adequately
unreal formulation is designed to "feed on" the mad surfaces of modern reality, to continue Lowell's oral imagery. What, one may well ask,
is the "something" that "unrealism" is purportedly "about"? I would
say that, at the very least, that "something" is the state of the poet's
mind at the moment of composition. In other words, the "unrealism"
results from the poet attempting not only to record his perceptions and
intuitions, but also to capture the curve of the instrument that records
them; unrealism reflects both modern reality *and* the force field it
creates in the poet's consciousness. Words are "loosely in touch with
reason" because the poet is in the same condition, at best; at worst, he
is testing that clinical hallucination or that rhetorical machinery available to him to see if its *version* of the order of things is not at least as
manageable, as true, as the derangements that are justified as "the way
things are."

Here is the passage from Ginsberg that formulates the problem a bit
differently, though there are striking similarities between the two
passages:

> I have to reconstitute by means of words, rhythms of course, and all
> that—but say it's words, phrasings. So, the problem is then to reach the
> different parts of the mind, which are existing simultaneously, the differ-
> ent associations which are going on simultaneously, choosing elements
> from both, like: jazz, jukebox, and all that, and we have the jukebox from
> that; politics, hydrogen bomb, and we have the hydrogen from that, you

see "hydrogen jukebox." . . . actually in the moment of composition I don't necessarily *know* what it means, but it comes to mean something later, after a year or two, I realize that it meant something clear, unconsciously. Which takes on meaning in time, like a photograph developing slowly. Because we're not really always conscious of the entire depth of our minds—in other words, we just know a lot more than we're able to be aware of, normally—though at moments we're completely aware, I guess.

Ginsberg's aesthetic has a more stochastic slant to it, relying as it does on a more explicit trust in chance elements, but Lowell's aesthetic may also be viewed as developing toward this sense of the need to register the depths of the mind, both its sensory surfaces and its more "bent" cognitions at the level of values and generalizations. Notice, too, how Ginsberg's formulation here trusts that there will be a future understanding, in contrast with the quote from Lowell's "91 Revere Street," with its emphasis on pastness and a world of memorial objects. Though Ginsberg's poetry has moments of reflection and enriching memory and Lowell's has moments of apocalyptic futurity, I still think that this difference in their temporal biases constitutes a key part of the difference in their poetic consciousnesses: Lowell is a poet haunted, and Ginsberg is a poet wishing.

It would be reductive to see Lowell's pastness and Ginsberg's futureness as different responses to their shared revulsion at the present America they see before them. But reading through Ginsberg's work, from the putatively ecstatic ending of "Sunflower Sutra" (1956) to "Wichita Vortex Sutra" (1966), one senses that the poet's faith is more and more sorely tested until, finally, in *The Fall of America* (1972) we have a volume of poems whose dominant mood is one of despair. In *The Fall of America* a feeling of defeat, a feeling that Ginsberg is "marking time," becomes stronger and stronger; the vivifying breakthrough in prosody, the sheer joy, of such earlier volumes as *Howl* and *Kaddish*, whose lamentations and protests were nonetheless life-affirming, fades when seen through the lenses of Ginsberg's loco-motion, his incessant travelling and journalizing. Occasionally a reflection, a rapt moment, or even a tirade in *The Fall of America* will ignite with a cresting fire, but the mood invariably reverts to the elegiac. Again, one is tempted to draw the too-easy comparison and see Ginsberg reaching the end of his career in the same mode, the same chastened temper, as Lowell. America, with her deep-rooted deceptions and her superficial madnesses, has defeated both poets.

Here is a passage from *The Fall of America*, the last stanza of "An Open Window on Chicago," which shows a fairly typical moment from the volume, with its quick shifts in perspective, its yearnings for an encompassing vision, its almost wan scatological musings:

Elbow on windowsill,
  I lean and muse, taller than any building here
Steam from my head
  Wafting into the smog
  Elevators running up & down my leg
Couples copulating in hotelroom beds in my belly
  & bearing children in my heart,
Eyes shining like warning-tower Lights,
Hair hanging down like a black cloud—
Close your eyes on Chicago and be God,
  All Chicago is, is what you see—
That row of lights Finance Building
  sleeping on its bottom floors,
  Watchman stirring
  paper cups of coffee by great Bronzed glass doors—
and under the bridge brown water
  floats great turds of ice beside buildings' feet
  in windy metropolis
    waiting for a Bomb

Every action and every person seem disoriented, despite the poet's attempt to take them in, even despite his offering of his metaphoric body almost as an alternate metropolis. "Close your eyes on Chicago" becomes a sublimated desire, given the following subjunctive, "and be God," to wipe away the world of objects and the field of vision at once. There is a suggestion here that if Chicago is "what you see," you can also choose not to see it, to wish it away and metaphorically complete with a slow dropping of the eyelids what seems the inevitable destruction of the urban stagnation. Indeed, almost all the poems of *The Fall of America* are written "on the road," and the jumpy spontaneity Ginsberg so much admired in Jack Kerouac becomes the only unifying principle of the book. The country gets crisscrossed repeatedly, but there is little sense of a discursive or accretive structure, and a reader might well end up thinking of the book as having occurred in a time warp, with only occasional flashes of some transcendent political hope to break the claustrophobic round.

Some political scientists would consider anarchy and liberalism reverse sides of the same coin, since both rely on individual moral awareness as the central element in the body politic. Lowell's classic liberalism, with its trust in rationality, shades into pessimism when that trust fails. Similarly, Ginsberg's utopian anarchy can dissolve into a personalist vision when the sustenance of fellow feeling is no longer available. As Ginsberg's affinity group has broken up in the course of his career, he has been driven back, in "Wichita Vortex Sutra," to lament and claim,

  I'm an old man now, and a lonesome man in Kansas

but not afraid
  to speak my lonesomeness in a car,
    because not only my lonesomeness
    it's Ours, all over America,
      O tender fellows—
    & spoken lonesomeness is Prophecy

The last line rings with a poignant hope reminiscent of Whitman, and Ginsberg introduces *The Fall of America* with a long prose epigraph from Whitman's "Democratic Vistas." This passage pleads the case of an America justified and redeemed from its crass materialism:

> It is to the development, identification, and general prevalence of that fervid comradeship, (the adhesive love, at least rivaling the amative love hitherto possessing imaginative literature, if not going beyond it,) that I look for the counterbalance and offset of our materialistic and vulgar American democracy, and for the spiritualization thereof.

From the beginning of his career, Ginsberg has constructed a poetry made up of a special blend of two voices: one, a putatively universal voice that would claim implicitly of its lonesomeness that "it's Ours"; the other, a frankly personal voice that insistently chronicled the growth and movement of a discrete, historically singular people. As the mores and life-styles of his affinity group came closer to the "mainstream" of American manners, or perhaps vice versa, since the early beatnik-hipster was eventually taken up by a later generation as an unspectacular, matter-of-fact alternative, Ginsberg's prophecy was fulfilled in all but the more meaningful ways. When drugs and drifting became almost commonplace, Ginsberg's daring use of these subjects in his defiant appropriation of a prophetic voice lost its force. This threw Ginsberg's poetry back onto its personalist voice, and concurrently his earlier technical breakthroughs and his insistence on a body-centered mysticism were being diversely adopted by other poets. We cannot say of Ginsberg what Auden said of Freud, that he became a climate of opinion, but what began as daring and distinctive had by the early 1970s become so widely assimilated as to be barely distinguishable. All the while, the "materialistic and vulgar" aspects of American life continued to exercise the fascination of the abominable.

In *The Fall of America*, we're told at one point that "grey twilight falls on rolling robotland," and it's as if Ginsberg's dedication to a poetry "composed directly on tape by voice, and then transcribed to page," has shaped his subjects and his attitude into this bleakly nontranscendent mood. At its weakest, Ginsberg's music has become the victim of its instruments.

The climactic moment in "Wichita Vortex Sutra" comes when the poet says,

I lift my voice aloud,
make mantra of American language now,
pronounce the words beginning my own millennium,
I here declare the end of the War!
Ancient days' Illusion!

It stands as a moment of poetic daring, an attempt to use the words of the language for their proper ends of communication and community, rather than for deceit and destruction. But in the roll call of deities that precedes this climactic moment, the names Ginsberg invokes are drawn predominantly from Eastern religion. It is hard to transplant Krishna and Shiva to Wichita, Kansas, as Ginsberg must surely know; the only way to "rectify" the geography is to correct the temporal order. But the putative start of a new millennium is cast in personal terms; as long as Ginsberg is forced, either by poetic "logic" or by a greater awareness to say "my" millennium, the poem must remain lyric rather than prophetical. *The Fall of America* is subtitled "poems of these states 1965–1971," thus it overlaps with *Planet News*, dated 1961–1967. In a note at the end of *The Fall of America*, Ginsberg says that "Wichita Vortex Sutra" belongs not in *Planet News* where it appeared, but in *The Fall of America*. If we place it there in our reading of Ginsberg's career, it might at first make *The Fall of America* a less grim book, as it surely makes it artistically more interesting. But finally this gives an even bleaker cast to *The Fall of America*, and the postlapsarian flavor of that book redoubles as the prophecy of "Wichita Vortex Sutra" is submerged by what follows it. The energy of Ginsberg's language has not, to this date, regained the force it had in "Wichita Vortex Sutra," but to expect another advance beyond *that* poem, as it was an advance beyond "America" and "Howl," is to ask for a great deal more than we are entitled to.

III

The pessimistic mood that had gathered force throughout *The Fall of America*—these "states of consciousness," as Ginsberg called both the poems and their subjects—was scarcely relieved by the dominant feelings of *Mind Breaths* (1977). This volume continues the spontaneous aesthetic of Ginsberg's later work; many poems are diarylike, and all are dated, sometimes with the hour as well as the month and day. But the spectre of bodily decay works against the book's other chief concern, the symbolic "breath" that is both physical and personal, as well as cosmic and spiritual. The title poem traces the course of a single breath around the globe, beginning in a village in the Tetons during a meditation period and returning there after crossing all the continents and being transformed into wind and breeze and puffs of smoke.

Decomposing ordinary conceptions of space, the mind exhales itself, and its passage through the world affects physical material (at least metaphorically); but the poem doesn't go far beyond a kind of tantric travelogue. If anything, it is a lament, not only for the fragility of breath but also for the briefness of the world itself; on the surface it's a celebratory poem, but beneath, it is difficult not to hear a plaintive note. There are other poems that stress a giving away, a surrender of all the *disjecta membra* of the poet's life, in preparation for an afterlife journey. And there is the directly despairing poem "Yes and It's Hopeless," in which even "the live corpse of Ginsberg the prophet" is declared hopeless.

As the physical energy has drained from his body, Ginsberg's faith in the antientropic forces of the universe has faded. Which is cause and which is effect is difficult to say, and perhaps unimportant. Occasionally *Mind Breaths* includes a hymn or a chant (with a musical scoring, usually restricted to simple chord changes). Most of these chants were composed when Ginsberg was part of the Rolling Thunder Revue, a travelling show of musicians and counterculture heroes that included Bob Dylan. In these chants the fellow feeling of the old affinity group revives, and the more optimistic, even utopian vision reasserts itself:

> When Music was needed Music sounded
> When a Ceremony was needed a Teacher appeared . . .
> When Shore was needed Shore met Ocean
> When Sun was needed the Sun rose east
> When People were needed People arrived
> When a circle was needed a Circle was formed

The ecstatic, communal Ginsberg has seldom been so firmly rhapsodic as this.

But again and again physical decay, and the concomitant cosmic entropy, haunts the book, and nowhere more thoroughly than in one of Ginsberg's more unusual poems, a lament for his dying father, "Don't Grow Old." The poem includes a section called "Father Death Blues," and it extends the breath symbolism to include the poet's father as the giver of breath, and as the spirit of time:

> Genius Death   your art is done
> Lover Death   your body's gone
> Father Death   I'm coming home . . .
>
> Suffering is what was born
> Ignorance made me forlorn
> Tearful truths I cannot scorn
>
> Father Breath   once more farewell
> Birth you gave was no thing ill
> My heart is still, as time will tell.

Here Ginsberg returns to the simple rhyming-ballad form he used in
The Fall of America and skillfully uses it to create an ambiguity by which
he speaks both for and to his own father. In fact, the use of such
traditional prosody is more prevalent in *Mind Breaths* than in any
earlier volume and is, among other things, a measure of the poet's
increased sense of threnody and grief. It is almost as if, faced with the
body-centered, spontaneous poetics he had earlier developed,
Ginsberg, his body now painfully aging, needed to call upon communal forms in order to complete his notations, his songs.

In his father's death, the poet sees his own:

> What's to be done about Death?
> Nothing, nothing
> Stop going to school No. 6 in 1937?
> Freeze time tonight, with a headache, at quarter to 2 A.M.?
> Not go to Father's funeral tommorow morn?
> Not go back to Naropa   teach Buddhist poetics summer?
> Not to be buried in the cemetery near Newark Airport some day?

The plaintiveness of the rhetorical questions expresses the inevitability
of time passing, the only consolation the poem can offer, as well as the
sense of physical weakness, the poem's central evil. For Ginsberg, the
only larger consolation posed by *Mind Breaths* is the breathing of the
mind itself, or as he puts it in "Manifesto" (a crucial poem for the later
Ginsberg), "There is Awareness—which confounds the Soul, Heart,
God, Science Love Governments and Cause & Effects' Nightmare." In
the end there is not enlightenment, certainly not rationality, but only
mental respiration, the taking in and giving out of consciousness. It is
the irreducible process out of which Ginsberg's poetics arose, and to
which it returned.

If awareness is a final, irreducible consolation for Ginsberg, it was
something like a final agony for Lowell.[4] In *Day by Day* (1977), the last
book he published before his death in the same year, he says in reply to
a doctor who wants to help him,

> I asked,
> "These days of only poems and depression—
> what can I do with them?
> Will they help me to notice
> what I cannot bear to look at?"

For Lowell, bodily decay was only part of his final vision. Much more
painful was the heightened awareness brought on by old age, an
awareness that became fixated on loss and the passage of time. His
historical eye seemed to lead Lowell into many discomfiting corridors,
and his last book is filled with images of uncomfortable nostalgia and a

kind of skewered seeing, a twisted vision in which the present is unfocused by the past. The book has several poems about an episode of mental illness, and the "modern" drugs of the chemotherapeutic revolution in psychiatry are the occasion and the metaphor for his peculiar sense of fixity:

> I am a thorazined fixture
> in the immoveable square-cushioned chairs
> we preoccupy for seconds like migrant birds.

Later, in the same poem, ironically called "Home," we see the characteristic temporal nullity experienced by the insane and the senile:

> The immoveable chairs have swallowed up the patients,
> and speak with the eloquence of emptiness.
> By each the same morning paper lies unread:
> *January 10, 1976. . . .*
> Less than ever I expect to be alive
> six months from now—
> *1976,*
> a date I dare not affix to my grave.

Haunted as he was by thoughts of death and futility, Lowell turned from the distinctive style of *Notebook*—and its final expansion and transformation into the three volumes of 1973, *History, The Dolphin,* and *For Lizzie and Harriet*—to the more familiar style of *Life Studies.* Though there are family "portraits" in *Day by Day,* Lowell also reminisces about friends, such as Robert Penn Warren and Peter Taylor, and about his boyhood in a Boston private school. But the deepest chords of the final volume are struck against three themes that were of major concern to Lowell throughout his career: the sense of a lost past that chides a failed present, where the wounds are inflamed by memories; the curious, painful ironies of the succession of generations; and the peculiar, almost scopophiliac fixation on seeing, through objects, snapshots, still lifes, what he calls "the photographer's sacramental instant."

The burden of the past becomes less historically weighty and more personally cumbrous in *Day by Day,* as the oppressive connotation of the title suggests. It is a complex, temporal sense that we find in the book, but part of the book's central tension can be found in a passage like this:

> Folly comes from something—
> the present, yes,
> we are in it;
> it's the infection
> of things gone. . .

The present "catches" the past like a sickness, a virus; or, to reverse the perspective, the feeling of present futility looks for some origin to help it reach an understanding of itself, and it fixes on the past. Men with a republican sense of time are subject to grave depression when the force of continuous purpose is lost. History and personal health, in the largest sense, feed on continuity; if the moments become merely serial rather than purposively linked, everything is at risk:

> We only live between
> before we are and what we were.

The "only" here is both a warning and an admission of the gravest defeat. This passage is from a poem, "For Sheridan," addressed to the poet's son, and it connects Lowell's sense of temporal nullity to the crucial question of the succession of generations. The poem ends with a sense of how each generation realizes its failures and at the same time, in the very awareness of failure, knows it must continue and hope for more:

> Past fifty, we learn with surprise and a sense
> of suicidal absolution
> that what we intended and failed
> could never have happened—
> and must be done better.

This sense of failure, combined with the unabated nagging idealism, becomes one of the limiting strictures of Lowell's poetic vision. As he sensed his own life drawing to a close, he felt the need to reflect, as he had before, on families and on the pain and joy of the ego delimited by familial structures. In "Realities" he speaks of what his current generation has cost its forebears:

> How little we cost then—
> and so many submitted to pain,
> and even joy, to bring us here—
> they now solid
> because we are solid,
> we their only outcome.

But the solidity has a double meaning, since it conveys both achievement and a sense of finality, the finality of intentions and dreams that have been concluded, "calcified," despite the desire to hang on for more time:

> Houses grew with them,
> increasing like the great conch's
> roselipped, steepled shell—
> left calcifying in gardens,

> where their children multiplied. . .
> I cannot believe myself them,
> my children more skeptical than I,
> misunderstanding those who misunderstood—
> hanging on to power by a fingernail.

The book is filled with this sense of insecurity, and of insecure resolution, this radical doubt about oneself and one's origins ("I cannot
believe myself them"), this "mis-fitting" history of personal time and
succession.

Such misfitting conditions the acts of vision in the book, throwing
them into the fog of insecurity and drugged submission. Lowell has
always been a highly visual poet, though often a poet of visual
distortions—or "irrealisms"—that measure the psychic strain. In
"Unwanted," he self-reflexively relates this "mis-fitted" seeing to his
own art, its peculiar aberrancies, as well as its insistencies:

> I was surer, wasn't I, once. . .
> And had flashes when I first found
> a humor for myself in images,
> farfetched misalliance
> that made evasion a revelation?

(Another important theme running through the book is that of the
aging poet setting the record straight, "confessing" that he hid his
faults under the guises of talent or genius: "I pretended my impatience
was concision"). But the flashes of skewered seeing begin at the most
mundane level, as in "Shaving":

> Shaving's the one time I see my face,
> I see it aslant as a carpenter's problem—
> though I have gaunted a little,
> always the same face
> follows my hand with thirsty eyes.

Here the theme of temporal nullity ("always the same face") intersects
the theme of uncompleted actions and failed hopes ("thirsty eyes"),
though the overtones are at least partially suicidal. In fact, in the poem
called "Suicide" we read these lines:

> Do I deserve credit
> for not having tried suicide—
> or am I afraid
> the exotic act
> will make me blunder,
>
> not knowing error
> is remedied by practice,
> as our first home-photographs,

headless, half-headed, tilting
extinguished by a flashbulb?

The bright flash of light blots out the subject and blots out the false or
"mis-taken" poses at the same time. *Day by Day* is about the difficulty
of seeing with a level glance, about keeping one's balance by looking
squarely at "Realities." "I am blind with seeing," the poet complains at
one point. In "Turtle" he awakens from a dream and sees a heap of
clothes as if it were the snapping turtles he had fished for as a child:

> They lie like luggage—
> my old friend the turtle. . .Too many pictures
> have screamed from the reel. . . in the rerun,
> the snapper holds on till sunset—
> in the awful instantness of retrospect,
> its beak
> works me underwater drowning by my neck,
> as it claws away pieces of my flesh
> to make me small enough to swallow.

Sight is often terrifying for Lowell because it can permit the past to
erupt into the present with more visual and emotional force than the
present has itself.

But these are as much artistic questions as they are moral quandaries.
Lowell, like Prospero, must not only address his own "age," and his
own aging, but also somehow come to terms with his own way of
seeing, his own magic. Again, as for Prospero, this final accounting
means giving up certain willful fantasies, means learning to see how
one was able "to notice/what I cannot bear to look at." It is part of
Lowell's vision that he acknowledges that such looking always takes
place in time, in the onward flow of successive instants; if our moral
wisdom cannot stand this irreducible truth, it can never reconcile the
fixed, "photographic" memory or the "object"-ified truth we find in
facts with the dialectical, "living" identity of ourselves and others.
Such reconciliation, between the pastness of the past—the pictures
taken—and the problematicalness of the present—the troublesome
self—becomes the highest goal of art. In Lowell's last poem in *Day by
Day*, "Epilogue," he summarizes his poetics, his skewered vision
thrust against the hope of something better. Here are the last lines of
that poem, which may be his most moving:

> But sometimes everything I write
> with the threadbare art of my eye
> seems a snapshot,
> lurid, rapid, garish, grouped,
> heightened from life,
> yet paralyzed by fact.

All's misalliance.
Yet why not say what happened?
Pray for the grace of accuracy
Vermeer gave to the sun's illumination
stealing like the tide across a map
to his girl solid with yearning.
We are poor passing facts,
warned by that to give
each figure in the photograph
his living name.

4

"With Your Own Face On"
Confessional Poetry

The confessional poets gathered their concerns from two cultural moments: the awareness of the emotional vacuity of public language in America and the insistent psychologizing of a society adrift from purpose and meaningful labor. This mode of poetry arose from the experience of the fifties in America, when the country first used its mass media to probe and lament the lack of cultural continuity. But public discussion of many issues, like a voracious consumer, seemed to thrive on new terminology, quick turnover, and sleek packaging. Analyzing (and often excusing or attacking) phenomena on the basis of the decade in which they occurred was to become a widespread habit. "These are the tranquilized *Fifties*/And I am in my forties. Ought I to regret my seedtime?" queried the temporally out-of-joint Lowell in *Life Studies* (1959). Sectioning personal and public growth calendrically suggests that historical impotence is at hand. The fifties also witnessed a new understanding of mass man and his futilities: now it was a society "beyond ideology" that provided his background, and the sociologist identified his prototype with such terms as *alienation, the lonely crowd,* and *inner-directed.* Poets went against the grain of this social atomizing yet inevitably reflected its distorted enlargement of individual psychology. In a sense, confessional poetry can be seen as a degraded branch of romanticism, placing the sensitivity of the poet at the center of concern. But in other terms, confessional poetry mockingly inverts the nineteenth-century ideal of "conversion" and "self-improvement," since an almost-Methodist notion of inner light flickers against the morbid self-voyeurism the mode exhibits. Individual "madness" under scrutiny finally becomes neither heroic nor pathetic, but simply clinical. Confessional poetry offers a personal vindication barely more sustaining than the social structure it implicitly scorns. The "long-haired Victorian sages accepted the universe,/while breezing on their trust funds through the world," said Lowell at his most acidulous, though we can almost hear a note of envy in the way faith in the universe and managing the world go together. But the confessional poet was often a failed sage, his wisdom gotten at the price of a debilitating pain, and any chance he had to become a spokesman for an entire community never received more than ironic consideration.

Moveover, a somnambulistic strain drifts through the tones of the confessional poet. This finds its fullest expression in Sylvia Plath, of course, where the voice of narcotic numbness mixes with a sort of slow-motion hallucination in poems like "Tulips" and "Yew Trees." But the strain is present from the opening of the mode, with Snodgrass's *Heart's Needle* (1959). This volume caused a considerable sensation when it appeared; though it was a first book, it won its author the Pulitzer Prize. (This rather sudden fame demonstrates how eager whatever audience there was for poetry had become by the end of the fifties for something other than the desiccated, argumentative ironies of post-Eliotic poetry.) Fifteen years later, however, only a re-creation of its immediate context can charge the book with much excitement. The long sequence that gives the book its title recounts in part a period of adjustment after the poet's divorce; during this time, he and his daughter try to hold on to a familial relationship, though it is clear that the strains of occasional visits and the presence of taboo subjects will defeat them. The implicit metaphors often turn mawkish as Snodgrass talks indirectly to the daughter and, glancingly aware of us as audience, wants his reveries to be on the one hand childlike and simple and on the other touching and controlled. The syllabic verse with its tight rhyme schemes helps in this cause but cannot overcome the limitations of the given situation. The poet looks around from object to object to fix the emotions he can't express directly, but this in turn induces his observations to take on a pathos that ends by courting the bathetic.

> Assuredly your father's crimes
>   are visited
> on you. You visit me sometimes.
>
> The time's up. Now our pumpkin sees
>   me bringing your suitcase.
>   He holds his grin;
> the forehead shrivels, sinking in.
> You break this year's first crust of snow
>
> off the runningboard to eat.
>   We manage, though for days
> I crave sweets when you leave and know
> they rot my teeth. Indeed our sweet
>   foods leave us cavities.

The strengths of this passage rest in its ability to focus the almost-neurotic concern with time and the briefness of the visit by means of the images of seasonal demarcation, which vibrate nervously against the images of decay that attend and undercut them. Argumentatively, the poem has an imagistic tightness reminiscent of a metaphysical lyric, though it leaps from image to image in a way that suggests a more modern aesthetic of re-creating psychological force fields. The speaker here, however, lacks the theatrical self-display of Donne; indeed, there is an almost Pre-Raphaelite wanness threaded throughout, so that the modern sense of fragmentation and alienation has, partly at least, a studied quality, almost a period feel to it. "We manage," the poem says, not with the resolution of Bishop's "we have come this far," but more as a whistling in the dark for the daughter's sake. When she leaves, the speaker will be lost among the images of decay that are all along bearing down on him. Again, it is important to consider the effects of the imagined audience here: the formal "addressee" of the poem is the daughter, but she is absent for most of the poem. In a way, the poem is a formalized musing aloud (this contributes to the period feel), a rumination too self-consciously protective of the speaker's emotional weakness to be totally private and too engaged with a barely warded off self-pity to be instructively public.

"Where but to think is to be full of sorrow/And leaden-eyed despairs": this formulation of Keats's might be taken as the leitmotif for most confessional poetry, and its recurrence bears down especially hard in the poetry of Sylvia Plath. Those oft-quoted lines from "Lady Lazarus" point up the equation of consciousness and pain as sharply as any:

Dying
Is an art, like everything else.
I do it exceptionally well.

I do it so it feels like hell.
I do it so it feels real.

To return to the feel of reality, to restore some sentiment of being, even at the cost of hellish pain, stood out as a major confessionalist goal. But the lines from Keats give us another clue, for the notion of "leaden-eyed" awareness seems to haunt Plath much more than does the pain that might result from plunging past the despair. In "Tulips," for example, the imagery of forced seeing, of vision itself as the source of the exacerbated sensibility, assaults us everywhere:

They have propped my head between the pillow and the sheet-cuff
Like an eye between two white lids that will not shut.
Stupid pupil, it has to take everything in.

The comic, almost spitting disgust of the assonance in the phrase "stupid pupil" adds to the allusive parody of Emerson's "transparent eyeball" from *Nature*. But this painful, forced seeing is still, one feels, better than the anesthetized drift that constantly threatens to overtake the poet. But whatever the reader might feel, Plath seems consciously desirous of either the drift *or* the pained fixation, as long as it provides her with an extreme experiential locus.

> I watched my teaset, my bureaus of linen, my books
> Sink out of sight, and the water went over my head.
> I am a nun now, I have never been so pure.

The openness to experience that some regard as one of the hallmarks of American literature becomes, in Plath's poetry, an ironically balanced pointer that can tip toward either salvation or annihilation.

> I didn't want any flowers, I only wanted
> To lie with my hands turned up and be utterly empty.
> How free it is, you have no idea how free—
> The peacefulness is so big it dazes you,
> And it asks nothing, a name tag, a few trinkets.
> It is what the dead close on, finally; I imagine them
> Shutting their mouths on it, like a Communion tablet.

These alternatives, salvation or annihilation, are here joined in a single image-turned-simile; and the toneless quality of the lines parodies the transcendent religious structure that lies behind them, just as "stupid pupil" parodies Emerson. "So big it dazes you" and "you have no idea how free" both originate in the vocabulary of schoolgirl intensification, and Plath built her language almost exclusively out of various forms of intensification. Condensation, catachresis, metonymy, and the verbal strategies of riddles and allusive jokes: all these and more are devices both to record and to ward off the numbing that results when ordinary consciousness is faced with an overwhelmingly fragmented objective world, a flood of facticity that simply will not submit to tenderness or mercy.

One of the standard critical clichés that sprang up around confessional poets was that the language itself provided their salvation, that the redeeming word could set right what the intractable world of egos, projects, deceits, and self-destructions had insidiously twisted. This axiom still putatively left room for individual poets to develop personal styles and remain recognizably confessional. Oddly enough, however, when thrown back on a radically personal axis, the poetry often ended up being simultaneously god-haunted and narcotized, as if narcosis and transcendence were mirror images of each other. In the poetry of Plath and Sexton, we find not only the subject matter but also the very structure of their imaginations returning again and again to an irreducible choice: the poet either must become God or cease consciousness altogether. Haunted by the failed myth of a human, or at least an artistic, perfectability, they turned to a courtship of nihilism. The suicides of Plath and Sexton, and that of Berryman as well, come into starkest relief not against the myth of the alienated modern artist, but rather against the ruptured gigantism of their own poetic egos. Plath says, in "The Moon and the Yew Tree,"

> This is the light of the mind, cold and planetary.
> The trees of the mind are black. The light is blue.
> The grasses unload their griefs on my feet as if I were God,
> Prickling my ankles and murmuring of their humility.

The poet who writes a paean to suicide and who can say "I eat men like air" identifies herself less as a feminist heroine than as an avenging deity wrenched out of some twisted Nietzschean self-hatred. There are no gods, Nietzsche said, for if there were, how could I stand not being one? "Need is not quite belief," says Anne Sexton, but the figuration of her needs always turns into either a reduction of the deity to a less than human level ("hung up like a pig on exhibit," she says of the figure on her crucifix in "For God While Sleeping") or a rather preposterous, ironic inflation of the human, as in "The Fury of Cocks":

> She is the house.
> He is the steeple.
> When they fuck they are God.
> When they break away they are God.
> When they snore they are God.
> In the morning they butter the toast.
> They don't say much.
> They are still God.

The question of orthodox belief doesn't arise, of course, in any rigorous context; instead, what we have is an attempt to appropriate the scope of religious awe while retaining the intensity of a personal, highly sensitized ego. The irony of Sexton's poetry is often bathetically broad; the line "In the morning they butter the toast" might have worked in Auden or even in Kenneth Fearing, but here it falls limp, creating most importantly the sense that the poet didn't really mean what she had said earlier. Also, as is often the case in Plath, Sexton echoes the language of children and children's games ("She is the house./He is the steeple.") in an attempt to suggest the broken world of childhood myth, a land where ego differentiation and fears of separation and dissolution are pervasively threatening. Sexton, of course, wrote *Transformations*, a book that retold the Mother Goose stories with a coarse irony; and the cyclical, almost litanylike structure of much of Sexton's and Plath's poetry mimics the semihypnotic patter of children's rhymes and songs. The somnambulism of Snodgrass gains a counterpart in Sexton's nursery language.

But in at least these four major confessional poets—Berryman, Plath, Snodgrass, and Sexton—we find one common denominator: a split between revealing intimate details in an unvarnished context and capturing the occult curve of their own dissociated, self-concealing emotional lives. This split produces the particular ironic texture we have come to associate with confessional poetry, a texture we can feel in *Dream Songs* as well as in *Heart's Needle*. The irony spins out of a mixture of self-pity and self-display, and it is woven into the poetry with a syntax that constantly holds out the affective center of its meaning for a dispassionate inspection, as if the language were asking us not so much to regard what we see, but rather to admire the speaker's ability to maintain an interest in words when the experience ought to result in incoherence or silence. Whether it is the twisted syntax of Berryman with its half-pathetic, half-comic evasions and stabs of honesty, or Plath wringing the neck of a compacted figure of speech (see, for example, "Cut," where a bleeding thumb exfoliates into several bizarre figures), the confessional poets were always stylish in their misery.

In Berryman's poetry, from the alexandrinism of his *Sonnets*, to the putative heroics of his *Dream Songs*, the major subject is literature itself, or more precisely, the insufficiency of life to literature in terms of our ability to control the outcome of things. In place of Malraux's museum without walls, in Berryman's work we have a kind of anthology without bindings, a gathering together of the figures, motifs, icons, and legends of the great writers of the past. The last half of *Dream Songs*, for example, becomes increasingly obsessed with the act of writing, in fact, with the act of writing the *Dream Songs*. It is almost as if after the exhaustion of the first hundred and fifty or so, the *Dream Songs* revealed their true subject: their author's attempt to establish his literary talent for the sake of posterity. Also worth noting is the tendency of the later *Songs*, when dealing with the trip to Ireland and the various accoutrements of the author's fame, which include a feature in *Life* magazine (that ultimate triumph of "image" over word), to settle for a more prosaic syntax. These later poems often lack the whipsaw irony of the earlier efforts; as Berryman's syntax unknots itself, as he abandons puns and dialects and crazy rhymes, we seem to arrive at the affective center of his world, at a desire to be enrolled among the "immortals," like Yeats, even if it means neglect and deprivation in his current life, as it did for Delmore Schwartz, Berryman's friend and increasingly his symbol of the intellectual poet with a burdensome sensitivity further encumbered by vast learning. Near the end of his life, Berryman was capable of beginning a talk with a college audience by saying, "Well, why don't you go ahead and ask me how it feels to be famous?"[1]

Part of the tension that makes Berryman's career interesting springs from the fact he surely must have known that the public who reads *Life* magazine was much less likely to maintain his poetry for posterity than was the audience of "younger" poets in the college writing classes. Many critics have pointed out that Berryman wrote an extremely literary antiliterature, fitfully trying to outwit culture at its own game of truthmaking by throwing in the *disjecta membra* of language: puns, dialects, allusions to figures from current events, all creating a sort of mass-media mix, a consciousness as scrambled as the six o'clock news, yet carefully wrought, ultimately upholding artifice as the highest value. Berryman's audience is comprised of would-be litterateurs, people who have at hand a ready recall of thousands of "savory" cultural tidbits, but who haven't spent so much time in libraries that they've forgotten to visit newsstands. The exhaustion of the culture and the exhaustion of the cultured individual are given their final threnody in Berryman's poetry. But to insure his salvation, Berryman was willing to risk all for art, willing indeed to risk his life to complete the last stroke in his self-portrait of the tormented artist in the half-willed grip of a crass age.

In an interview published in the *Harvard Advocate*, Berryman was asked why he bothered to write poetry, especially since he himself had said that you must sacrifice everything to be a poet, yet your reward is never money and only very limited prestige.

He answered this way:

> That's a tough question. I'll tell you a real answer. I'm taking your question seriously. This comes from Hamann, quoted by Kierkegaard. There are two voices, and the first voice says, "Write!" and the second voice says, "For whom?" I think that's marvellous; he doesn't question the imperative, you see that. And the first voice says, "For the dead whom thou didst love;" again the second voice doesn't question it; instead it says, "Will they read me?" And the first voice says, "Aye, for they return as posterity." Isn't that good?[2]

This answer is instructive on many points, each of which illuminates the *Dream Songs*, and other confessional poetry as well. Notice that the real answer must be singled out, that the fact that the question is being taken seriously needs special testimony. The habits of irony, concealment, and defensiveness have made it necessary for confessional poets to expend part of the available artistic energy qualifying the status of their language. Also, the answer quotes another writer, showing how often the confessional poet traps himself in the context of another's saying, despite his attempts to be forthright. Also, of course, the story itself invokes "voices," characterless forces of authority who also happen to speak in a literary dialect but who have no fixed social or historical dimension. The confessional poet wants in some sense to be his own muse, to do for himself what Rodin did for Balzac, to make of the individual artist a type of genius, the grand culmination of an epoch, an artistic style, and a vision of life. Only then can the poet take his place with the immortals, only then will the rules of discourse be recast; thus, the poet's audience will always be made up of the dead and the not yet born.

In the ironic balance between display and evasion, Berryman's Henry appears a master. Here, in a late *Dream Song*, he talks to himself about himself, an occupation the confessional poet is often at pains, though unsuccessfully, to avoid:

> —Oh, I suffer from a strike
> & a strike and three balls: I stand up for much,
> Wordsworth and that sort of thing.
> The pitcher dreamed. He threw a hazy curve,
> I took it in my stride & out I struck,
> lonesome Henry.
>
> These Songs are not meant to be understood, you understand.
> They are only meant to terrify and comfort.
> Lilac was found in his hand.

Here Berryman is simultaneously Casey at bat and the poet laureate; self-parody and self-glorification jostle each other with knowing wit. The offhanded irony of "and that sort of thing" occurs often in the *Dream Songs* and is the extension of the mixing of modes that becomes the work's characteristic signature. The inversion of "out I struck" allows Berryman to have the anticlimax become, by means of the sort of punning linkage through syntax that is the major artistic breakthrough of the *Songs*, a triumphant announcement of new heroic ventures. The not-quite-sentimental reference to "lonesome Henry" is then followed by a direct and fairly unironic "message" to the reader, like those moments when the comedian cuts into his own patter to say, "seriously, folks." So Berryman lets us know he wants to be identified with the mainstream of literary fame ("Wordsworth and that sort of thing"), yet he doesn't want to lose the common touch altogether, as the baseball figure makes clear, especially when he can play with the literary and mock-dramatic aspects of the national "pastime." The suffering and the loneliness suggest the terrifying purpose of the *Songs*, while the ability of the poet to take fate's hazy curveballs in his stride suggests he can also be comforted by his art. Adrienne Rich has suggested that only two men in this age know what the American language is, in all its fullness and impurity, and they are Bob Dylan and John Berryman.[3] I would amend that to say that both men have been very successful at creating a private language out of the cultural confusion of the age and at finding an audience (though, since Dylan's is obviously so much wider, the comparison is rather strained) of the believers who are willing, almost before the fact and despite the repetitiousness of the art, to see in the mock-casual defiance of respectability an artist who belongs at the top of the list, an artist who merits his fame by flaunting it. Unlike Dylan, however, Berryman ends up with a limited audience, smaller than that of baseball, and smaller too than that of Wordsworth, since it must be made up of those who "follow" both baseball and Wordsworth with a disinterested, yet animated, curiosity about their ultimate reputability.

Berryman's art, then, thrives on what we might call the "dirty little secret" of our desire for fame, the secret so bluntly and artlessly revealed by Norman Podhoretz in *Making It*. But, if Berryman was intent on making it, Sylvia Plath seemed equally intent on not making it, indeed on undoing her own selfhood with all the fierce artistic attention on concealment and mystery that Berryman lavished on fame and self-display. When I speak of Plath's concealment I want to stress the counterforce of her confessional impulses, of the part of her poetic temperament that makes her turn a poem about the hatefulness of her father into a quasi ritual, a Freudian initiation into the circlings we create around our darkest secrets.[4]

> There's a stake in your fat black heart
> And the villagers never liked you.
> They are dancing and stamping on you.
> They always knew it was you.
> Daddy, daddy, you bastard, I'm through.

Strangely Transylvanian and oddly chthonic, the father in "Daddy" is one only someone under analysis, or perhaps an adept in advanced comparative mythology, could easily identify. But so great is the pain borne by the poet's exacerbated sensibility that only the appropriation of the greatest crimes against humanity will serve as adequate counters for it:

> I may be a bit of a Jew.
>
> I have always been scared of you,
> With your Luftwaffe, your gobbledygoo.
> And your neat moustache
> And your Aryan eye, bright blue.
> Panzer-man, panzer-man, O You—

> Not God but a swastika
> So black no sky could squeak through.
> Every woman adores a Fascist.
> The boot in the face, the brute
> Brute heart of a brute like you.

Here the repetitions, the insistent rhyming on the *ou* sound, and the tone of mixed contempt and fascination all serve to mimic and perhaps to exercise a child's fixation on authority, self-hatred, and guilt. Who but a supreme egotist could take the plight of the victims of genocide as the adequate measure of her own alienation? Perhaps if we didn't know the comfortable bourgeois background of Plath's family, we could say the poem was about authority "in general," about the feminists' need to make clear the far-reaching power of chauvinist "enemies." But instead we hear the tones of a spoiled child mixing with the poem's mythical resonances. Indeed, the petulance of the voice here, its sheer unreasonableness masked as artistic frenzy, found wide and ready acceptance among a large audience. This audience widened considerably when Plath's novel, *The Bell Jar*, became a best-seller. The novel hardly breaks through anything like the linguistic barriers the poetry crosses with such seeming ease, though late in the novel the descriptions of the onset of a schizophrenic breakdown are extremely effective, and one wonders if they were influenced by the theories and writings of R. D. Laing, so well do they capture the mode of mental operations described in *The Divided Self*.

But Plath's art remains a considerably private affair. In "You're," for example, she obsessively describes a fetus through a series of metaphors and linked, appositive clauses, with few active verbs (the participle is Plath's favorite part of speech), all in the space of two stanzas, each with a symbolic nine lines. Here is the second stanza:

> Vague as fog and looked for like mail.
> Farther off than Australia.
> Bent-backed Atlas, our travelled prawn.
> Snug as a bud and at home
> Like a sprat in a pickle jar.
> A creel of eels, all ripples.
> Jumpy as a Mexican bean.
> Right, like a well-done sum.
> A clean slate, with your own face on.

The forward but incompleted thrust of the poem's title finds completion in the last image of the poem, with its flat irony that at one and the same time celebrates and deflates individuation, as if human identity were both an unlimited possibility and an encumbering curse. Again, as in Berryman, the irony generates a mixing of modes, a deliberate flaunting of propriety in favor of a higher logic of connectivity ("Bent-backed Atlas, our travelled prawn") that suggests Auden at his camp-iest. But the structure of the poem portrays the mind of someone obsessed with a recurrent image, some psychological template that persists throughout many metamorphoses into objects both mundane and literary. The unborn child here achieves something like a mythological status, but one drawn in secular terms, a kind of arche-typal definition by inclusive, fortuitous resemblances. (George Her-bert's poem "Prayer" may have been Plath's model here, though the texture of her poem also recalls Hopkins, the Jesuit priest in Victorian England who could easily serve as the prototype of the confessional poet.) The poem could also, of course, be read as a comic takeoff on the penchant of Freudians, especially those of a debased sort, to see mother or father images everywhere. The metaphors spray out into a crazed freedom and an unrelenting enclosure.

The things in the world of Plath's poetry have a status resembling that of either totems or scoriae, sacred emblems or excremental junk, since whatever cannot release the psychic energies with the force of an obsessive icon must be seen as a cheapened, vulgar impediment to the imagination. This split status avoids the reductive dullness it might produce in a lesser talent, because in the foreground of the poetry looms a quality of consciousness, often imaged as a "blue light," which can, by turns and simultaneously, represent the frigid glow of con-trolled hate or a sublime, purifying, predawn clarity. Here is a passage from "Lesbos":

> Meanwhile there's a stink of fat and baby crap.
> I'm doped and thick from my last sleeping pill.
> The smog of cooking, the smog of hell
> Floats our heads, two venomous opposites,
> Our bones, our hair.
> I call you Orphan, orphan. You are ill.
> The sun gives you ulcers, the wind gives you T.B.
> Once you were beautiful.
> In New York, in Hollywood, the men said: "Through?
> Gee baby, you are rare."
> You acted, acted, acted for the thrill.
> The impotent husband slumps out for a coffee.
> I try to keep him in,
> An old pole for the lightning,
> The acid baths, the skyfulls off of you.
> He lumps it down the plastic cobbled hill,
> Flogged trolley. The sparks are blue.
> The blue sparks spill,
> Splitting like quartz into a million bits.

The poem confuses the identity of the speaker, though we are always sure it is one of two women, both of whose lives are models of frustrated desire. Plath's poetry throws up a welter of concentrated images made even denser by her elliptical, allusive syntax, again recalling a kind of half-structured association used by people in analysis, as one after another of the layers of pretense and psychic scar tissue is stripped away. Her images dazzle like Berryman's, since both poets are writing a highly skillful poetry for an audience of self-conscious initiates who have developed a codified language of symbol, suggestion, and recognition. Again as in Berryman's poetry, the tension created by Plath's oscillation between a language that carefully blocks out and discriminates its audience and a language that suggests full and shameless disclosure tightens the poem into a brittle, artificial construct. Instead of the tightly rhymed stanzas of Snodgrass's *Heart's Needle*, we have severely dense metaphors in which the metamorphosis from image to metaphor to symbol (see, for example, the lines above with the lightning rod, the acid bath, and the skyfulls) takes place kaleidescopically.

In one of the few of Anne Sexton's poems that continue to be interesting, "Eighteen Days Without You," we also see this split between a voyeuristic public revelation and a hermetic constellation of private memories. Here are the last two stanzas of "December 18th," a section of that poem:

> Draw me good, draw me warm.
> Bring me your raw-boned wrist and your
> Strange, Mr. Bind, strange stubborn horn.
> Darling, bring with this an hour of undulations, for
> this is the music for which I was born.
>
> Lock in! Be alert, my acrobat
> and I will be soft wood and you the nail
> and we will make fiery ovens for Jack Sprat
> and you will hurl yourself into my tiny jail
> and we will take a supper together and that
> will be that.

We saw in Snodgrass a desire to be at once childlike and simple as well as touching and controlled; likewise, the run of the verse here awkwardly bumps against the rhymes, as the colloquial love talk becomes part enticement, part celebration. The spinning out of various metaphors for the anticipated copulation presents us with a shower of nursery-rhyme figures and ironic conjunctions, along with a tired metaphor or two (the wood and the nail) swept up in the excitement. But seldom is Sexton this successful in generating a childlike, playful tone; often the very proclaiming, histrionic prosaism of her language keeps her poetry from having the artistic "rightness" of Plath's or Berryman's, and her reliance on a flattening irony ("that/will be that") becomes increasingly less rigorous. In a sense she was from the first the most "confessional" of the four poets discussed here, if by that word we mean a commitment to recording as directly as possible the shape of a private pain and an intimate sickness, without regard to artifice or aesthetic transcendence. If Plath seems to exhaust the verbal possibilities of the exacerbated sensibility, Sexton bears witness, perhaps unwittingly, to the same exhaustion at the level of subject matter, as one more psychotic episode, one more terminally ill relative, one more horrendous familial crisis becomes just another trauma. On a shelf of such horrors as her books present, it becomes impossible to find a title or a line that will rivet us; finally, the poetry is read more out of a duty to at least listen to the maimed than out of a sense of discovery or of artistic energy, let alone of tragedy. The public clutching of her awkward language becomes its own reproach.

Berryman and Sexton were often occupied with denying the direct, autobiographical basis of their poetry. But the recourse they had to theories of "personae" and the inescapability of artistic fabrication grew less sheltering as their careers progressed. Behind much of this, of course, were Eliot's famous dicta about the impersonality of the author and the need to separate the "man who suffers and the mind that creates." But the practice of most confessional poets went sharply counter to Eliot's reserve; as the modernist breakthrough seemed to be at once assimilated and inconsequential (or at least no longer as forceful), poets felt a continuing need to see their art as a challenge to the calcified surfaces of emotional life, "an ax for the frozen sea within us," as Sexton said, quoting Kafka. But confessional poetry flourished in the early and midsixties, and rather suddenly the wide-ranging developments in America's cultural modes and life-styles quickly overtook the "new" manner. For a middle class on the way to socializing the use of marijuana, the revelation of a postdivorce bout of depression carried little weight. What had seemed to Snodgrass and Sexton in the late 1950s as the most taboo subjects became the objects of widespread and ordinary, if not always well-informed, discussion. Emotional irregularity became a virtual commodity, advertised and marketed; cultural instability and faddishness generated their own growth cycles. Berryman, with his obsession with fame and an alcoholic self-destruction, began more and more to look like a carry-over from the generation of Hemingway and Fitzgerald, or to seem like a Norman Mailer with considerably less presence on a television talk show. America could only be titillated by an author who made a great deal of money while he was busy excoriating public mores, and very few lyric poets fitted that description.

So what had started with considerable fanfare died out rather quickly, as the confessional mode perhaps became American poetry's first casualty of a publicity blitz. Actually, many of the marks of confessional poetry persisted, though some people, like Erica Jong, returned them to their natural habitat, the roman à clef. The speaker in confessional poetry continues to survive, but now often in a surrealist cloak; and the secrets revealed are likely to come draped with an imagery borrowed from South American poets. "The tulips are too excitable," says Plath at the opening of her poem, and that same note of a near-hysterical, exacerbated sensibility, threatened by a world of objects and possessed of a narrow range of perfervid emotions, sounds again and again in contemporary poetry.

> The carnation in my buttonhole
>
> precedes me like a small
> continuous explosion.

This is from one of the poets in Paul Carroll's anthology *The Young American Poets* (1968), and it can be nearly matched by any of the following samples, each from a different poet but all carrying a common stamp:

> When I eat pork, it's solemn business.
> I am eating my ancestors.
>
> * * *
>
> Like lemon jello in a dream-
> child's hand, here is my heart,
>
> I don't know what to do with it. . .
>
> * * *
>
> I am one man, worshipping silk knees,
> I write these lines to cripple the dead,
> to come up halt before the living. . .
>
> * * *
>
> I am not anyone in particular.
> A chewing-gum wrapper.
> A streetlight.
>
> Still, somehow I manage to exist.

What we have here is an idiom of poetry that will, that must, appropriate anything it can find in its desperate attempt at self-definition. It is also a poetry that often relies on a thin and fragmented narrative structure in order to energize itself; and this bare-bones narration combines with bizarre, frequently razor-sharp imagery, with little or no weight or social definition, to produce lyrics that might be called surrealist parables. Though they have several other important literary determinants as well, these surrealist parables are in some measure the heirs of confessional poetry. They differ from their predecessors in being more disjunctive in their structures and their images; the psychological world of the confessional poet has been denuded to a X-ray clarity as most of the socially identifiable or personally individuating details have been removed. (Mark Strand clearly represents the high-water mark of this idiom, and the near-solipsistic nature of his work resembles John Berryman without publicity.)

But these surrealist parables share at least one important trait with confessional poetry: they are keenly divided between the impulse to tell "all" and the impulse to whisper to a band of initiates in its special psychological code. Part of the (perhaps unwitting) irony in this sort of poetry comes from the realization that the mere impulse toward a radical honesty fails to insure its realization, since, as Irving Goffman demonstrates, there can be no meaning for the self without a social frame. Contemporary poetry, like its predecessor modern poetry, more often than not seems to be overheard rather than spoken. It might be added that, as confessional poetry lost its tendency to public display, a poetry of the "interior life" replaced it, with an impulse to etch rather than to proclaim, a need to suck imagery dry with the thirst of egoism. Many contemporary poets convey the impression that they would like to revel in their own sensibility and free the resources of language from any ideational or discursive purpose. In trying to explore this sensibility, they often resort to artistic strategies that resemble those of confessional poetry: they take a tepid, defensively ironic attitude, they often try to be winsomely childlike in their honesty, and they accept their own pain and glory in it, almost as if poetry were a kind of alienation sweepstakes.

Many of the traits exhibited in common by surrealist parables and confessional poetry are, of course, endemic to most American contemporary poetry; the two modes discussed here simply isolate and concentrate these traits. The use of a toneless first-person speaker; a relatively dense but discontinuous imagery; a constant, one might almost say a willed, preoccupation with alienation and emotional dislocation; an interior life rendered in terms of bizarre figures or ironic parables: these traits can often be traced, in part, to a writer–audience nexus that is extremely threadbare, and they imply, despite their pluralistic attitudes, a fairly limited but homogeneous audience of readers who generally accept psychological maladjustment and social impotence as the given, if not the "norm."[5] The poetry of moral enervation, whose master spokesman was J. Alfred Prufrock, has become, successively, a poetry of plangent egoism and a poetry of psychological vacuity. Pried asunder from both an audience and a social value, many contemporary American poets have become caretakers of their own obsessions, tending a ground both desiccated by defensive irony and overgrown with psychologized imagery, but seldom visited by outsiders. The concern with craft, with "workshops," and with the enclave theory of poetic schools and critical camps seems somehow woefully beside the point when the reader looks for vision or music or grandeur or even pleasure among the magazines and anthologies almost too readily available today. A reader can sometimes avoid this condition of limited promise simply by reading a single poet's work in depth, for, although what I have tried to describe has become a nearly dominant idiom in our poetry, widespread and pervasive, it is certainly not the only alternative. It results, as do most poetic idioms, from many poets working in an uncritically accepted vocabulary. Those few poets who became known as "confessional" drew on a deep source of disaffection, to be sure; but they also relied on a contradictory aesthetic with neither the energy to accept the terms of its forebears nor the determination to reject them in favor of a newer, more truly public discourse. What we may be seeing, in people as otherwise diverse as Sylvia Plath and Mark Strand, is the culmination of the poetry of the oversensitized ego, the final statement of the exacerbated sensibility.

Interchapter

The Poet and the Poet's Generation

Poetry, or so the comfortable cliché has it, is universal, free of the petty concerns of time and place. But now and again readers discover with something of a shock that poets feel trapped in their contemporaneity. Even Alexander Pope, with all his Augustan detachment, had real eighteenth-century enemies (and a few friends), and, though he often formally disguised their names, he put them into his poetry with many of their recognizably distasteful traits sharply rendered. There is little successful satire in contemporary American poetry, but the residue of the problems and advantages of contemporaneity can be found there. How does it look to an American born, say, in 1926 when he glances to either side as his career reaches fruition? Is there, or was there, anything like a common sense of mission among poets born in the third decade of this century? How did they see their possibilities, their encumbrances? Literary history doesn't usually get around to asking such questions about a group of poets until most of them are deceased, and probably with good reason. It is difficult to see at the time how the "forces in the air" are shaping the poetic language of the day. But it might be worthwhile to speculate, even if a little idly, on some of what was at stake in the contemporary poet's sense of his time and place.[1]

Many people are familiar with William Carlos Williams's lament that with the publication of *The Waste Land*, Eliot returned poetry to the classroom, just as Williams thought he and others had made it safe for the streets. And Hart Crane wrote his *Bridge* in part to answer Eliot's despair. Eliot, in his turn, along with Pound, had earlier made it quite clear how little was available to a serious poet by way of a "life model" in 1913 or thereabouts. Frank Kermode, in *Romantic Image*, has demonstrated rather convincingly that Eliot went about rewriting literary history in order to supply himself with a few such models, however distant in time and locale. Can we see in Eliot's use of Baudelaire the pattern for Robert Bly's adoption of Pablo Neruda, that is, the pattern of selecting a morally superior, albeit distant, father with which to correct the follies of epigones? Bly has also felt the need to step outside the American grain, at least what he saw as its North American parochialism. What was it in Bly's career that led him to attack Southern Agrarian poets and to refer to "the Tate-Ransom nostalgia for jails," as if writing in rhymed verse were equivalent to taking an advanced degree in penology? Could it be Bly failed to see that there was much in Neruda's work that simply couldn't be translated, in the fullest, most productive sense of the word, and thus made available to the Chilean's northern neighbors? Of course Bly did see this, since he is a conscientious and excellent translator. But he assiduously continued to redefine the guild of acceptable "influences" to include not only Trakl and Rilke, but also Li Po. His conviction grew in part out of a sense that his contemporaries were almost self-congratulatory in their narrowness, and no doubt he was partially right. But how to explain his fervor? Or how to account for W. S. Merwin's interest in primitive Mexican poetry? Or John Ashbery's predilection for a French idiom, a Gallic sensibility closer to Valéry and Roussel than to Whitman or Frost?

There are at least two obvious answers to such questions. First, we can rely on the axiom that the style is the man; taste and destiny are imponderables, and they seek their own completions, with or without our assent. Secondly, we can point to the lack of any cultural hegemony in this country and make the point that when no single mode is the standard, and when innovation and individuality are unquestioned positive hallmarks, the plurality of styles will need many "traditions" to give the styles ballast. These answers are correct in large measure, and they explain the small curves and the large pattern very well. But I think the influence of contemporaries has a pervasive, though perhaps less visible, effect on how men and women see the possibilities and necessities for developing new poetic discourse. The anthology "wars" of the early sixties were clearly a manifestation of this kind of influence at work. Several of the poets included in the Donald Allen anthology *New American Poetry* have spoken of the effect that seeing several kinds of poetry placed together had on their work, and on their sense of where they fit into the "landscape."[2] Surely some poets in 1965 had to decide, more or less consciously, whether to ignore the sudden flood of "breath-line" poets as just another fad or to use the example of Olson's projective verse to help them out of what had clearly become the impasse created by the desiccation of academic poetry. Donald Hall, in the introduction to his anthology *Contemporary American Poetry*, speaks forthrightly about the clotted, densely over-ironic poetry he had come to realize he must escape, and the selective anthology is clearly one agency to help in this enterprise.

Consider for the moment some dates. Bly, Kinnell, Ammons, O'Hara, Ginsberg, and Creeley: all these poets were born in either 1926 or 1927. They were to approach their twenties just as the Second World War ended; when President Johnson expanded the war into North Vietnam, they were reaching forty. (Except for O'Hara, of course, whose untimely death occurred in 1966.) The transvaluation of values we associate with modernism was beginning to reach masses of people just as these poets were arriving at "adulthood"; when they might have been expected to be enjoying the fruition of their careers, America entered a period of social unrest that not only challenged its cohesiveness but also revealed many of its values as false pieties. Perhaps Ginsberg felt he had history on his side when he began his "beat" period, for the mores of American officialdom were clearly decades out of date. Bly, upon receiving the National Book Award in 1967, donated the check to people set upon a policy of defying the illegitimate authority of their government. For Bly and Ginsberg, and their more or less exact contemporaries, the language of poetry had to be "against the grain," not in any tepid sense of the "loyal opposition," but in the most radical way they could manage. In the meantime, many of the critics, and poets as well, who had solidified their tastes and their careers just a few years earlier were busily espousing the tenets of "New Criticism" and condescendingly dismissing poetry with any hint of an "activist" stance or content. In reaction to this, Robert Creeley has often spoken against the most widely used college textbook for teaching poetry, Brooks's and Warren's *Understanding Poetry*, because its bias is in favor of a rational, paradoxical, but always self-contained meaning for poetry. Creeley, of course, has gone on to explore the furthest reaches of a personalist, spontaneous, gestural poetics, where thematic coherence or imagistic development is not so much difficult to locate as totally irrelevant. Creeley's poetic forebears would include Charlie Parker, but never Eliot or John Crowe Ransom; culture was something you survived or tested on your pulse, not something for "understanding" that had come down through the ages in some disinterested public "forum."

Yet the generation of 1926–1927 at a certain point took over the public leadership of poetry, as is inevitable with each generation whether it wants to or not. As Bly and Creeley and Ginsberg—to concentrate a while longer on these three—knew in 1975, their work had already been done; the vindication of their vision, their "purpose," must have been aided in large measure by the way in which they had watched each other develop. In the meantime, what might they, or their followers, who were more likely to think about such things, value in the work of A. R. Ammons, whose dedicated integrity never included, indeed actively shunned, any public role for himself, while his poetry grew more and more distinctive? The value of Ammons, in other words, might have to be seen as epicyclic, that is, as a circle of self-protective integrity inside another circle that starts "off center" but ends up being focal. Yet Ammons's style is determined in part by his adaptation of just so much of Williams's demotic diction and no more; in other words, Ammons is only as modern as he has to be, but just how modern *that* is depends on how willingly his contemporaries push ahead and on when they choose to fall back into *their* traditions. This is not to suggest that Ammons is a trimmer, but simply to indicate that any poet who is temperamentally not completely in the vanguard must still have some sense of where the line of battle is drawn.

Place can have as much to do with these questions as timeliness, for each generation forms vortices of interest in a geographical as well as an ideological sense. Ammons's long tenure at Cornell contrasts sharply with Creeley's moves in the last ten years from Placitas, New Mexico, to Buffalo, New York (in part to join Charles Olson there), and then on to Bolinas, California, to be a tutelary spirit to a group of younger poets, but also no doubt to return to a landscape in which he feels comfortable. The spareness of Creeley's poetry, the absence in it of any but psychological space-coordinates, results, perhaps, from his peculiar rootlessness combined with his consistent return to a certain type of landscape—Majorca, Placitas, Bolinas. Ammons, on the other hand, writes a poetry dense with natural observations, exhibiting a familiarity with local flora and fauna that comes not from guidebooks but from hours in the fields. Yet might not both poets sense that their sense of place was a necessary way of marking their own work off from that of their contemporaries? It is as if Ammons is always staking out his private tract, while Creeley is pushing in on his own singular mental spaces. In turn, their sense of place might be drawn up as an answer to the preceding generation of poets, who tended to overuse a kind of psychologized mythical exempla and hence to produce a picture-book sense of landscape in their poems. Again, a sense of how much detail is too much, or what kind of force can be noted and what "local color" ought to be expunged (Creeley has spoken sharply against what he calls "description"), takes its measures in part from the prevailing idiom, the current excesses and deprivations.

With each generation there are elements of support as well as cases of definition by negation. The contemporary scene frequently seems to feature the latter, however. Take the disheartening case of James Dickey, who authored a book called *The Suspect in Poetry*, a collection of diatribes, parodies, and negative reviews of virtually all his contemporaries.[3] For years Dickey was in advertising; he then wrote a very stylized kind of academic poetry for about a decade. Suddenly, it seemed, he was writing a kind of free verse, something he had earlier excoriated; and, while his criticism was filled with high-minded calls to lofty ideals, his poems began to appear in such places as *Life* magazine, on such topical items as the Apollo moon-landing. After his novel

Deliverance became a best-seller, his fame drew him out even further. His poetry was often about violence and social malcontents, and he seemed to be vague about who the enemies of art were, hating advertising agents, avant-garde poets, and academic critics with equal gusto. Then, in the September 1972 issue of *Esquire*, he offered his contemporaries a poem we might imagine he felt *they* wanted to write but wouldn't because they were too fainthearted, too corrupted by their elite aesthetics. It was called "For the Death of Vince Lombardi" and contained, among others, these suspicious, unenviable lines:

> Vince, they've told us;
> When the surgeons got themselves
> Together and cut loose
> Two feet of your large intestine,
> The Crab whirled up, whirled out
> Of the lost gut and caught you again
> Higher up. Everybody's helpless
> But cancer. . . .
> A boy wraps his face in a red jersey and crams it into
> A rusty locker to sob, and we're with you
> We're with you all the way
> You're going forever, Vince.

Dickey was right in his criticism, it takes more than a knowledge of where to break lines to write honest verse. This passage shows that execrable line breaks can be but the superfluities of truly false poetry. Perhaps only some perverse sense of what it is still possible to do to stand out as distinctive can explain why such a poem gets written. If the editors of *Esquire* were his audience, Dickey is a slick hack; if football fans were who he had in mind, then he is a hopeless exploiter; but if he had one sly eye cocked for his fellow poets, he may be flaunting his corn-pone crassness as the last ironic refuge for his failed talent.

   Theodore Roethke was born in 1908, almost twenty years before James Dickey. For Roethke, as we can see looking back on his career, the problem might have been one of being suspended between generations. Eliot, Pound, Stevens, Moore, Williams: these poets were twenty years older than Roethke, and their work must have loomed over him with increasing stature as he grew older, since the acceptance of their accomplishments by the academy occurred only after the Second World War. Roethke, in his pseudonymous mask of "Winterset Rothberg," lambasted his contemporaries and the succeeding generation as well, and he clearly received little support from the bulk of them. Yet he went about the task of developing his language and his talent with assiduous care, taking from the tradition what he needed and from the avant-garde what he could use. But it is almost touching to read in his essay his sense of "indebtedness" to poets like Elinor Wylie, not that he overestimates their final worth, but because he has a historical "lateral vision," as it were, and knows the limits of what he can ask from his fellow practitioners. Roethke, of course, is a great poet by other measures, and he has other sources of talent, but his final patience with the commonality of effort that poetry requires explains why his career is in many ways exemplary.

There has been one especially problematic case of contemporary influence in recent American poetry: the question of whether W. D. Snodgrass convinced Robert Lowell to try his hand at "confessional" subjects. Lowell is evasive on the point in his *Paris Review* interview, and some have even argued that it was Lowell who influenced Snodgrass. Such questions may never be solved conclusively, and they only obfuscate the more interesting question, namely, was the confessional mode good for Lowell's poetry? Many people would rank *Life Studies* as his most innovative, hence his best book. Others insist he needed to pass through the "family secrets" of that book so he could muster the authority for larger, more public statements. But part of the pleasure of reading *Life Studies* may derive from our sense that Lowell is sloughing off the dead skin of his agrarianlike rhetoric in quest of a surface less varnished; yet, paradoxically, the emotional center of the book lies in the faded, lost gentlemanly air of its frozen gestures. In other words, what Lowell "confesses to" is not some painful divorce or psychotic episode. Rather, the confession is built right into the language, as if the words had stayed on one stop past their destination, to adapt one of the images from the book. Where Snodgrass always seems satisfied with his verse, we sense in *Life Studies* that Lowell realizes the language is enervated, that it is a sad but fit instrument for someone who knows he "hogs a whole house on Boston's hardly passionate Marlborough Street." In this enervation, we can almost hear Lowell telling Tate and Ransom, and perhaps even Snodgrass, that questions of shapeliness, of "order," don't take precedence over the available supply of energy. Lowell has also explained that *Life Studies* was originally composed in rhymes, but under the pressure of giving public readings, he decided to use a looser line, a more flexible sense of structure. Again, the "simple" pressures of the contemporaneous situation shaped the poet's language.

Confessional poetry might be the most obvious example of how looking at one's contemporaries can shape one's view of things. Many poets don't like to admit it, but finding interesting subjects in America is difficult, not that there are so few, but that so many seem to have been damaged beyond use, while others are indistinguishable from one another and hence unattractive. But, once it was permissible, even potentially heroic, to poeticize your personal shortcomings, it didn't take long for people to *expect* confessions from every poem. Oh, the poets seemed to say, if you think that's neurotic, wait till you hear what *I* did! No one likes to be a holdout in a circle of truth tellers. After a while, of course, poeticizing personal shortcomings paled, and the whole question about the aesthetic rightness of, or need for, personae and masks seemed bogus. Once a certain poet was widely known to have spent time in an asylum, to hear him or her insist the poem was only a "version" of the truth was disconcerting or boring; the aesthetic theories from the preceding generation about the "impersonality" of art had become woefully hollow.

Which raises another question about contemporaneity: how soon and for how long can a well-articulated or widespread theory affect the writing of poetry? Is it fair to say that a polemicist like Bly will have a very limited effect on his exact contemporaries, who admit the problems but must formulate their own solutions? Further, can we say that his influence will be greatest on the next immediate generation—those who are, say, fifteen years younger than he—because they will need the issues stated clearly when they first begin writing, but that the succeeding generation will have lost the contextual understanding of his polemical terms? This seems to be the case, judging from the many Bly-like poems that flooded the little magazines in the late sixties and early seventies. Again, what I mean by *Bly-like* are those poems, often with a pastoral subject, that rely almost exclusively on an imagistic intensity achieved through a bareness of diction and an "associative" structure, poems, that is, typified by the work of Bill Knott, Gregory Orr, Charles Simic, and William Matthews. Often, these poems have all the requisites for being successful "deep-image" poems, but they lack just that element of wisdom and mystery that Bly's own poetry manages to convey so often and so powerfully. Could it be that once the generation after Bly loses the polemical, "against the grain" edge of his (often self-dramatized) struggle against a prevailing idiom, once the members of that generation all end up working together and sounding alike, the next "wave" must break against *their* orthodoxy? It is a simplistic formula, but occasionally such simplified approaches to literary history operate *at the time* they are being made. Only later do more comprehensive literary historians discover that the simplistic issues were in fact containers or even sublimations of a host of other forces only faintly present in the workaday consciousness of the group.[4]

But the contemporary is by definition antihistorical; it can't be charted, it can only be suffered. The suffering need not be totally negative, of course; if some generations feel trapped in their contemporaneity, others revel in theirs. Needless to say, the members of any generation don't feel its burdens and possibilities equally. But we can arrive, eventually, at some rough consensus of how a generation saw itself, and so far the evidence is lacking that many poets born in 1926 felt America was safe for poetry—at least for any kind of poetry they were compelled to write. There seems to have emerged from the somewhat polarized discussions of the early sixties an uneasy truce, based more on weariness than on any substantial conclusions or victories. A feeling of laissez-faire prevailed in the mid-1970s, as if most poets felt there were a lot of lieutenants and very few generals and hence the battle lines were vague—after all, didn't the avant-garde turn up everywhere, always with the same report?—but with so much left to conquer, perhaps it was best to move steadily ahead and not dwell too long on the casualty lists.

"The Clear Architecture of the Nerves"
The Poetry of Frank O'Hara

Frank O'Hara's poems, as profuse in their inventiveness as they are pervasive in their influence, demand that we attempt to judge their place in American poetry. It is not only because these poems skirt the edges of such contiguous but opposed aesthetic qualities as artless simplicity and dazzling elaboration that they are hard to judge. These poems outline their own territory by operating with a high degree of consciousness about themselves as literature and simultaneously flaunting the notions of decorum and propriety. Just when they seem placed, or placeable, in some historical or theoretical classification, they are off again, saying that such classifications don't matter and that it's clearly wrongheaded of people to ask any poem to maintain an attitude long enough to be labelled. For all we can say about them, they yet remain chastely irreducible, as if they wanted nothing so much as to beggar commentary. But if read in bulk, the poems leave us with the peculiar sensation that we've been listening to a manic waif, someone for whom any audience becomes the most charitable therapy; for as soon as the poems stop talking, stop chatting, their speaker will fall dead. The chatter registers the *frisson*, the stimulation, but it also hints at the shiver of fear, the *gouffre*. Like all great improvisational artists, O'Hara thrives in the realm of nostalgia, in a looking back that can never for a moment become true regret. Like the Steinberg drawing of the hand holding the quill pen that has just created the profile of its own face, O'Hara's poetry startles, as does any utterance clearly self-begotten.[1]

Self-begotten in more than one sense, for these are the most autobiographical poems we have; they make "confessional" poetry seem alexandrine or allegorical by comparison. The friends, the places, the objects, the very reverie: they are all his and all there for us to rummage through. Just by writing them down, just by taking note of them, O'Hara has won for his personal ephemerals another status. "Save him from the malevolent eyes of/spiders but do not throw him to the swans," he begs in "Words to Frank O'Hara's Angel," wanting neither gothic terror nor fruity sublimation. This poem ends with a simple, a necessary plea: "Protect his tongue." His tongue assumes the duties of his soul, of course; it is the principle of his individuation. An ordinary biography of O'Hara would be a distraction from the poems. Yet, reading the poems in an autobiographical, chronological order, we're struck by an early despair, by the hint of a habit of mind that could have been crucial in the determination of the poetry's final texture. Frank O'Hara may well have despaired of ever escaping himself.

This early despair took the form of a fear of his own selfhood. Persistent emotional demands and the ability to be haunted by his own irremovable privacy characterize the fearful self, and it can be conquered only by turning over to the world of contingent actions all hope of finality. The solipsist must be conquered by the improvisor. Once the solipsist is conquered, it is as if O'Hara never allowed his own self to become the subject of the poetry. His self might be, almost always was, the *occasion* of the individual poems, but the poems' focus is rarely on that self as subject matter. His self is the great given of his poetry; it is what memory was for Wordsworth or moral excellence for Milton, that concern without which his poetry, the very idea of his poetry, would be unspeakable. Unlike Whitman, O'Hara never sings *of* his self; rather, his self is the instrument *on* which the poet sings. It is more than an instrument, though, for his various selves form an ensemble whose central organizing subject is always problematical, as in "In Memory of My Feelings":

> I have lost what is always and everywhere
> present, the scene of my selves, the occasion of these ruses,
> which I myself and singly must now kill
>   and save the serpent in their midst.

There are several relatively early poems that record intimations of this despair, this many-selved situation that could be burdensome if it weren't possible to metamorphose this problem into the very means of escape from an even worse one. This is the end of "Poem ('All the mirrors in the world')":

>   I
> cannot face that fearful usage,
>
> and my eyes in, say, the glass
> of a public bar, become a
>
> depraved hunt for other re-
> flections. And what a blessed
>
> relief! when it is some
> disgusting sight, anything
>
> but the old shadowy bruising,
> anything but my private haunts.

> When I am fifty shall my
> face drift into those elongations
>
> of innocence and confront me?
> Oh rain, melt me! mirror, kill!

If this came later in his work, rather than in the Hopwood Award
manuscript submitted at the University of Michigan in 1951, its tone
might register as less sincerely grim. Here the problem is a self that is
fixed yet longs to confront some chaos, some "disgusting thing," so
that it might again become an Emersonian "transparent eyeball," some
self with no private identity, nothing to contain or protect but the
activity of its own indiscreet peering. But it must never look inward,
nor must it see itself in the faces in the mirror. To do so would be to
become a mere object in the world of objects, rather than the sustaining
principle of the observed world. These poems are often personal in
subject matter but seldom intimate in tone. Notions such as Laing's
"ontological insecurity" might be applied here as well, since the speaking subject in O'Hara's poems often loses domination of himself to the
surrounding objects. John Ashbery remarks that O'Hara would have
been amazed to see his *Collected Poems* run to over five hundred pages,
but surely the very dismemberment of O'Hara's consciousness has no
rational limits, and once the dispersal of its contents starts there is no
way to stop or even slow it.

Such dispersal reaches its characteristic limits in O'Hara's long
poems, sustained flights of improvisational inclusiveness in which a
Whitmanesque voice seems intent on driving through the detritus of a
surreal world in order to celebrate and assume whatever it finds at
hand. This is from "Biotherm (for Bill Berkson)":

> extended vibrations
> ziggurats ZIG I to IV stars of the Tigris-Euphrates basin
>   leading ultimates such as kickapoo juice halvah Canton chinese
> in thimbles
>   paraded for gain, but yet a parade kiss me,
>   Busby Berkeley, kiss me
> you have ended the war simply by singing in your Irene Dunne foreskin
> "Practically Yours"
>   with June Vincent, Lionello Venturi, Caspar Citron
> a Universal-International release produced by G. Mennen Williams
>   directed by Florine Stettheimer
>   continuity by the Third Reich
> after "hitting" the beach at Endzoay we drank up the liebfraumilch
>   and pushed on to the Plata to the Pampas
>   you didn't pick up the emeralds you god-damned fool you got
>   no collarbone you got no dish no ears

O'Hara wrote a friend to say he was pleased he had kept this poem " 'open,' and so there are lots of possibilities, air and such." Seen in the light of avant-garde poetics, this poem is successful as an experiment—it is nothing if not open—but at the same time it is a failure as anything but a closed, nonreferential object. The allusion to Hemingway and the parody of his style aren't illuminated by the juxtaposed reference to Hollywood "gossip-fame"; rather, the poem is a tour de force only if we disregard all referential frameworks of meaning that it might momentarily generate. Like an "action paint-ing," it might have begun as an attempt to register the energy that could accrue or discharge in any mind possessed of myriad contents in all their rigorous denial of hierarchy. But it ends as something else: a collocation, a collage that seldom rewards lingering attention or com-pels an energized response. Somehow the poem manages to bring the marvellous and the humdrum together, not so much as fragments of heterogeneous values jostling together, but as an aleatoric set of tran-scriptions, the recording of many merely different things. The things, of course, are not the objects referred to by the words but rather the words themselves, for language here is not employed to transmit information or express states of mind. In this poem, as in many of O'Hara's, the words possess an almost archeological status: they are the thrown up or thrown in phenomena of a particular sociocultural mix. Look, the words say, this is how we came out, this is how we were used *for the moment*. We may indeed have been used to point to something else, but whatever that is, or was, is surely gone now, and it couldn't have been ascertained or possessed in any case. "I hope the poem to *be* the subject, not just about it," O'Hara said. Here he has supplanted the fearful vacuum of a changeless, irreducible, yet contin-gent self with the screen of a jumbled, particularized, but impermeable language.

O'Hara may well have composed by lines, but it is more likely that the poems grew by phrases. The typography of the long poems isolates these phrases, or spurts of phrases, and it's hard to see any other architectonics at work. In the short lyrics this is also true, and the erratic syntax or arbitrary stanzaic patterns present no handicap to reading the lyrics, since we have to get the phrasing right on our own, regardless of line breaks or any traditional sense of poetic measure. Performance, that special quality of an individual self flashing forth in gestures and sudden turns, is crucial here and can be seen, dominant and offhand, in such poems as "Why I Am Not a Painter." O'Hara talks about it most humorously in his manifesto, "Personism":

> I don't believe in god, so I don't have to make elaborately sounded structures. I hate Vachel Lindsay, always have; I don't even like rhythm,

assonance, all that stuff. You just go on your nerve. If someone's chasing you down the street with a knife you just run, you don't turn around and shout, "Give it up! I was a track star for Mineola Prep."

It may help if you *were* a track star, even if it wouldn't help to announce it. This is supremely an American trait, this trust of activity over words, the sense that thought or cognition is a degraded form of motion. Going "on your nerve" requires something almost like a contempt for language, or at least an impatience with its discursive possibilities. This sensibility best registers itself in transcription, the literal recording of what is going on at the moment. Urban life, however, fragmented, skeptical, and alienated as it is, creates a feedback in the recording apparatus. It begins to skip, miss, and jump. The pieces of the pattern challenge the cohesiveness and ask only to be recorded as pieces. Performance and preservation becomes synonymous. "You had to be there," says the observer, for the gesture remains as unique as the moment of expression that allowed it to be witnessed. When words are asked to witness the unique, to become unduplicable, they may very well cling to a few neighboring words and then fall silent.

Many of O'Hara's short poems begin in one of the several modes and then continue in the same mode without development or variation; as such, the short poems present alternative (though similar) versions of the longer poems that surrealistically mix voices and levels of attention. These shorter poems manifest O'Hara's technical inventiveness as it shows forth both in challenging syntactical verve and, even more immediately, in the distinctive offhandedness so central to his sensibility. Take, for example, the openings of poems where this wit begins with such daring casualness. Here is what might be called the "personal madcap" mode:

> Diane calls me so I get up
> I wash my hair because
> I have a hash hangover then
> I noticed the marabunta have walked into the kitchen!
> they are carrying a little banner
> which says "in search of lanolin"
> so that's how they found me!

The flat quotidian voice drops to the confessedly antiheroic only to raise the spectre of urban terror, till quickly we realize the terror exists only as the bizarre, salvaged from the realm of popular culture. The only thing to fear is that our momentary disorientation might make us discover how irrational the surfaces of life have been all along.

Then there's the more directly surrealist mode, where common objects perform fantastic maneuvers, where transformed memories and bizarre projections erupt in counterpoint against an almost relaxed, reflective structure:

> I watched an armory combing its bronze bricks
> and in the sky there were glistening rails of milk.
> Where had the swan gone, the one with the lame back?
>   Now mounting the steps,
> I enter my new home full
> of grey radiators and glass
> ashtrays full of wool.
> Against the winter I must get a samovar
> embroidered with basil leaves and Ukranian mottos
> to the distant sound of wings, painfully anti-wind. . .

This mode, employed often by O'Hara's friends and imitators, from Kenneth Koch to Michael Benedikt, obviously satisfies a desire, felt by many modern poets, to include both armories and Ukranian mottoes in the poem if it is to maintain a level of interest commensurate with the world of objects. Owing much to use of collage and *objets trouvés* by modern painters and sculptors, this might be called the mode of "surreal serendipity." It resembles very strongly the "paranoiac–critical" method enunciated by Salvador Dali; in attributing occult and protean abilities to everyday objects, it has the same mixture of theatricalized terror and whimpering playfulness as do Dali's paintings. At the same time it spins off such delightful accidents as the notion of the wings of "anti-wind."

A third mode arises from O'Hara's fascinated interest in personality, especially as it is revealed in the lives of artists and the interrelationships of his own circle. This mode provides much of the tone that has caused many of O'Hara's followers to become known as the "gang-and-gossip" school. Here the quirkiness of human actions replaces the quirkiness of objects, and the quotidian finds itself suddenly redeemed by uniquenesses of temperament and gesture. The "Bill" in this typical opening is probably Bill Berkson:

> He allows as how some have copped out
> but others are always terrific, hmmmmmm?
> Then he goes out to buy a pair of jeans,
> moccasins and some holeless socks. It
> is very hot. He thinks with pleasure that
> his first name is the same as deKooning's.
> People even call him "Bill" too, and
> they often smile. He feels rather severe
> actually, about people smiling without a
> reason. He is naturally suspicious, but
> easily reassured, say by a pledge unto death.

The offhand approach to the extremism of a death pledge typifies the humor of this sort of poem, where endearing traits are simultaneously exaggerated and excused. This mode of praise must never be sentimental; even a sudden plunge into bathos or the absurdly inconsequential will be used to prevent any sentimental tone from developing. Camaraderie remains on guard against slack soppiness. This mode might be called "mock-ironic praise." (Provocative resemblances with mock-heroic satire suggest themselves. See especially Swift's "Description of a City Shower," a poem I imagine would have delighted O'Hara.) The attitudes of the speaker must shift as quickly as the facades in a cityscape, and everything is both available and vanishing.

Related in part to each of the preceding modes, yet occurring often enough in its own distinctive way, the fourth mode concentrates on sentiment itself. Often seemingly surprised at his own ability (or should we say liability?) to experience sudden occurrences of ordinary or even banal emotions, O'Hara writes many poems where he confronts his own reserves of sentiment. This confrontation veers sharply and quickly, however, into the ambiguous. Such poems can often be either the most frustrating or the most intriguing of O'Hara's to read, and they often seem the most unstable, bearing most visibly the marks of conscious turns, labored leaps, and manifest evasions. Here is an opening, from "Nocturne," where the first six lines promise something they never deliver:

> There's nothing worse
> than feeling bad and not
> being able to tell you.
> Not because you'd kill me
> or it would kill you, or
> we don't love each other.
> It's space. The sky is grey
> and clear, with pink and
> blue shadows under each cloud.
> A tiny airliner drops its
> specks over the U N Building.
> Everything sees through me,
> in the daytime I'm too hot
> and at night I freeze; I'm
> built the wrong way for the
> river and a mild gale would
> break every fiber in me. . . .

Traditionally, the poet finds counters in the landscape to measure his "inner weather," but that process visibly malfunctions here. (O'Hara's play with forms and formats reflects his inability to leave them alone; he was as much a tinkerer as an explorer.) The natural backdrop and the events that occur upon it have taken up the coloration of the poet's mood, even down to the quaint "tiny" that modifies "airliner," yet the poet refuses to maintain an attitude, either of constructive reflection or of purgative expressiveness. This sort of poem offers the illusion of development or variation, but the inconclusiveness recurs so constantly that after a while it's implicit in the very forthrightness with which such poems announce their mood. Characteristically direct at the opening, they always finish off with a zany nonsense (this poem concludes: "the Pepsi-Cola sign,/the seagulls and the noise."), signalling O'Hara's tacit admission that enough has been said or that words have to be put in their proper place. Their place, of course, is to be free wheeling through the consciousness, looking for random meanings, but mistrusting any discursive demands on their formal or syntactical possibilities. They are poems in the mode of "fitful sentiment." This mode presents the residue of that fear of selfhood mentioned earlier. John Ashbery says that O'Hara "talks about himself because it is he who happens to be writing the poem." But this is also why the poems are often evasive and fitful: O'Hara is as concerned to escape as he is to reveal himself.

As was suggested above, these modes, though distinguishable, combine in varying degrees with one another and are often mixed in erratic ways in the longer poems. Each has close affinities with the others, yet they can be viewed separately as dominant influences on various poets who have chosen to emulate O'Hara's style. Anne Waldman, for example, often uses the "personal madcap" mode, mixing it with that of "fitful sentiment," while the other two occur much less frequently in her poetry. James Schuyler's poetry overflows with examples of "surreal serendipity" and "mock-ironic praise," but he never tosses off revelations and incidents just to reflect disorder and hence seldom indulges in "personal madcap." Bill Knott, on the other hand, alternates among all of the modes, using now one and then another in different books, changing styles (within a fairly narrow range) as the fashion dictates. Obviously, O'Hara's influence cannot be attributed simply to the fact that he developed certain stances or tones that would allow personal inventiveness to assimilate large hunks of mundane material. (These modes were employed concurrently by Ashbery and Koch, and all three men form the fountain of the influences that make up what is now all too tiringly, and resentfully by the poets themselves, known as the New York school.) Though his mastery of the low style in comport with the attitudes of high camp composes a significant portion of O'Hara's peculiar genius, I think his poetry reveals the stresses and offerings that arise out of larger, less easily named forces in contemporary poetry.

It could be argued, for example, that O'Hara's poetry, viewed in the context of the 1950s, formed a severe reaction against the "academic" poetry then in the ascendancy by mounting a challenging return to the true spirit of modernism. The breakthroughs of Eliot and especially of the earlier Williams (of *Kora in Hell*, say) had been allowed to calcify, so the argument runs, into the prettified ironic set pieces so beloved by anthologizers and New Critics. What was needed, or in any case what would be most interesting, was a reassimilation of the first energies of modernism bolstered by an infusion of the cosmopolitan, surrealist sensibility. Poetry would once again have a chance to get in touch with the crazily energized surfaces of modern life, but only by abandoning once and for all any lingering notions as to what constituted proper "poetic" subject matter. Something similar, but more polemical, can be presented as a further argument, namely, that the English and American traditions never really secured the attacking front of modernism. Eliot and his peers flirted with the more readily assimilated parts of the European avant-garde but withdrew when they realized what was really at stake. Stevens's hermeticism and Auden's conversion in the forties gave evidence that retrenchment was inevitable. What else might a young poet have done in 1950? It was only in the plastic arts that development seemed steadily exciting, that the forms had not set and the gestures had not stilled. Jackson Pollock and Willem de Kooning and other abstract expressionists were the only American artists as interesting as the Continental giants of the early years of the century. You simply had to sidestep the current literary scene in the States, a plunge not backward to recover something lost or fading, but a jig sideways to pick up the floating currents in other forms. The poetic idiom available to O'Hara was not so much depleted as simply irrelevant.

O'Hara's relations with his circle of painters and poets were the fruition, then, not only of a singular temperament but also of a larger national cultural need. Robert Creeley was listening to the improvisations of Charlie Parker, still digging out a native American idiom from the seemingly disreputable, chaotic cadences of a dispossessed class. Robert Bly was beginning to discover the European and South American surrealists; and voices from the San Francisco renaissance, such as Ginsberg and Snyder, were turning to Eastern mysticism and their own version of the beatified lunacy of William Blake. O'Hara's work was just one more of the freaky alternatives thrown out by the pressures of growing up absurd in the American society of the 1950s. Such a construction of literary history, however skeletal, may go a long way toward normalizing O'Hara's poetics, and allowing it to share the banner of innovation with others both qualifies and increases our appreciation of it. But I would hold out for a more radical formulation of its literary value, both intrinsic and extrinsic. For this formulation we must bear in mind several things, but perhaps most especially the course of O'Hara's influence on the second and third generations of poets to follow his lead. Hardly any young poet today has not written at least a dozen poems in one of the four modes outlined above, and I would argue that no poet born since 1920 has had more of an impact on American poets today than Frank O'Hara. His role in shaping the current idiom challenges overstatement.

His work, as we have seen, resonates more fully when seen in the context of the plastic arts than when seen in comparison to the work of his contemporaries who wrote poetry. This is because O'Hara wanted his poems to assume the status of things, and he was even willing to run the risk that they would sink to the level of commodities. His refusal to mark off clear aesthetic patterns in his work, his insistence that the poems bear all the marks of their occasional nature, and his deliberately nonpurified language reaffirm this commodity aspect of his poetry. In many important senses, O'Hara's poetry takes on the prospects of being the perfect expression of an industrialized world: it is the highest poetic product of commodity-market capitalism. In the two decades between the Second World War and O'Hara's death in 1966, American economics and society began to face, and some would say to resolve, the problems of capitalism at its highest stages of development and production. America did this with its own peculiar, but trend-setting, innovations, or set of innovatory social-engineering techniques: it created the consumer-oriented society. At its simplest level this can be seen as capitalism's enormous and pervasive effort, when faced with the prospect of shrinking industrial growth rates, to "manufacture" the one element that could sustain an expanding economy, namely, consumer demand. In order to do this, and in part as a result of attempting to overdo it, capitalism invaded areas of human activity it had previously left untouched, and their products were monetized and marketed. Activities usually regarded as nonutilitarian, or set apart as ludic and arbitrary escapes from the pressures of a market system, were transformed in both their productive and consumptive aspects. This happened most visibly in the plastic arts, where a pool of palpable objects lay ready for merchandising. Here is how Harold Rosenberg describes it:

> In the reign of the market, the intellectual role of the artist, in which is embodied his social or philosophical motive for painting, is cancelled, and his public existence is restricted to the objects he has fabricated. . . . Today, art exists, but it lacks a reason for existing except as a medium of exchange, a species of money. Art as a commodity does not even exist for

art's sake, since that implies existence for the sake of aesthetic pleasure.[2]

Such socioaesthetic formulations are fairly commonplace, but they are seldom applied to contemporary poetry. Very few people would deny that this is what happened to modern painting in America, but I would extend the argument to include O'Hara's poetry as well, with certain important reservations. Unlike paintings, poetry has no market value (if we exclude the "market" of grants and awards), but its striving to remain autotelic and nonreferential raises the possibility that it can be considered as a kind of species of commodity. O'Hara's impulse to depersonalize his most intimate utterances, to see his poems as possessing their own status as objects, conflicts with his equally strong desire for spontaneity and freedom.

O'Hara's poetry, in seeking to reduce itself to the status of objects, wants above all to avoid what Susan Sontag calls the "curse of mediacy," that is, it will not serve as a reservoir of truth or value, created by an artist and offered to an audience in order to question, clarify, and reaffirm those values. O'Hara's poems point to nothing else; they are absolutely immediate. This flight from the referential uses of language has many modernist exemplars and many explanations; in novelists such as Joyce it is a final form of artistic heroism, an attempt to make the book suffice for the world, or even supplant it. In the fifties and early sixties, O'Hara was, I think, fascinated by this myth, the last viable myth of modernism. His poetry would be sufficient unto the day, in all its dailiness, mundane and fallen and inclusive. But it would also, as both a preliminary to and a result of its dailiness, not have to answer to anything but the poet and his own fantasies. If indeed the poems would take on a "currency" outside these strictures, they would do so by paying their own way, by being taken up as the lingua franca and used by other poets in their commerce with the world of objects and words.

This aspect of O'Hara's work, of course, can be viewed under a different aegis. Some would call O'Hara a modern Whitman, the poet of the celebratory list, the praiser of the ordinary, the embracer of contradictions. We can agree with this view without denying or weakening the other view. As if overdetermined in a Freudian sense, O'Hara's poetic compulsions represent the confluence of several large movements; and this welter of possibilities that he both tosses up and mockingly refuses to choose among provides the richness his followers continue to tap. But central to O'Hara's poetics is the absence of any idealizing impulse, or any clash of opposing values; all is levelled into an ever more inclusive "yea," and the meretricious mixes easily with the meritorious. As Herbert Marcuse describes it, "works of alienation are themselves incorporated into this society and circulate as part and parcel of the equipment which adorns and psychoanalyzes the prevailing state of affairs. Thus they become commercials—they sell, comfort, or excite." It isn't simply that O'Hara's poems decline to oppose the current "state of affairs," rather it is that their particular mode of celebration leaves little room for any truly personal statement, any possible alternative vision. By using the language of fantasy in a flat, commonplace way and by projecting mundane reality onto a level occupied by the fabulous, O'Hara flattens his words into a scrap heap of nonsyntactical, nondiscursive fragments that can do little beyond record—or reify—a world of objects and objectified sensations. Again, Marcuse:

> For the expression of this other side [different from the established order], which is transcendence within the one world, the poetic language depends on the transcendental elements in ordinary language. However, the total mobilization of all media for the defense of the established reality has coordinated the means of expression to the point where communication of transcending contents becomes technically impossible. The spectre that has haunted the artistic consciousness since Mallarmé—the impossibility of speaking a non-reified language, of communicating the negative—has ceased to be a spectre. It has materialized.[3]

O'Hara was fitfully aware of this possibility, this sense that the fullest statements had all been said and, having been said, were now only capable of being fractured; but no countervailing statement, no alternative myth was comfortably possible. (See such poems as "How to Get There" and O'Hara's essay on Pasternak.) What has happened, I think, is that his imitators and followers have not possessed the same agonized tension between this desire for objectification and the need for spontaneity that O'Hara felt, therefore their poetry is increasingly threatened with inconsequentiality. The winners of the O'Hara Memorial Award published by Columbia University amply demonstrate this.

Finally, O'Hara's poetry reflects a needed vision and must be judged as work of a valuable consciousness because it is strung between two poles, each of which offers liberating possibilities and yet defeats them. These poles are the exaltation of sensibility and the celebration of a world of things. As the poems veer toward these polar extremes, their language faces its problematic limits: words reflect order, though sensibility is whimsical and chaotic; words are fleeting when things are stable and dense when things are evanescent. In his greatest poems, such as "The Day Lady Died," the "personal madcap" mode vivifies the "mock-ironic praise," and the sense of "surreal serendipity" ("I buy/an ugly NEW WORLD WRITING to see what the poets/in Ghana are doing these days") never totally obliterates the "fitful sentiment."

Such fortuitous combinations of the various modes are rare in his work, and even rarer in that of his· followers.

Overloaded with gestures and attitudes as they are, O'Hara's poems are so fraught with their insistent personality that their status as objects never fully belies their existence in a special class. They reflect their humanness in a special way; they flaunt it and defy it at the same time. They flaunt it by their very availability (the "personal madcap"), heaving themselves forth, indiscriminately asking for recognition, yet careful to retain their idiosyncrasy. Personal and allusive, like an "in" joke, they say you can't know me fully unless you accept all the particularity of my context ("fitful sentiment"), yet simultaneously they promise that such intimate knowledge is worth more than any merely "objective" reality (the "mock-ironic praise"). You, too, can be in, they seem to say, and by accepting me fully in all my quirkiness, you will find that the value of your own quirkiness will become clear. Don't sell yourself cheap, the poems whistle irrepressibly,

>   And
>   before us from the foam appears
>   the clear architecture
>   of the nerves, whinnying and glistening
>   in the fresh sun. Clean and silent.
>   ("Early Mondrian")

At the same time the poems defy their humanness by their levelling of all values. A sort of falling rate of idiosyncrasy sets in, and the poetry becomes nearly anonymous, like the scraps of printed matter in a Schwitters collage or the *disjecta membra* of a Cornell box (the "surreal serendipity"), floating between the ultimately arbitrary and the ultimately determined. A sharp dialectic of freedom and obsession energizes the poems; in spite of their desire to be objects, they retain numinous possibilities. For all their playfulness, the poems finally do affirm a set of values or, at least, by reflecting certain values in their high resplendence, allow affirmation without ever urging it. These values, of course, are insouciance and improvisation: though the poems want an objective structure, a clear architecture, they yet, inescapably it would seem, act out of a boundless trust of their own nerve. Hearing so many words and phrases that could apply to O'-Hara's poetry—pragmatic; Adamic; individualistic; insane energies revolving around a calculated center; for sale and yet priceless—it should be no wonder if we settle for calling them, and judging them as, completely American.

6

"The Rank Flavor of Blood"
The Poetry of Galway Kinnell

When Ezra Pound called for the "direct, objective treatment of the thing itself," he was in some sense echoing the historicism of late nineteenth-century thought. Historicism implicitly rejects systems, whether of an ideological or a theological sort; and, in attempting to understand historical events without the benefit of any transcendent framework, it tacitly accepts the end of absolute value and absolutist authority as signalled by the French Revolution. Though Pound's polemic addressed itself to eradicating the "emotional slither" he identified with late Victorian poetry, it inadvertently limited the poet almost exclusively to the ironic mode. Since mythical statements, and expressions of direct sentiment, would be curtailed by any rigorous adoption of "direct, objective treatment," the lyric poem might well lose the chief sources of its resonance. One way for the poet to render some justice to the complexity of experience is by turning to his own divided consciousness as his chief subject and presenting the consciousness directly while ironically qualifying the mind that observes it. Or the poet might take different, fragmentary, but conflicting values inherent in an experiential situation, relate them one to another, dampening his own intentions and judgments, and energize the poem through an ironic interplay of multiple but partial "truths." Poets, especially ironic poets, became in some sense historicists of imagination.

From such impulses we can trace the development of the typical American poem of the two decades that span the Second World War: Eberhart's "The Groundhog," Nemerov's "The Goose Fish," and Shapiro's "Auto Wreck." Few poets produced much work outside this dominant mode, marked as it was by logical structure, "tension," and ironic verbal surfaces. The two major exceptions are Randall Jarrell and Theodore Roethke, though both of these, with poems like "Death of the Ball-Turret Gunner" and "Elegy for My Student Jane," respectively, showed they had mastered the ironic idiom. But changes began to occur: Olson's "Projective Verse" and Allen Ginsberg's "Howl" were clear signs, at least with the comfort of retrospection, that a new poetics was developing. It might be instructive to trace some of the lineaments of this new idiom by focusing on one poet's career for a certain period, namely that of Galway Kinnell in the 1960s.

Kinnell's poetry of this period involves itself with a virtual rediscovery of how to view objects intensely, while continuing to avoid any prescribed system. Even as early as his long poem "The Avenue Bearing the Initial of Christ into the World," which falls outside the scope of the present study, though it deserves an essay of its own, Kinnell's poetry has been celebratory and inclusive in its characteristic attitude toward the world of objects. "There are more to things than things," says one modern French philosopher, and the contemporary poet instinctively agrees; but how to discover that "more" without falling into mere attitudinizing remains problematic. Pound taught his successors, who include most American poets, that no authority could replace personal testament, especially when such testament involved accurate perception and attentive apperception. But poets could still remain estranged from things; they might fall into a glorified listing of the mundane, or make the operations of the mind so dominant that the poems would lose their subjects in a welter of "impressions." Pound's influence dominated developments in American poetry so completely that poets as diverse as, say, Robert Creeley and William Meredith could easily refuse to yield to each other in their admiration for Pound's accomplishments. Kinnell took from Pound, however, only so much as could fruitfully be grafted onto the traditions of Blake and Whitman; and, though for some Pound's concern with "technique" might seem inimical to inspiration, such need not be the case. Pound's concern with objective "vision" on the physiological level corrects rather than replaces the concern with the "visionary." But Kinnell was still faced with the problem of how to bring his poetry out of the modernist cul-de-sac of irony into a postmodernist aesthetic. He did this in large measure by two actions, which may appear contradictory but are in fact complementary: self-discovery and self-destruction, the heuristic and the incendiary actions of poetry.[1] Kinnell became a shamanist, rather than a historicist, of the imagination.

The first volume to contain poems Kinnell wrote in the sixties was *Flower Herding on Mount Monadnock* (1964), a book divided into two parts, the first heavily concerned with cityscapes and urban consciousness, and the second almost totally rural in its subjects and locales. The last poem of the first section, "For Robert Frost," offers a convenient transition into the second section, a transition important for the next volume, *Body Rags* (1969), filled as it is with a poetry of nature rather than of history. Such a reductive distinction can be misleading, of course, and it may help to look briefly at the poem for

Frost to see in part how Kinnell views America's most famous "nature poet." The pastoralism of Frost both echoes and disjoins Kinnell's sensibility:

> When we think of a man who was cursed
> Neither with the mystical all-lovingness of Walt Whitman
> Nor with Melville's anguish to know and to suffer,
> And yet cursed. . .A man, what shall I say,
> Vain, not fully convinced he was dying, whose calling
> Was to set up in the wilderness of his country,
> At whatever cost, a man, who would be his own man,
> We think of you.

The qualified praise here may well bring to mind Auden's elegy for Yeats, a typically modern poem in the way it refuses to follow the ordinary "rules" for elegiac praise and insists on an honesty that threatens to dislocate the very discourse of the poem and move down to the level of verse epistle or even satire. Still, Kinnell sees Frost as "cursed," not perhaps as the same sort of *poète maudit* as Melville, but as someone tied to, perhaps bound down by, his bourgeois virtues of self-reliance and rugged individualism. The obverse of those virtues reflects the loneliness, the alienation, in Frost's life, the "desert places," against which confusion the poems offer only a "momentary stay." This surely is the side of Frost that most attracts Kinnell (as the third section of the poem makes clear), and he almost appears to be exorcising those other, civilized virtues of Frost that made him such a master ironist. When we look back on this poem from the perspective of Kinnell's two latest books, the most stringent criticism of Frost he proposes may be when he says that the older poet was "not fully convinced he was dying." Such an affirmation of life *against* death will become for Kinnell a weakness, a mark of the weak self-love, an unwillingness to accept the "last moment of increased life." As he says in "The Poetics of the Physical World,"[2] "The poetics of heaven agrees to the denigration of pain and death; the poetics of the physical world builds on these stones."

Along with death, Kinnell places pain at the base of his poetics, and pain plays a large part in the poems of *Flower Herding*. The first section of the book is concerned with pain as a subject, or at least as a surrounding condition of other subjects. Chief among these subjects, Kinnell places an awareness of time's ongoingness, an intense awareness that this particular moment, this *now* is isolate, thrown up by itself to baffle and defeat human expectations. Here is a passage from "The River That Is East," the first poem of the book:

> We stand on the shore, which is mist beneath us,
> And regard the onflowing river. Sometimes

> It seems the river stops and the shore
> Flows into the past. Nevertheless, its leaked promises
> Hopping in the bloodstream, we strain for the future,
> Sometimes even glimpse it, a vague, scummed thing
> We dare not recognize, and peer again
> At the cabled shroud out of which it came,
> We who have no roots but the shifts of our pain,
> No flowering but our own strange lives.

All New York poems with bridges in them, such as this one, must recall Hart Crane, though part of the success of this poem lies in how effectively it uses its poetic forebears without being strangled by them. This is true of much of Kinnell's poetry and is one of the several ways in which he resembles Theodore Roethke. The images here of mists, scum, and shrouds should remind us of how early Kinnell was involved in a poetry obsessed with death and pain, a product of a consciousness in which sharp juxtapositions and sudden changes of perspective appear endemic. The root and the flower of his experience exist without any system except what they may discover for themselves in an existential framework.

It is in section II of *Flower Herding* that we find the first seeds of Kinnell's "poetics of the physical world," as that poet concentrates on natural, as opposed to urban, objects, moments, and landscapes. Here, too, pain and death are present, almost omnipresent. But the isolate moments, the "leaked promises" of continuity, or of wholeness, become, in the rural setting, moments of ecstasy. The perspective of the future as "a vague, scummed thing/we dare not recognize" fades into a more empty perspective, perhaps; but it is that very emptiness that constitutes such promise for Kinnell. As Kinnell suggests in "The Poetics of the Physical World," death represents the last, absolute perspective; its very finality makes it a magnificent possibility, or rather, the source of magnificent possibilities.

> We may note that the desire to *be* some other thing is itself suicidal; it involves a willingness to cease to be a man. But this is not a simple wish for extinction so much as it is a desire for union with what is loved. And so it is a desire for more, not less, life.

Reading *Flower Herding* as part of a putative spiritual autobiography, the reader will decide that it is only when Kinnell escapes the city for the country that the possibilities of mortality become positive rather than negative. When we regard *Flower Herding* as the barometer of other, larger currents at work in American poetry in the sixties, it clearly stands with Bly's *Silence in the Snowy Fields* (1962) and Wright's

The Branch Will Not Break (1963). These three books can be seen as developments away from the ironic mode practiced and perfected by, among others, Ransom, Tate, Nemerov, and Wilbur, and toward a poetic mode first announced by Theodore Roethke as early as 1950, but largely unheeded until ten years later. Here is Roethke characterizing the lyric poet in "Open Letter," from *On the Poet and His Craft*:

> He must scorn being "mysterious" or loosely oracular, but be willing to face up to a genuine mystery. His language must be compelling and immediate: he must create an actuality. He must be able to telescope image and symbol, if necessary, without relying on the obvious connectives: to speak in a kind of psychic shorthand. . .He works intuitively, and the final form of his poem must be imaginatively right.

Such phrases as "psychic shorthand" and "telescop[ing] image and symbol" illuminate the shifts in perspective and the imagistic density that make the typical Kinnell poem. Here are the final lines of the title poem of *Flower Herding*:

> It burns up. Its drift is to be nothing.
>
> In its covertness it has a way
> Of uttering itself in place of itself,
> Its blossoms claim to float in the Empyrean,
>
> A wrathful presence on the blur of the ground.
>
> The appeal to heaven breaks off.
> The petals begin to fall, in self-forgiveness.
> It is a flower. On this mountainside it is dying.

Heaven and the void vie with each other to be the flower's proper domain; the flower makes claims it cannot demonstrate, and yet it forgives itself; it needs its covertness in order to survive, and yet it must utter itself, make known and articulate its "invisible life." All of these contradictory impulses suggest that we can "interpret" the flower as an image from the processes of nature and as a symbol for the act of writing the poem, or even for the psychic paradoxes of the poet himself.

Nowhere are such leaps from the imagistic to the symbolic made clear; in fact, the tone of the poem occasionally works against such leaps, especially in the last line. But the pain and the ecstasy of the consciousness that employs such telescopings tell us that aspiration and acceptance are two aspects of the same intentionality. We might even say that the dialectic between aspiration and acceptance provides the central energy of the poem and that that dialectic reveals its terms most clearly in the tone of a line such as "A wrathful presence on the blur of the ground," where overtones of an almost biblical phrasing terminate in the flatness of the final five words. But the flatness of such a termination, along with phrases like "breaks off," can't be called ironic, at least not if we use irony to mean a kind of qualifying defensiveness. If anything, the variations in texture in these lines reflect quite openly the actuality of the circumscribed transcendence in the poem, circumscribed because it sustains itself only through an acceptance of death. And the persistence of fire and death imagery throughout Kinnell's poetry forces us to disregard, or at least to minimize, the habitual expectation of ironic distance that we bring to much modern poetry. His obviously attempts to be a poetry of immersion into experience rather than of suspension above it.

Kinnell's next book after *Flower Herding* presents several difficulties; these result in part simply because several of the single poems in *Body Rags* are difficult ("The Last River" and "Testament of the Thief"), but also because the mode of expression throughout can seem half-formed, occasionally alternating between the densely remote and the flatly commonplace. At least seventeen (out of twenty-three) of the poems are constructed in "sections," and the section becomes the organizing principle of *The Book of Nightmares* as well as of the best poems in *Body Rags*: "The Poem," "The Porcupine," and "The Bear." But eight of the poems in *Body Rags* contain only two sections each, and these represent, I think, some of Kinnell's least successful poems. At the same time, the concentration of imagery and attention that they contain, along with the multiple and shifting perspectives, eventually culminates in what remains Kinnell's typical strength. Here is one poem that has some strength but finally fails to be as powerful as several others in the same format:

Night in the Forest

1
A woman
sleeps next to me on the earth. A strand
of hair flows
from her cocoon sleeping bag, touching
the ground hesitantly, as if thinking
to take root.

2
I can hear
a mountain brook
and somewhere blood winding
down its ancient labyrinths. And
a few feet away
charred stick-ends surround
a bit of ashes, where burnt-out, vanished flames

absently
waver, absently leap.

Postmodernist poetry insofar as it rejects or moves beyond irony, runs
the risk of sentimentality on the one hand and of being "loosely
oracular" on the other. Here, the "blood winding/down its ancient
labyrinths" is susceptible to either charge, though perhaps especially
the latter. Such resonance as the poem does have originates in the
subtly controlled tone and syntax of the last few lines. But, considering
the total statement of the poem as a dialectic between its two "sections"
doesn't particularly increase our appreciation of it. The poem goes
beyond descriptive prettiness only by hinting at emotions that would
probably be mawkish if further explored.

But it is ungracious to consider at too great a length any failings in
Body Rags when that volume contains at least three poems that have
already come to enjoy a wide and deep esteem: "The Poem," "The
Porcupine," and "The Bear." These are the three poems in which
Kinnell moves most clearly beyond the suspension of irony toward the
immersion of empathy, and they are, I believe, sure indicators of a new
postmodern aesthetic in contemporary American poetry. By empathy I
mean something other than Keats's "negative capability," though that
concept forms part of Kinnell's poetics. Empathy in Kinnell's poetry,
however, results in an important way at the edges of experience, that
boundary along which the organism and the environment become
interdefinitional. Irony occurs at the center of opposing vectors, at the
point of greatest cumulative tension. On the other hand, empathy
results from a systemic consciousness, an awareness of the field on
which and through which the forces of experience act and make themselves visible. In some ways this accounts for Kinnell's feelings that the
self, the ego, hinders true poetry, since the ego so often defends itself
rather than adapt to new experience, thus effectively delimiting the
consciousness instead of surrendering it to new forms. Such a poetics
of empathy, however, stops short of aesthetic anarchy by insisting that
reality itself has forms inherent in it, or at least that the mind will
instinctively develop such forms for itself, out of its own powers, its
own thirst for order. Robert Creeley quotes Allen Ginsberg as saying
"Mind is shapely." And Denise Levertov gives the following definition
of organic poetry:

> It is a method of apperception, i.e., of recognizing what we perceive, and
> based on an intuition of an order, a form beyond forms, in which forms
> partake, and of which man's creative works are analogies, resemblances,
> natural allegories. Such poetry is exploratory.[3]

In order to complete its explorations, such a poetry must avoid an entrapping irony and make maximum use of empathy.

Each poet's method of exploring will be different, and the various forms of control he exercises will be based on his own method of apperception. For Kinnell, this reflexive act of sensory consciousness often takes shape, as I have suggested, along the edges, the margins of perception. Such consciousness need not be purely spatial in form, either; and Kinnell often uses a temporal marginality, a sense of the "just occurred" or imminent event as crucial in the discovery of the "form beyond forms, in which forms partake." As he says in "The Poem":

> On this hill crossed
> by the last birds, a sprinkling
> of soil covers up the rocks
> with green, as
> the face
> drifts on a skull scratched with glaciers.
>
> The poem too
> is a palimpsest, streaked
> with erasures, smelling
> of departure and burnt stone.

Along with the images of burning, "build-soil," and painful scars that occur frequently in Kinnell's work, this poem has two other images: the human face and a written text. Both of these latter figures recur with increasing frequency in Body Rags and The Book of Nightmares, and their resonances are indicative of Kinnell's attempts to "register" experience with the most sensible recorders available. In his essay "Poetry, Personality, and Death,"[4] Kinnell offers the following observations on the American face, a face he thinks has literally been marked and transfigured by the technological age:

> Contrast the ancestral faces one still sees in Europe, contrast the faces in old paintings and photographs. Is it just my imagination that the American chin has thickened, its very bones swollen, as if to repel what lies ahead? And those broad, smooth, curving, translucent eyelids, that gave such mystery to the eyes—is it my private delusion that they have disappeared, permanently rolled themselves up, turning the eyes into windows without curtains, not to be taken by surprise again? And that the nose, the feature unique to man, the part of him which moves first into the unknown, has become on our faces a small neat bump?

Concern with the face in large part springs from a concern with sensuous experience, with receiving the primary data of our environment,

with exploratively moving "into the unknown." The face offers a force
field of sensitively registered changes and dispositions; it also provides
a collection of "edges" that take shape according to our willingness to
immerse ourselves in our experience. Speaking in "The Porcupine" of
the "clothespins that have/grabbed our body-rags by underarm and
crotch," Kinnell describes the animal in these terms:

> Unimpressed—bored—
> by the whirl of stars, by *these*
> he's astonished, ultra—
> Rilkean angel!
>
> for whom the true
> portion of the sweetness of earth
> is one of those bottom heavy, glittering, saccadic
> bits
> of salt water that splash down
> the haunted ravines of a human face.

Physiognomy takes on the scope of geography, and again, in proper
Rilkean fashion, the transcendence of the poem's desires springs from
contact with the earth, as the human face becomes the source of the
porcupine's intensely craved salt and becomes of more interest than
"the whirl of the stars." The larger systems of signification are replaced
by pain.

Kinnell had begun *Body Rags* with a poem called "Another Night in
the Ruins," which has the following terminal section:

> How many nights must it take
> one such as me to learn
> that we aren't, after all, made
> from that bird which flies out of its ashes,
> that for a man
> as he goes up in flames, his one work
> is
> to open himself, to *be*
> the flames?

The volume ends with "The Bear," a shamanistic immersion in the
unknown, a "dance of solitude" that describes in great detail the
hunting of the animal with "the chilly, enduring odor of bear." I think
one phrase that might adequately hint at how the poem achieves its
power over us is Denise Levertov's *natural allegory*. Pursued so intensely, the bear must end up "meaning something else," but only the
briefest of analogical touchstones appears at the end of the poem, after
the speaker has killed the bear and is watching a dam bear give birth to
her cubs, "lumps of smeared fur":

the rest of my days I spend
wandering: wondering
what, anyway,
was that sticky infusion, that rank flavor of blood, that
    poetry, by which I lived?

Exploration and attentiveness provide the grounds of existence for the hunter of bear, for the poet; and those grounds are both the occasion and the subject of his most insistent questionings.

The hunter kills the bear by coiling a bone and freezing it in blubber; when the bear ingests it, the bone uncoils and pierces his inner organs. The resultant internal bleeding dominates the images of the poem, and the speaker eventually tracks down the bear, hacks "a ravine in his thigh," tears him "down his whole length," and climbs inside. Once the hunter is inside, his empathetic identification with the bear becomes literal, and the poet recapitulates by dreaming the bear's death. The final death agony of the poet-shaman-dreamer can easily be read as the moment of greatest artistic risk, when the flux of experience yields to the stasis of form.

    and now the breeze
blows over me, blows off
the hideous belches of ill-digested bear blood
and rotted stomach
and the ordinary, wretched odor of bear,

blows across
my sore, lolled tongue a song
or screech, until I think I must rise up
and dance. And I lie still.

Only by digesting the blood that leaked into his stomach, that is, only by destroying himself, could the bear have lived; and such self-transcendence, Kinnell seems to be saying, can only be achieved by someone tracking down and recording the experience. Such evidence as becomes available for this act may only be a carcass, a remnant of what has "just occurred"; but, through empathetic dream-work, through poetry, such exploration and attentiveness can be the source of new life. Again, from "Poetry, Personality, and Death":

The death of the self I seek, in poetry and out of poetry, is not a drying up or withering. It is a death, yes, but a death out of which one might hope to be reborn more giving, more alive, more open, more related to natural life. . . .For myself, I would like a death that would give me more loves, not fewer. And greater desire, not less.

The song may be no more than a screech, but it still expresses the organism's need to come to terms with its environment, and for Kinnell such a coming to terms involves growth. Throughout his poetry there flows the awareness that growth involves a kind of dying, and *The Book of Nightmares* becomes the fullest statement of this theme. Though the theme itself might be expressed as a paradox, the mode of its expression in the poems remains that of empathetic immersion, rather than that of ironic suspension.

Empathy as Kinnell employs it in *The Book of Nightmares* makes most statements about his "themes" appear reductive. In a poem that uses ironic tension suspended throughout a logical structure, the thematic argument still constitutes a weakened paraphrase of what the poem "really says," but this difficulty of determining what the poem "says" is geometrically increased when the poem uses an affective structure, articulated more by associative links than by a deductive sequence. When Susan Sontag called for an "erotics rather than a hermeneutics" of art, she was asking for a method much more suited for a postmodernist, nonironic literature. Such an approach might best lead us into this book of Kinnell's, a book densely palpable in its concern with the suffering flesh and peaked with frequently climactic longings. As Robert Bly says, "in poems ideas lie curled under tree roots, only a strong odor of fur indicating anything is there," though we should add that this is certainly truer for the poems of which Bly approves than for other, more "thematically consistent" poetry. It might be possible to indicate the change from a thematic, "argued" poetry to an associative poetry, of which *The Book of Nightmares* represents such a brilliant example, by considering as symptomatic the change from a predominant use of visual imagery to a more and more frequent use of olfactory and gustatory images. "The rank flavor of blood" in "The Bear" controls the affective energies in that poem much more strongly than do any of the visual images it contains. But perhaps the best way to appreciate *The Book of Nightmares*, or rather our experience of it, is to plunge into it, gathering and sorting ideas only as they become dominant.

There are ten poems in *The Book of Nightmares*, each with seven sections. Like the Commandments with alchemical glosses, the poems are about holiness grossly apprehended in a world charred by ignorance and intensity. The titles of the individual poems—"The Dead Shall Be Raised Incorruptible," "The Call Across the Valley of Not-Knowing," "Lastness"—are like titles of religious tracts or gnostic testaments; yet enough narrative fragments and images recur and develop from poem to poem to make the book a considerable whole. Inside each of the ten poems, the sections vary in texture, pace, intensity, and mode. Some are exacting transcriptions of climactic moments; others are quiet, loving exempla, or mysterious, mystically symbolic constructs. The subtile syntax, often articulating the curve of a perception or the morphology of an emotion, echoes the sort of thing that we saw at the end of "Night in the Forest."

Complex and rich as all this is, the voice that sustains itself and discovers itself throughout the poems remains somehow straightforward. It's almost as if Kinnell constantly and innocently surprises himself, finding, "as he obeys the necessity and falls," that "the dead lie,/empty, filled, at the beginning,/and the first/voice comes craving again out of their mouths." The young daughter who "puts/her hand/into her father's mouth, to take hold of/his song" is the initial addressee of the book (if such a spirit can be described by that rhetorical term), and her innocent grasping after the human voice stands for the central mystery that is both the cause and the occasion of Kinnell's book. Again, the human face and the work of art are the key traces of emotion.

In Kinnell's poetry, deeply human utterances are like animals. They are best witnessed as expressive gestures. The bear that concluded *Body Rags* makes several reappearances in this book, in several guises. Nowhere does he speak, but he is witness to human speech whether he "sits alone/on his hillside, nodding from side/to side" or is "floundering through chaos/in his starry blubber" as Ursa Major. Notice too the shifting perspective, the sudden awareness of infinite extension for the bear, something that happens frequently in these poems. Other images besides the bear recur, each equally part of the failed flesh of the world as well as of its fulfillment. A decapitated hen becomes a hen-flower, filled with a "mass of tiny,/unborn eggs, each getting/tinier and yellower as it reaches back toward/the icy pulp/of what is." An unborn child can "rouse himself/with a huge, fishy thrash, and resettle in his darkness."

The Book of Nightmares, filled with obsessive images, carries back from the darkness a "languished alphabet." But this set of characters can spell more than objects; it speaks as well of people and events. The daughter who appears in the first and the son who hears the final reflections of the poem are just two, though the two most important, of the people with whom Kinnell converses. Indeed, if one were to formulate a thematic statement equivalent to the poem's energies, that statement would have to recognize the daughter's birth and the poet's own imagined death as the terminal points of the work. There is also a "stranger extant in the memory" though extinct from the palpable world, perhaps a suicide, but certainly a possessed individual who defines for the poet not only the limits of pain but also the body that suffers, "all bodies, one body, one light/made of everyone's darkness together."

Again, it should be pointed out that the book succeeds beautifully as a whole; but what makes the total more than the sum of the parts is the tough, but complexly responsive, sense of form that Kinnell has discovered for his own voice. Each of the ten poems is variously incendiary and heuristic. The poet's attention burns through level after level, each vision catching up sparks and flashes from other sightings. The fires of the world must be met with fire if the poet is to truly discover all the edges of his possibilities. "Somewhere/in the legends of blood sacrifice/the fatted calf/takes the bonfire into his arms, and *he*/burns *it*."

Destructive though the element of fire may be, Kinnell's forms are always instructive. There is an almost didactic tone in some parts of this book, a didacticism close to the evangelical. (That alone should make the book distinct from the dominant modern mode of irony.) But the poet draws back from priesthood because he continually rediscovers himself, and discovers in himself "the hunger to be new." Proposing new visions, like Adam he awakes to find them true: "The witness trees heal/their scars at the flesh fire." Nightmares are incendiary, but the book is heuristic. Or, to put it another way, what we see in our nightmares will surely char us unless we can transcribe it. The shaman-speaker of the last poem in *Body Rags* ends his days wondering; but in this later book, the shaman-speaker is closer to the answer to that question, "what. . .was the rank flavor of blood. . .by which I lived?" Again, it is through dream that the answer is formulated:

> a face materializes into your hands,
> on the absolute whiteness of pages
> a poem writes itself out: its title—the dream
> of all poems and the text
> of all loves—"Tenderness toward Existence."

Once more the human face and the poetic text coincide to register the vision. Learn, he tells his child, "to reach deeper/into the sorrows/to come," anticipate the "still undanced cadence of vanishing." Then, with the child soothed and put back to sleep, he adds a promise. The promise is to learn, even if the lesson is preceded by destruction, and the promise constitutes Kinnell's testament.

> Little sleep's-head sprouting hair in the moonlight,
> when I come back
> we will go out together,
> we will walk out together among
> the ten thousand things,

> each scratched too late with such knowledge, *the*
> *wages of dying is love.*

Kinnell has discovered his own way of looking at things here, and though irony may be weakened, certainly American poetry is the stronger for it.

"Rejoice in the Gathering Dark"
The Poetry of Robert Bly

Since *Silence in the Snowy Fields* appeared over fifteen years ago, Robert Bly has steadily accumulated a poetry of secrecy and exultation, that most difficult of combinations. While excoriating the destructiveness of false public values, he insists on a silencing solitude as the primary poetic discipline. Diving into the stillest mythical recesses, he resurfaces with thrashing energy, intensely unwilling to settle for any but the most blinding light. His body of work is relatively small—certainly smaller than that of others of his generation such as Levertov, Snyder, and Ashbery—and this sharpens the sense of a patient accumulation. In describing his contemporary Robert Creeley, Bly uses the prose poem to simultaneously heroize, domesticate, and totemize:

> The beak is a crow beak, and the sideways look he gives, the head shoved slightly to the side by the bad eye, finishes it. And I suppose his language in poems is crow language—no long open vowels, like the owl, no howls like the wolf, but instead short, faintly hollow, harsh sounds, that all together make something genuine, crow speech coming up from every feather, every source of that crow body and crow life.
> The crows take very good care of their children, and are the most intelligent of birds, and wary of human company, though when two or three fly over the countryside together, they look almost happy.

Though not the total picture, this offers a good grounding in Bly's poetics. For him, authentic language arises out of a depth, "coming up from. . .every source," and is never to be thought of as floating or being passed around aimlessly. All artistic intuition is body centered, all "thou-saying" becomes a way of being-in-the-world. Articulations of the tongue are simply higher forms of the organism's exploration and control of the environment: adjustments, like the tilt of the head, to assure the proper perceptual thrust. But physical harmony provides for moral equilibrium, and we have a moral obligation to be intelligent for the sake of the species. We ought not to seek to illumine nature so much as to make her dark energies the source of our own. The health of the individual's interior life measures the higher truths, for if we are concealed from ourselves, we will destroy everything that doesn't blend with our own ego.

You will notice, of course, how the poetics have become an ethic. But the highest virtue, aesthetically and morally, is patience:

> Beneath the waters, since I was a boy,
> I have dreamt of strange and dark treasures,
> Not of gold, or strange stones, but the true
> Gift, beneath the pale lakes of Minnesota.
>
> This morning also, drifting in the dawn wind,
> I sense my hands, and my shoes, and this ink—
> Drifting, as all of this body drifts,
> Above the clouds of the flesh and the stone.
>
> A few friendships, a few dawns, a few glimpses of grass,
> A few oars weathered by the snow and the heat,
> So we drift toward shore, over cold waters,
> No longer caring if we drift or go straight.

It may seem odd to think of patience in connection with Robert Bly, when for many he remains a master polemicist, a "self-advertising" publicist (Allen Tate's view), or an intemperate dissenter. Bly has touched and often irritated virtually every poet and every issue in contemporary poetry in at least one of his roles: editor, satirist, theorizer, organizer, translator, regionalist, prizewinner, and iconoclast. One might well say, as Eliot said of Pound and Chinese poetry, that Bly has invented South American poetry for our time. No literary history of the last twenty years would be complete without reference to Bly's magazine, *The Sixties*. And few social aestheticians would ignore Bly's acceptance speech at the 1968 National Book Awards ceremony: "I know I am speaking for many, many American poets when I ask this question: since we are murdering a culture in Vietnam at least as fine as our own, have we the right to congratulate ourselves on our cultural magnificence? Isn't that out of place?"[1]

As a critic and as a poetic theorist, Bly has contributed much to the recent shift from a tightly ordered, highly structured verse, with irony as its dominant mode, toward a poetry more open in form, associative in structure, and ecstatic in intention. When people attempt a balanced assessment of his accomplishments, though, his criticism all too often outweighs his poetry. It has become almost necessary to right this situation and concentrate for a while on Bly's poetry, placing, where possible, his criticism in relation to *it* rather than picking at the poems through the grid of the polemics. What follows is an attempt to do just that; but before proceeding, it will be useful to have before us at least two of Bly's critical assumptions, assumptions unavoidably central to his work and almost invisibly dispersed throughout it. The first, from a

review of David Ignatow's poetry, argues for a proper sense of the
position of ideas in poetry:

> In the most nourishing prose or poetry, I think, we always find ideas. But
> an essay and a poem are different in the way an idea lies inside them. In an
> essay, obviously, the idea must be clear—every inch of the idea's skin
> should be visible. The idea should be laid out flat—like the skin of a
> goat—we should be able to walk around it, tell the head from the tail. Ideas
> in poems don't appear that way—in poems ideas lie curled under tree
> roots, only a strong odor of fur indicating anything is there. . . .To learn to
> read poetry in fact we have to learn to reach in and uncover ideas, which
> actually are so much fresher than the ideas in prose precisely because they
> have been lying curled.

As several people have pointed out, William Carlos Williams did not
say "no ideas, only things," but rather "no ideas but in things."
Likewise, Bly doesn't exclude ideas or choke them into submission or
dilute them into mere fancies when he writes his poems. Instead, he
places himself differently in relation to the idea, approaches it differently, than would a writer of expository prose or more traditional
poetry. Ideas lie close to the source of nourishment and support in his
poems, but they must work their way in almost by stealth. Bly's use of
animal imagery, his emphasis on olfactory and kinesthetic sensation,
tells us more about his "thinking" than any paraphrase can. His
thought aspires to a form in which gesture and intention are the same,
to an integrity that ties together perception and conception, object and
subject. His psychology and epistemology are clearly much closer to
those of the phenomenologists (such as Merleau-Ponty) than those of
the classical materialists or idealists.

The other principle in Bly's poetics creates more heat than light in his
polemics but vitalizes his poetry in ways that are very important: it
claims that technique is the work of rationality, ego, and hence suffocation:

> I refuse to say anything at all about prosody. What an ugly word it is! In the
> true poem, both the form and the content rise from the same place; they
> have the same swiftness and darkness. Both are expressions of a certain
> rebellious energy rising in the psyche: they are what Boehme calls "the
> shooting up of life from nature to spirit." What is important is this rebel-
> lious energy, not technique. If I write a bad poem it is because I have
> somehow taken the thought from someone else—I haven't really lived it: it
> isn't my energy. Technique is beside the point in this matter.

Such a doctrine, in the hands of unskilled enthusiasts (critics as well as
poets), might easily spell bathos. But the theories of Eliot and Pound
had begun to do the same when Bly wrote this. Few phenomena need a
clarifying historical context more than literary theories do; we can

identify what past and established theories these words are attacking more easily than we can see, precisely, where they will lead. Thus, Bly's poetics resembles his populist political sentiment: it is rooted in deep feeling, intimately "known" but seldom analyzed, and often more vigorous in its denials than its affirmations.

The positive aspects of Bly's poetics revolve around his concentration on the image. In a series of reviews and essays in *The Sixties*, Bly, in conjunction with James Wright, erected a theory concerning the "subjective image," produced by the workings of the transrational mind, charged with mythical resonances, and bearing the major responsibility for organizing the poem's energies. This image, as the passage above suggests, resulted more from a special gathering of consciousness than from any purely verbal manipulation; it came from a region beyond syntax, and it had powers more than grammatical. To write such poetry, one needed a carefully plotted surrender, and to read it required a discipline less passive than deeply meditative. "But at last, the quiet waters of the night will rise,/And our skin shall see far off, as it does under water." Bly's own images are often liquid and cold, like lake waters soundless and dark, and the poems are often filled with gazes and deep snow. They end with suddenly opened vistas, consoling with something like infinite regress ("Our ears hear tinier sounds,/Reaching far away east in the early darkness.") or vague, indefinable threats ("The doors are open, many are called to silence"). Obviously, the poetry needed the theorizing to clear space for what might otherwise have been a scant, febrile, and barren order.

II

Bly draws up his poetic sensibility out of at least three obvious sources: the heritage of imagism, with its brevity at once precise and evocative; the argumentative diffidence, especially in metaphysical matters, associated with the haiku; and the body-centered mysticism perfected by such Protestant writers as Jakob Boehme. This relatively wide-ranging literary mix both precedes and results from Bly's interest in translation, for he is quick to appropriate structures of feeling and thought from whatever region or epoch he finds necessary and usable. "We reason with a later reason," as Stevens says, and few writers are more aware that they are drawing on an extensive, multivalent jumble of traditions than is Bly. For all his emphasis on cutting against the grain of too readily accepted poetic modes, and for all his antipathy to questions of technique, Bly demands of himself an unequivocally *centered* sense of his vocation—it is only because his aesthetic geometry seems eccentric to others that his polemics become necessary. What critics might view as the limitations of various modes, he insists on regarding as poetic necessities. For example, I spoke above of the diffidence associated with the haiku; but Bly argues that only when the forces of rationality are stilled, or at least dampened, can the configuration of emotions rightly shape the poem's truth. What some might see as a poetry based on modesty or exclusion, he sees as daring and assertive. Far from reluctant to address ideas in prose argument, Bly makes his own poetic statements turn aside from the ease of identifiable cognitive patterns and plunge instead into dense, pathless areas of experience and darkly associative pools of feeling.

Such a sensibility as Bly has developed could easily lead to a host of predictable enactments and debilitating excesses when the time came to write individual lyrics. A memorable life-style, or even a reassuringly human conscience, as Bly's critics rather smugly repeat, cannot guarantee verbal magic. My sense of Bly's poetry is that it exhibits the skill it does because of its author's high seriousness, but such a sense can only be averred, not demonstrated. However, we can register the characteristic energy of Bly's lyrics by exploring them as resolutions (not solutions, in the sense of problems disposed of, but resolutions, in the sense of a consciousness articulated) through which two apparently opposing compulsions redefine one another. One of these compulsions is most visible as theme, the other as style. Thematically, the concerns of meditative poetry, namely the structures of consciousness and the relation of fact and value, outline the range and subject of these poems. Poetry for Bly offers a criticism of life, but a criticism available only through discipline, by a rectification of thought and feeling. Bly's antiwar poetry doesn't settle for expressing humanistic values; rather, he alleges that the grossest forms of false consciousness are necessary for such inhumanity as a war to occur and that only through a fundamental relearning of the world can it be prevented. This accounts for Bly's aggressive, sometimes intemperate modernism: he sees the poet simultaneously as a solitary craftsman and as a moral scourge.

With regard to style, the language of ecstasy and spiritual autobiography energizes Bly's exploration of his themes. Resembling voices employed by authors as distinct as Thoreau and Mailer, this style employs a dialectical structure as it oscillates between ecphrasis, or heightened description, and a schematizing impulse akin to allegory. Bly insists that the reader surrender to the moment, the intensely peculiar conjunction of sensations stripped of any mediating common circumstances. On the other hand, any satori can be equivalent to any other; the hidden world constantly surrounds us, and any breakthrough, despite and almost by virtue of its arbitrariness, can serve as a template to reassure and instruct readers in the abiding presence of that hidden order. The sacred, masked by the ordinary, escapes our vision, trained as it is to look for the wrong significances. Neither strictly transcendental nor existential, Bly's style owes much to these "methods," especially in their American guises.

This apparent disjunction of theme and style may explain the difficulty many readers have with Bly's poetry. Meditative poetry often conveys a highly developed discursive sense, willing to be patiently self-correcting, never totally sundered from its framework of ideas, though never subsumed by it. To know our own minds or the landscapes that surround, shape, and support us, we must open out deliberately, intent and almost passive, like a snowy field. Autobiographical or ecstatic poetry, on the other hand, proceeds by what Bly calls "leaping," a nondiscursive, elliptical process that stakes everything on the momentary verbal gesture. All accumulative or qualified judgments are untrustworthy; we must be willing to jump from our bodies (or drop, renewed, back into them), as anxious as the silent dark itself to blanket the false lights of the rational mind. Fully responsive readers of Bly's poetry need to undergo long preparation, disciplined and meditative, and yet be willing to undo it all at a moment's notice. This, too, explains why Bly resorts to polemics and chafes at technique: the protective space around his poetry has been laboriously cleared, though he chooses to conceal the evidence of axe and plumb.

Running as an almost silent current beneath this part of Bly's work is a strain of prophetic or chthonic music, a response to very large rhythmic pulses, caught in a vision that can zoom from a nearly microscopic to an archeological measure. This, too, can be confusing, sometimes even toneless, as in "Looking at Some Flowers":

> Light is around the petals, and behind them:
> Some petals are living on the other side of the light.
> Like sunlight drifting onto the carpet.
> Where the casket stands, not knowing which world it is in.
> And fuzzy leaves, hair growing from some animal
> Buried in the green trenches of the plant.
> Or the ground this house is on,
> Only free of the sea for five or six thousand years.

The one word "only" conveys almost all the emotion of the poem, though of course its placement and its context make such emotion available to it. But this is often part of Bly's effect, a sense that we are sharing some secret, glimpsing some long concealed vista that closes shut as soon as the poem ends. In the political poetry this often causes people to complain that Bly is preaching to the converted, but of course such people seldom admit that no poetry built on political vision has much *persuasive* power, whatever its strengths and reassurances. When we call Bly a "nature" poet, we must remember that visions of nature are as various as political opinions and are often the result of an ineffable mixture of temperament, experience, and self-discipline. Also, Bly's political poetry earns some of its most moving successes when he adopts the viewpoint of his political enemies, as in the bizarre "Counting Small-Boned Bodies":

> If we could only make the bodies smaller,
> Maybe we could get
> A whole year's kill in front of us on a desk!

Bly's political poetry plunges past the metaphysical tenuousness of imagism and symbolism into a hidden order. But this hidden order he openly declaims. Like the Marxists with their notions of false consciousness, Bly posits a common awareness of mundane reality as something to be altered, and if necessary smashed, if we are to uncover the true (and truth-revealing) relations that shape the polis and the psyche. Bly's hidden order differs from, say, Mallarmé's because we can trace it from the dailiness of the world—we needn't slip into a world of albums and fauns and cabalism to discover it. On the other hand, it also differs from Stevens's, since we need no patient dialectic, no tone-juggling irony, to coax it from the welter of physical sensations that flood our thirsting eyes. His politics insistently slice along an emotional bias that is essentially populist, though without the xenophobic isolationism of the populists, and tolerate no analysis, no "party structure," no compromised platform.

> The time for exhortation is past. I have heard
> The iron chains scraping in asylums,
> As the cold bird hunches into the winter
> In the windy night of November.
> The cold miners rise from the pits
> Like a flash flood,
> Like a rice field disintegrating.
> Men cry when they hear stories of someone rising from the dead.

Official culture and the State work for the oppression of the spirit, but so pervasive is their success that the evidence of their crimes hides everywhere, and hence is visible only in dreams or trances.

> Ministers who dive headfirst into the earth
> The pale flesh
> Spreading guiltily into new literatures
>
> That is why these poems are so sad
> The long dead running over the fields
> The mass sinking down

The light in children's faces fading at six or seven

The world will soon break up into small colonies of the saved

Bly's political poetry thus arrives repeatedly at a crux: though the language must be hushed or ecstatic, appealing to suprarational truths, the evils must be squarely, almost pictorially, addressed. Part dream-vision, part diatribe, the poems seem laughable to anyone who is unsettled by all-embracing pathos or all-damning bile. Satire and ecstasy make strange bedfellows and often produce a tonelessness, a cancelling out of affect, in the service of an ineffable wisdom.

> The crane-handler dies, the taxi-driver dies, slumped over
> In his taxi. Meanwhile, high in the air, executives
> Walk on cool floors, and suddenly fall:
> Dying, they dream they are lost in a snowstorm in the mountains,
> On which they crashed, carried at night by great machines.
> As he lies on the wintry slope, cut off and dying,
> A pine stump talks to him of Goethe and Jesus.
> Commuters arrived in Hartford at dusk like moles.
> Or hares flying from a fire behind them,
> And the dusk in Hartford is full of their sighs;
> Their trains come through the air like a dark music,
> Like the sound of horns, the sound of thousands of small wings.

Because Bly mastered the idiom of pastoral ecstasy in *Silence in the Snowy Fields* before the directly political poetry appeared in *The Light around the Body* (1967), many people will continue to regard his political writings as deviant, as a falling away from a purity of diction and viewpoint that was perhaps too intense for its own good. The voice, however, is a seamless garment, and the "leaping" imaginativeness operates in both field and city, imprinting victim and villain with a distinctive animism.

III

In some instances Bly clearly separates his political poetry from his poetry of pastoral ecstasy, as when he entitles a section of *The Light around the Body* "The Vietnam War." On the other hand, the two small collections of prose poems, *The Morning Glory* (1975) and *Point Reyes Poems* (1974), are completely without political content, yet they contain some of Bly's most moving and intensely rhetorical writing. His full-length collection, *Sleepers Joining Hands* (1973), though largely ignored by reviewers, contains both sorts of poems (though without being divided into distinct sections). This collection also includes an extended expository prose essay, "I Came Out of the Mother Naked," related directly to the longest poem in the book, "The Teeth Mother

Naked at Last," which is the longest poem Bly has written. Concluding this volume is the long poem-sequence that gives the book its title, and it stands as Bly's most challenging and most beautiful poem to date, one that merges perfectly his pastoral and political obsessions and mythologies. "Sleepers Joining Hands," with its five sections and long, loosely cadenced lines, is Bly's celebration of himself, a poem that attempts to reconcile the chanting openness of Whitman with the mythical intensity of Rilke. Before considering it closely, however, we might linger a while on that medium Bly has slowly, unobtrusively, and patiently mastered: the prose poem.

Most readers think of the prose poem in connection with Rimbaud's *Les Illuminations*, in other words, as a series of aggressively scintillating but fragmentary insights spilling from a deranged mind, perhaps the devil's work, perhaps not. Then, too, there is Mallarmé with his imposingly rigorous sophistication, in love with and caused by its own etiolation (Eliot's "Hysteria" obviously belongs to this part of the tradition), while more modern still are the interiorizations of material objects perfected by Francis Ponge speaking "on the side of things." In any case, the prose poem appears decidedly French, a rather bourgeois invention and hardly suited to a Minnesota poet intent on breaking through to mythically resonant images. Yet if his first books showed Bly working with an essentially pastoral poetry, his prose poems illustrate how he has moved closer to a poetry of natural history. The pastoral remains resolutely literary, always conscious of tradition and audience, always at some important level an *exercise*, an attempt to test and redefine the limits of its own saying. Natural history, on the other hand, cultivates a prosaic idiom, it is concerned with observing precisely and labelling tentatively and yields little to its audience by either addressing its emotional needs or reaffirming its metaphysics or even its properties.

In the earlier brief collection, *The Morning Glory*, Bly introduces his prose poems with this short apologia:

> There is an old occult saying: whoever wants to see the invisible must penetrate more deeply into the visible. Everything has a right to exist. If we examine an animal carefully, we see how independent it is of us. Its world is complete without us. We feel separated at first; later, joyful.
>   Basho says in his wonderful poem:
>   The morning glory—
>   Another thing
>   that will never be my friend.

This becomes the central theme and the recurrent strategy of these poems: the exclusion of the human. Emotion and subjectivity are not totally removed, certainly not denied in these poems, but the phenomena under scrutiny displace ordinary human reactions and relegate them to a subsidiary or marginal role. (This, of course, makes these poems more like Ponge than Rimbaud, but they are quite distinct from either.) We are on the outside, or at the edges, looking in, and our curiosity might exfoliate into any of several emotions. But this perceiving energy dwindles if we lose our curiosity, our reverence, or our patience. Though never directly about "seeing" as both a psychical and physical harmony, these poems presume and demand it as our most human activity. This is the second half of "The large starfish," from *Point Reyes Poems*:

> How slowly and evenly it moves! The starfish is a glacier, going sixty miles a year! It moves over the pink rock, by means I cannot see. . .and into marvellously floating delicate brown weeds. It is about the size of the bottom of a pail. When I reach out to it, it holds on firmly, and then slowly relaxes. . .I suddenly take an arm and lift it. The underside is a pale tan. . .gradually as I watch thousands of tiny tubes begin rising from all over underside. . .hundreds in the mouth, hundreds along the nineteen underarms. . .all looking. . .feeling. . .like a man looking for a woman. . .tiny heads blindly feeling for a rock and finding only air. A purple rim runs along the underside of every arm, with paler tubes. Probably its moving-feet. . . .
>
> I put him back in. . .he unfolds—I had forgotten how purple he was—and slides down into his rock groin, the snail-like feelers waving as if nothing had happened, and nothing has.

All the ellipses here are Bly's, and he uses them frequently in the *Point Reyes Poems*. These poems occasionally recall the sensibility of Marianne Moore, or of A. R. Ammons, in their loving care, their careful hovering that sustains itself by shifting from one tack-sharp observation to another. Bly's seeing has seldom been more precise than it is in his prose poems: we are shown gulls "with feet the color of pumpkin" or the orange belly of a salamander that is "the color of airplane gasoline on fire," a seeing that refracts rather than parades the emotional, as in the case of the starfish, "a delicate purple, the color of old carbon paper, or an attic dress."

But the overriding impression of these poems reveals itself as diffidence, almost as if the prose were used to protect the speech act, because formal verse patterns might announce too much of a shaping impulse or initiate a solemnity that could disrupt the ruminative spell. The use of ellipses, along with phrases like "as if" and "a kind of," reinforces the sensation "that we are sailing on skeletal eerie craft over the buoyant ocean," as Bly concludes one of these self-effacing performances. Tentativeness of structure is heightened by similes and metaphors proposed but not pursued, their wayward or incidental charm left to do the work: a wave has the "gentleness of William Carlos Williams after his strokes"; a heron "slowly ascends, each wing as long as Holland"; we see several sea lions "looking neither arrogant nor surprised, but like a billfold found in the rain." In some cases the comparisons are relatively extended, but never to serve as logical support or thematic underpinning: watching the light come through a white bird's nest, "we get the feeling of those cloudy transoms above Victorian doors, or the manless hair of those intense nurses, gray and tangled after long nights in the Crimean wards." Human emotions and human weaknesses, though submerged, are omnipresent. Humility of format has its purposes, for it tends to reveal its own vulnerability, to get close to those moments of connectivity and insight that ordinarily we quickly dismiss with an antisentimental jab at our reverie.

Closely related to this tentative sense of structure, a thematic concern with various kinds of movement and growth makes itself felt throughout these poems. The variety extends from motility to glaciation, and the "leaping," associative energies of Bly's poetic attentions test themselves against a world where surprise, spontaneity, immeasurably slow drifts, or immense geological transformations are the order of the moment. These various modes of motion become evident to the human senses only at moments of great stress or utter freedom; they are avilable only to a haptic or body-centered consciousness, an awareness that cuts across perspectives and breaks down discursive categories. You can well read these poems with a sense of Bly's pragmatism in regard to form, as though a primer course in developmental biology were a prerequisite. The scale can be either macro- or microscopic, focusing on life at either end of the spectrum, exploring the growth of cells or of galaxies. Our vision must learn a different pace and a new frame of reference, until, like the moon, it "moves slowly southward as the clouds flow past. It is an eye, an eye-traveller, going so alone. . .sturdy as an orphan. Bold and alone and formed long ago."

Here is "Walking among Limantour Dunes" (the *Point Reyes Poems* are topographical, even incipiently chthonic in their pursuit of the genius loci):

> Thinking of a child soon to be born, I hunch down among friendly sand-grains. . .And the sand grains love us, for they love whatever lives with force not its own, a young girl looking out over her life, alone, without horses, with no map, a white dress on. . .whatever is not rushing blindly forward, the mole blinking at the door of his crumbly mole Vatican, the salmon sensing in his gills the Oregon waters crash down, or this planet abandoned here at the edge of the universe, the life floating inside the Pacific of the womb, near the walls, feeling the breakers roaring.

Bly's objective here clearly is to create something resembling those evanescent moments of sudden expanded consciousness he rendered so often in the early books, as in the following example:

Driving to Town Late to Mail a Letter

It is a cold and snowy night. The main street is deserted.
The only things moving are swirls of snow.
As I lift the mailbox door, I feel its cold iron.

There is a privacy I love in this snowy night.
Driving around, I will waste more time.

However humble these early poems may be, however concerned to defeat their own ambitions and lose the ego in the momentary sensations and prevailing drift of the scene, they remain vaguely "confessional," lyric celebrations of an exacerbated, private sensibility. But the later prose poems develop a different consciousness, one no less emotional but much more impersonal (if that distinction will stand), in which the ego is always measured against contexts capable of rectifying our obsession with it. Here is the end of "The Turtle," from *The Morning Glory* sequence, where Bly inverts the animal and sees:

The bottom is a pale, washed-out, rose from being dragged over the world—the imagination is simplified there, without too much passion, business-like, like the underside of some alien spaceship.

This clearly sounds a note not heard in *Snowy Fields*. The prose poems speak more self-sufficiently, with less protection from the sometimes hectoring theory of the deep image; they clear their own ground as they go, or rather float like fog "over soaked and lonely hills." Bly continues to use many of the strategies of the earlier poems, such as those deep images, sprung loose from Jungian depths; the barebones narratives, exemplumlike in their simplicity; and the heightened descriptions. But Bly has realized that the image alone can't do the work of the poem, that the ego and pseudorationality will make themselves felt in any surrealist attempt (especially a programmatic one) to escape them. If we trust too much in the theory, "mind" will be there anyway, not necessarily supplying significant form, but more likely having designs on *us*; and the only way to keep the possibilities of discovery open is to acknowledge the presence of the intellect but relegate it carefully from the seat of control. Much of the putatively surrealist poetry spawned by Bly's theories comes out clichéd and conceited, in both senses of the term, as the farfetched and the self-advancing merge histrionically. But Bly, especially in his prose poems, manages to skirt the foolishness of his students. Here, as coda to these points, is the conclusion of "The dead seal near McClure's Beach":

He raises himself up, and tucks his flippers under, as if to keep them warm. A wave comes in, touches his nose. He turns and looks at me—the eyes slanted, the crown of the head like a leather jacket. He is taking a long time to die. The whiskers white as porcupine quills, the forehead slopes, goodbye brother, die in the sound of waves, forgive us if we have killed you, long live your race, your inner-tube race, so uncomfortable on land, so comfortable in the sea. Be comfortable in death then, where the sand will be out of your nostrils, and you can swim in the long loops through the pure death, ducking under as assassinations break above you. You don't want to be touched by me. I climb the cliff and go home the other way.

IV

If somewhere behind his prose poems stands Francis Ponge or even Robinson Jeffers, the tutelary spirit of *Sleepers Joining Hands* is surely Pablo Neruda. It is odd, but beneficially so, that a Norwegian immigrant meditating in the snowbound isolation of Minnesota should, in part, extend his resonance by way of the tropically surreal imagination of a Latin diplomat. Though there are only ten short poems included in *Sleepers Joining Hands*, the language is whittled out of a sense of distance and anguish, and the poems tell of a natural world almost preternaturally capable of storing and releasing great depths of human emotions. Some of these poems are like Neruda's early work, such as *Twenty Love Poems and a Song of Desperation* (1924), and they make us realize the poetic value of constant separation working in consort with the hope of ultimate possession. This passage is from "Water under the Earth," and the lines in which the poem describes itself recall Neruda's self-conscious modesty, born of a desire to create an organic language at home in the world of growth and decay:

Everything we need now is buried,
it's far back into the mountain,
it's under the water guarded by women.
These lines themselves are sunk to the waist in the dusk
    under the odorous cedars,
each rain will only drive them deeper,
they will leave a faint glow on the dead leaves.
You too are weeping in the low shade of the pine branches,
you feel yourself about to be buried too,
you are a ghost stag shaking his antlers in the herony light—
what is beneath us will be triumphant
in the cool air made fragrant by owl feathers.

In the surrealism of the long antiwar poem "The Teeth Mother Naked at Last" we can again hear the influence of Neruda, as here, where the central image might have come from a carnival fairgrounds, but its new context renders it anything but entertaining:

> There is a black silo inside our bodies, revolving fast.
> Bits of black paint are flaking off,
> where the motorcycles roar, around and around,
> rising higher on the silo walls,
> the bodies bent toward the horizon,
> driven by angry women dressed in black.

This dissociating juxtaposition of images with associative complexities alternates with straightforward connections between mundane surfaces and horrifying realities:

> It's because the aluminum window shade business is doing so
>   well in the United States that we roll fire over entire villages
> It's because a hospital room in the average American city now costs $90
>   a day that we bomb hospitals in the North. . .
>
> It's because we have new packaging for smoked oysters that bomb holes
>   appear in the rice paddies
> It is because we have so few women sobbing in back rooms,
> because we have so few children's heads torn apart by high-velocity
>   bullets,
> because we have so few tears falling on our own heads
> that the Super-Sabre turns and screams down toward the earth.

Some will mutter in disbelief at these lines; others will think of Sidney's "The poet, he nothing affirms, and therefore never lyeth" and wish that Bly had heeded the advice. But like Neruda's anti-imperialist poems in *Canto general* (1950), I think Bly's antiwar poems will become even clearer and more striking in time, and their "excess" will be recognized as Blakean.

"The Teeth Mother Naked at Last" is followed, and its title image explained, by an essay Bly wrote and included in the midst of *Sleepers Joining Hands* to outline his theories and his method of "psychic archeology." The tone of his argument is, by turns, allusive, hectoring, suggestive, definitive, and exploratory. The essay shows Bly at his rhetorical best and at the same time shows how far beyond even Neruda his search has carried him.

> Whenever a man enters the force field of a Mother, he feels himself being pulled toward mothers and childhood, back toward the womb, but this time he feels himself being pulled *through* the womb, into the black nothing before life, into a countryside of black plants where he will lose all consciousness, both mother and father. The teeth in the vagina will strip him as he goes through. He is dismembered while still alive. The job of this Mother is to end the intensification of mental life that the Ecstatic Mother began, to end ecstasy and spiritual growth. The alcoholic has seen the Stone Mother, and he drinks to dull the fear that his inner rivers will turn to stone. He avoids looking at the Mother and the alcohol turns him to

stone. The Stone Mother stands for numbness, paralysis, catatonia, being totally spaced out, the psyche torn to bits, arms and legs thrown all over: Poe's "Descent into the Maelstrom" suggests the horror of the descent. My Lai is partway down; hard drugs that leave the boy-man permanently "stoned" are among the weapons of this Mother.

Though virtually every aspect of this argument can be traced to some previous writer—the dichotomy between "mother consciousness" and "father consciousness" echoes and parallels Lawrence's "blood consciousness" and "mind consciousness"; Bachofen's *Mother Right* is openly acknowledged as a source; the interest in force fields and the archaic consciousness as energizing templates for contemporary poets recalls Charles Olson—the essay is distinctive and revealing for Bly's poetry. Bly continues to favor images and associative structures over ideas and logical distinctions, and he continues to see good poetry as being a result of disciplined consciousness, not so much a criticism of life (though it is that, too) as a search for almost lost origins, a patient surrender almost Christian:

> I see in my own poems and the poems of so many other poets alive now fundamental attempts to right our own spiritual balance, by encouraging those parts in us that are linked with music, with solitude, water, and trees, the parts that grow when we are far from the centers of ambition.

But the most praiseworthy achievement in *Sleepers Joining Hands* is the title sequence, a five-part dream-vision deserving comparison with the best of contemporary poetry. As I suggested above, this sequence has affinities with Whitman, especially as it announces a new consciousness founded on a new sense of the ego, and also with Rilke, for it develops a complex symbolism in its search for a transcendent vision, a desire "to see things from the other side." Bly attempts to formulate a special sense of space and time in this poem; although his predecessors are apparent and many, he succeeds, and succeeds largely in his own terms. Simply put, Bly's temporal sense places the perspectives of a floating present, such as we experience in dreams, within an archeological, even a geological framework. At the same time, this temporal sense accompanies and is supported by a spatial sense, really an awareness of "inwardness" in which, again, a dreamlike space is modified by a consciousness directed toward the inner reaches of the body.

Thematically, discussions of the poem are apt to be clumsy, for reasons that should now be obvious. Yet the sequence does offer vague outlines for its "argument," and careful readers can sense a "plot" rising and falling with the speaker's energies, with his trust and doubt concerning his own visionary powers. The point of simplest and most

intense affirmation comes in the third section, "The Night Journey in
the Cooking Pot":

> Leaves slip down, falling through their own branches.
> The tree becomes naked and joyful.
> Leaves fall in the tomby wood.
> Some men need so little, and even that I need very little.
> Suddenly I love the dancers, leaping
> in the dark, jumping
> into the air, and the singers and dancers and leapers!
> I start to sing and rove around the floor,
> singing like "a young Lioun."
>
> I want to rise far into the piney tops
>
> I am not going farther from you,
> I am coming nearer,
> green rain carries me nearer you,
> I weave drunkenly about the page,
> I love you,
> I never knew that I loved you
> until I was swallowed by the invisible

This acceptance, however, is much more problematic than it appears in
this passage, and the poem goes on to record self-hatred and despair.
Slowly the necessity becomes clear: we must accept our mortal bodies.
But the necessity can be cruel long before it is kind:

> I fall into my own hands,
>   fences break down under horses,
> cities starve, whole towns of singing women carrying to the burial fields
>   the look I saw on my father's face,
> I sit down again, I hit my own body,
> I shout at myself, I see what I have betrayed.
> What I have written is not good enough.
> Who does it help?
> I am ashamed sitting on the edge of my bed.

Like many dream-visions, "Sleepers Joining Hands" unravels the
speaker's vocation, his being called to the knowledge of a higher,
hidden order. Though his guides announce their otherworldly origins,
the speaker must finally conduct his own initiation:

> I have been alone two days, and still everything is cloudy.
> The body surrounds me on all sides.
> I walk out and return.
> Rain dripping from pine boughs, boards soaked on porches,
> gray water awakens, fish slide away underneath.
> I fall asleep. I meet a man from a milder planet.

I say to him "I know Christ is from your planet!"
He lifts his eyes to me with a fierce light.
He reaches out and touches me on the tip of my cock, and I fall asleep.

The sleep within sleep, the savior who rejects our recognition, and the symbol of assertive power rendered weak by gentleness: we are clearly closer to Jung than to Freud, to hermetic rather than rational knowledge.

Some savior appears to have come, but the arrival is on a different scale, in a different world, than we expected:

The barn doors are open. His first breath touches the manger hay,
and the King a hundred miles away
stands up. He calls his ministers.
"Find him.
There cannot be two rulers in one body."
He sends his wise men out along the arteries,
along the winding tunnels, into the mountains,
to kill the child in the old moonlit villages of the brain.

The body politic merges with the transfigured body, for this poem wants a new consciousness and a new world, and it will settle for nothing else, even if it must live in dreams and fantasies:

Sometimes when I read my own poems late at night,
I sense myself on a long road,
I feel the naked thing alone in the universe,
the hairy body padding in the fields at dusk. . . .

I have floated in the eternity of the cod heaven,
I have felt the silver of infinite numbers brush my side—
I am the crocodile unrolling and slashing through the mudded water,
I am the baboon crying out as her baby falls from the tree,
I am the light that makes the flax blossom at midnight!
I am an angel breaking into three parts over the Ural Mountains!
I am no one at all.

Whether passing "under the earth through the night-water" or "all alone, floating in the cooking pot/on the sea," the speaker remains isolate, selfless, lost through his own irresolution or defeated by false energy. But if he is "the last inheritor crying out in deserted houses," he also sees himself as "an eternal happiness fighting in the long reeds."

The poem spills out images, it gathers toward clarity, it moves through thickets of association, and through it all develops an emotional force field, a sense of temporal simultaneity and spatial diffusion. Quotations, even frequent and lengthy, will not convey this force, and with associative poetry this critical axiom becomes freshly true. We must become patient readers, for the lyric bursts of the shorter poems are here protracted, though with no dampening of the lyric intensity. The poem *is* lyrical, its audience is a better, secret part of the speaker, or of someone willing to assume that role. The speaker imagines himself joining an Indian tribe; and, as "the suppressed race returns," Bly resembles Thoreau, another spokesman for solitude who desperately wanted to be inside the body of the redskin. Echoing the poet-naturalist, the transcendentalist, Bly waits to give birth to the new man:

> There is another being living inside me.
> He is looking out of my eyes.
> I hear him
> in the wind through the bare trees. . . .
> That is why I am so glad in fall.
> I walk out, throw my arms up, and am glad.
> The thick leaves fall,
> falling past their own trunk,
> and the tree goes naked,
> leaving only the other one.

One can hear some Thoreauvian puns here as the tree and the man uncover their common state. The poem ends with the following lines, and their utter difference from the rest of the poem recalls the end of Eliot's "Prufrock" with its two three-line stanzas, but the mermaids and the solitude and the destroying waves are replaced by something shared, a joy, and by the waters of release:

> Our faces shine with the darkness reflected from the Tigris,
> cells made by the honeybees that go on growing after death,
> a room darkened with curtains made of human hair.
>
> The panther rejoices in the gathering dark.
> Hands rush toward each other through miles of space.
> All the sleepers in the world join hands.

V

The publication of *This Body is Made of Camphor and Gopherwood* (1977) signaled a decisive change in Bly's poetry. Though continuing to use the prose poem as he had in *The Morning Glory* (1975), in the later work Bly concentrates his vision more directly on ecstatic moments and writes what must be described as religious poetry. These moments, or nodes of psychic energy, have only a fleeting relation with the subjects of natural history over which Bly lingered so lovingly in *The Morning Glory*. That earlier collection was dominated by a sense of animal delight and keen observation. Its middle section, "The Point Reyes Poems" (earlier printed as a separate volume), struck me as Bly's finest work: a celebration of presence and vision, a peripatetic delight in the evidences of process and system that avoided both the disappointments of self-conscious closure and the overreaching of the glib sublime. But Bly, ever aggressive, was obviously not content to rest there. The publication of *This Body is Made of Camphor and Gopherwood* moves Bly beyond *The Morning Glory*, just as *The Light around the Body* (1967) moved him beyond *Silence in the Snowy Fields* (1962). In both instances, a continuity of idiom and style contrasts with a shift in the central subject matter. To simplify the matter grossly, Bly first went from midwestern pastoral to antiwar polemic, and now he has gone from natural history to religious vision. However, what looks ostensibly like a change in subject can be read as an intensification in style (taking *style* in the largest sense, as the intersection of temperament and vocation), since the pastoral can readily turn into polemic, as with Vergil's first eclogue and Milton's "Lycidas." Likewise, celebrations of natural history are often possible only through a sublimated religious yearning, as is apparent in Lucretius, Erasmus Darwin, and, in some senses, even in Whitman.

Of course this schematizing of Bly's work ignores much detail and overlapping. To take the most obvious point, *The Light around the Body* has both pastoral and political polemics as its subject matter. Also, there are in *Camphor and Gopherwood* moments of sheer pastoral delight, and even domestic relaxation, that are not directly religious. And my scheme ignores *Sleepers Joining Hands* (1973), which is best assimilated as a "transitional" volume (what would any scheme do without its transitionals!), part way between the antiwar polemics of the late sixties and the religious–ecstatic poetry of the seventies. In fact, *Sleepers Joining Hands* gathers together Bly's highest utterances in both the polemical and the religious modes: "The Teeth Mother" and the title poem, respectively. But the general shape of Bly's growth exhibits at least the outline I have sketched. I would argue further that the continuity of idiom, contrasted with the shift in subject matter, makes Bly's development both dramatic and instructive; moreover, such change with continuity is in fact a working out of poetic problems that remain central to contemporary poetry.

What is distinctive about *Camphor and Gopherwood* is the persistence and dominance in it of the religious impulse. Or, to put it in broader terms, Bly exemplifies the curious persistence of theological modes of experience and feeling in our present-day, secularized culture. This persistence often poses a scandal for criticism. For many readers, especially those with secularized imaginations, Bly's work strikes a thoroughly false, and what is worse, an utterly outmoded, note. For others, the religious is simply assimilated to that other category, the supercharged "poetics," a post-Arnoldian preserve of the literary, where we safely store away all that is not marketable, all that is not "operative" in today's society. These readers are likely to overpraise Bly, to read him with little critical or historical awareness, and to accept his religious yearnings simply as a sort of Jungian compensation and corrective to technocratic thought. It is difficult to know a way other than these two alternatives, the dismissive and the obsequious. The former often degenerates into ad hominem attacks, while the latter becomes a twisted form of condescension.

But some middle ground might be claimed. Bly, like some of his contemporaries, can be seen as fighting (a rearguard action? a border skirmish? or the start of a pitched battle?) against the too-pat assumptions of late modernism. In this view, Bly wants to move beyond irony, past the fourth stage of Vico's historical cycle, past the low-mimetic irony of Frye's system, into some challenging affirmation. If we put Bly's work in this sort of context, we can treat its religious impulses seriously and still see how the poems remain essentially poetry and not sacred texts. In other words, Bly writes in such a way as to reaffirm the value of spontaneity, the emphasis on process and sudden illumination often associated with certain trends in modernism (from surrealism to John Cage). But he also wants out of the modernist trap of autotelism, the sense of poetry as "just another" language game. His poetry registers a desire to move beyond what we can call the problem of the symbolic, the modern notion that since reality is constituted by language, everything is (or can be read as) a text. To borrow terms from linguistic theory, in modern consciousness generally there is no signified, and hence there can only be an excess of signifiers; in which case, each code must do what it can to claim autonomy, or else poetry must surrender any claim to a special linguistic status (hence, we have "found poetry," the lingua franca campiness of the epigones of the New York school, and so forth). But one way out of the traps of autotelism and excessive self-consciousness is the insistent affirmation of some indisputable "signified," a "beyond," a realm where value is generated and confirmed. This realm becomes the ground of ultimate concern, a place where irony must fall silent or else change into celebration. But how can Bly hope to find a language that will take him beyond the ironic, especially when irony often seems the only language?

One key to Bly's latest volume lies in his fascination with the medium of the prose poem. Baudelaire described the "miracle of a poetic prose, musical, without rhymes and without rhythm, supple enough and rugged enough to adapt itself to the lyrical impulses of the

soul, the undulations of the psyche, the prickings of consciousness."
Impulses, undulations, prickings: with this category of gestures, each
bordering suggestively on half-liberated, half-choked releases of the
unspoken, we begin to sense why Bly has turned to the prose poem.
His needs and vision have led him to the point where spontaneous
revelations must be somehow both respected for their contact with the
marvellous and incorporated into an everyday idiom, a language both
supple and rugged. Bly, in other words, wants to domesticate the
sublime.

> We love this body as we love the day we first met the person who led us
> away from this world, as we love the gift we gave one morning on
> impulse, in a fraction of a second, that we can still see every day, as we love
> the human face, fresh after love-making, more full of joy than a wagon-
> load of hay.

The spontaneous ("fraction of a second") becomes the quotidian ("every day"), as the palpable flesh ("this body") is equated with transcendence ("away from this world"). For such eruptions of the marvellous
and such blessed sinkings-back into the everyday no strict verse form
will suffice. Verse, even intense lyric poetry, has traditionally had a
public dimension; it cannot be whispered. It can pretend to be overheard, as "Prufrock," but it almost always has its eye on the larger
audience. (Think of Donne, even Catullus, winking at *us* over the
shoulder of his mistress.) But prose poetry sets up a different writer–
reader contract by asking the reader to surrender his or her sense of
regular measure. Verse promises a return to some unit of measure that
implies, however weakly, a mediation between the cry of a revealing
truth and the closure of a presentable argument. By their very irregularity, prose poems *suggest*; the best of them almost always are master-
pieces of insinuation. They are less achieved mediations than a sort of
self-erasing indicator of something beyond themselves, hushed point-
ers to the ineffable.

Many of the prose poems in *Camphor* include passages that announce themselves as dreams; still others suggest a dreamlike structure, as does "Galloping Horses." Even "Walking Swiftly," which
begins "When I wake. . . ," has the characteristics of a dream-vision,
where impulses, undulations, and prickings are the dominant kind of
occurence. Such concern with the texture and the ultimate moral
meaning of dreams has been crucial to Bly's poetry from the beginning.
Articulating such concern in prose poems seems natural; besides, Bly
has never had an ear that was musical at the level of the poetic line. One
sensed from the first that he composed by phrases and clauses, that he
wanted more a suggestive cadence than a measured rhythm. So the
spontaneous "gesture" of the prose poem has been suited to the

"word" of the dream-vision. Falling into holes, leaping through and by images: both types of motion are made possible by the spontaneous, insinuating discursiveness of prose poetry. We can summarize this sort of movement as "motile," defined as having the power to move spontaneously, like certain spores and microorganisms. (A secondary meaning of motile is drawn from psychology, where the word describes a person whose mental imagery consists of his own bodily motion. This word thus relates the movement of Bly's sentences to his "body-centered" mysticism.)

For Bly, motility represents more than a stylistic tic. It stands for the particular form of heuristic discovery that alone can do justice to his religious imagination. Central to this imagination is the belief, itself a vital part of the Protestant mystical tradition from which Bly borrows much of his imagery, that conversion is most strong when it is most sudden. In *The Varieties of Religious Experience* (1902) William James discusses this phenomenon of sudden conversion. By using the then new notion of a "field of consciousness," James analyzes sudden religious conversions as resulting from a change in relative importance between what had been centered in the "field" and what had been only marginal to consciousness. To illustrate such repolarized fields, or " 'uprushes' into ordinary consciousness of energies originating in the subliminal parts of the mind," James refers to cases of posthypnotic suggestion. This persistence of mental energies and their eventual irruption into a waking state of mind, though originally discovered in a sleeplike state, is, of course, at the center of Bly's poetic project.

James then goes on to discuss (in the same lecture) the difficulty of ascertaining the "class-mark distinctive of all true converts." James concludes that such identification is difficult, if not impossible. Spontaneous conversion leaves no specific evidence; as such, it is indistinguishable from conversion occurring over a protracted period. Likewise with Bly's poetry. Its religious intensity leaves no mark except its own spontaneous, motile discoveries. Bly's political poems, for example, strike many as unsuccessful because they are based on no apparent understanding of social cohesiveness. For Bly, the only important ingredient in the *social* is the ecstatic; the ordinary demands of social mediation and historical necessity go largely unregistered in his poetry. This raises a problem that many readers face with Bly, both in his political and in his religious visions: they feel that his salvation is less suffered than willed. Since there is little social experience in his poems, little evidence of how his conversion affects his daily intercourse with others, the reader must react from inner, subjective criteria. Bly's is essentially a utopian vision. Furthermore, the negative element of his vision, his sense of satiric correction, can hardly extend beyond labelling the unawakened as unawakened. On the positive side, he preaches not simply to the converted, but to the transformed. The social does not necessarily obliterate the spontaneous, but it remains a fact that when American poets glorify the spontaneous and inner life, then the programmed and exterior life—and hence inevitably society itself—becomes the undesirable.[2]

Now, generally, religion (as the root of the word tells us) has a social, communal element: one is "bound" not only to a higher force, but also with others. (Wittgenstein's argument against a private language would apply equally strongly against a private religion.) But Bly's religious intensity has no immediate social content; it is a religion of one. Throughout *Camphor* Bly addresses a "friend." This "friend" can be viewed as the polar opposite of Baudelaire's "hypocrite lecteur," but as with some polar opposites, there are strange resemblances. Bly's friend is an interlocutor, a psychological necessity that permits communication to continue; such interlocutors are necessary when the very status of the lyric voice has been called into question. As Walter Benjamin says of Baudelaire, he conceived of his poems as being written for an audience that no longer read lyric poetry. So Bly writes his religious meditations for a public that is no longer ostensibly religious. But a more positive perspective on this "friend" would relate him to the friend addressed by George Herbert in *The Temple*. In this sense the friend is not merely a rhetorical crutch, or a way to domesticate the sublime, but the very divinity made companionable. In other words, the friend is the savior, or us, or the savior-in-us, less a social force than a private, inner healer.

> My friend, this body is made of camphor and gopherwood. Where it goes, we follow, even into the Ark. As the light comes in sideways from the west over damp spring buds and winter trash, the body comes out hesitatingly, and we are shaken, we weep, how is it that we feel no one has ever loved us?

The Ark is the vessel of love, both the covenant that demonstrates we will be saved and the body scented with eros. (Gopher wood is traditionally the wood Noah used to construct the Ark. The camphor tree is aromatic, and its gum has legendary ritual uses. Although the Song of Songs clearly uses camphor in an erotic metaphor, it developed a certain reputation as an anaphrodisiac. But whether used erotically or ascetically, its odor is sensuous.)

Such religious feeling exists, however, only in a "sideways" light, in the subliminal or marginal consciousness. (This is perhaps why Bly often uses olfactory imagery.) As soon as the feeling is called into the light it may begin to petrify and die:

> Then what is asked of us? To stop sacrificing one energy for another. They are not different energies anyway, not "male" or "female," but whirls of different speeds as they revolve. We must learn to worship both, and give up the idea of one god. . . .

Does Platonism lead inevitably to pantheism? Even without tackling that question, we can see how Bly's trust in a realm beyond matter leads him to "recontain" things material as suffused with divinity. Because faith, the "evidence of things that do not appear," is so strong, it can only be located in *every-thing*; and because every thing is thus (at least potentially) sacred, no institutionalization of religious feeling is permissible. The temple always leaves something outside, something "pro-fane," but Bly cannot accept this. Before any temple he prefers the upright heart, but the upright heart must be prepared to cast down its glance—and its attachments—to the lowliest things. Like many American poets before him, from Whitman to Roethke, Bly believes that what Stevens called "the malady of the quotidian" must be rescued by and for the poetic consciousness. As Emerson argued, "The poet, by an ulterior intellectual perception, . . .puts eyes, and a tongue into every dumb and inanimate object." So a wagonload of hay can be full of joy.

But in this religion without priest or hierarchies, what and how should the poet celebrate? If, as Emerson says, "Small and mean things serve as well as great symbols," isn't the worshipful act indistinguishable from the casual, unthinking acts of everyday consciousness? An answer is offered by Emerson:

> Here is the difference betwixt the poet and the mystic, that the last nails a symbol to one sense, which was a true sense for a moment, but soon becomes old and false. For all symbols are fluxional; all language is vehicular and transitive, and is good, as ferries and horses are, for conveyance, not as farms and houses are, for homestead. Mysticism consists in the mistake of an accidental and individual symbol for an universal one. . . .The history of hierarchies seems to show, that all religious error consisted in making the symbol too stark and solid, and, at last, nothing but an excess of the organ of language.

The poet then becomes a priest of process; he must constantly throw off his own symbols and perceive "the independence of the thought on the symbol, the stability of the thought, the accidency and fugacity of the symbol," as Emerson goes on to say. What better instrument to use for such throwing away than the motility of the prose poem, that most protean of forms? What better divinity than the yet to be disguised as the castoff, the fugitive cloaked in the forgotten? Bly says:

> The dream said that The One Who Sees The Whole does not have the

senses, but the longing for the senses. That longing is terrible, and terrifying—the herd of gazelles running over the savannah—and intense and divine, and I saw it lying over the dark floor. . .in layers there.

It is also possible to see here how Bly escapes the problem of the symbolic. As for a true Emersonian, language is for him transparent, even fugacious. The opacity of language, which has long provided one basis for the autotelic theories of modern poetry—"a poem should not mean, but be"—is simply willed away. Language, for Bly, always offers a way of encapsulating the longing for the senses and is therefore a way of going beyond the senses.

All this might be taken as another way of saying that Bly is a typical postromantic poet, that he faces the same problem the symbolists faced, namely, how to discover an entrancing language without a binding social myth, or how to write a liturgy without a theology. In part, Bly's response has been to join that sector of the modernist movement that sacralizes the unconscious. (His closest *poetic* forerunner may be D. H. Lawrence, especially in the "Preface" to the 1923 volume of his poems.) But the most important aspect of the unconscious is that it is a process. *Camphor* is filled with revealing processes, appearances, the comings-on of a guide or the discoveries of a traveller, a catalogue of Poundian *periploi*. But it records slower processes as well, like falling snow and rising smoke, pilgrimages in a slow, protozoic time frame, "the sweetest pools of slowly circling energies." To anchor his sense of a nonbinding religion of process, Bly rewrites the Freudian "return of the repressed" as an activity best registered by the body, not sublimated into the "beautiful" or the therapeutic. This is, among other things, Bly's way of avoiding the "religion of art," that other tendency in modernism that would aestheticize all experience and thus render religion superfluous.

> We take our first step in words each day, and instantly fall into a hole in the sounds we make. Overly sane afternoons in a room during our twenties come back to us in the form of a son who is mad, every longing another person had that we failed to see returns to us as a squinting of the eyes when we talk, and no sentimentality, only the ruthless body performing its magic. . .

It is the body, the individual human body, that best incorporates both the spontaneous discoveries and the longer, slower processes. If the body becomes "the field of consciousness," then bodily ecstasy becomes a sort of sacred unconsciousness, that is, a something beyond that can suddenly become central and in turn redefine all value.

I would offer a formulation at this point. What Bly's religion does is substitute the body for the soul as the privileged term in the traditional body–soul dichotomy. (The negative term then is not soul, but conscious rationality.) This dichotomy has been traced by Paul Ricoeur, in *The Symbolism of Evil*, back to orphic religion. It was in Orphism that the "body" was first named, and it was there regarded as "an instrument of reiterated punishment." Once the body was termed evil, the next step was inevitable: the soul is not a part of the body, it "is not from here; it comes from elsewhere; it is divine." At this crucial point in Western culture, myth is not yet separated into religion and philosophy, but a lasting assumption is made about experience:

> Other cults taught enthusiasm, the possession of the soul by a god. What seems to be original in Orphism is that it interpreted this sudden alteration, this rapture, as an excursion from the body, as a voyage in the other world, rather than as a visitation or a possession. Ecstasy is now seen as manifesting the true nature of the soul, which daily existence hides.

Ricoeur goes on to argue that Greek philosophy was to take this body–soul dichotomy as the basis of its definition of the soul, as that essence that remains identical, the same as itself. Thus, the body is seen as change, as the subject and locus of decay, while the soul is eternal and immutable. But for Bly ecstasy is not an excursion from the body; it is an excursion *with* and *into* the body. Ecstasy manifests the true nature of the body, which is to be the evidence of the divine.

Bly's poetry, in *Camphor* especially, is best understood as an attempt to get back to a preorphic sense of the body. The body is sacred for Bly because, as the subject and locus of change and process, it becomes the perfect universal symbol. The body, in *Camphor*, provides the stability, while it is thought that bears the burden of "accidency and fugacity." Paradoxically, it is the body-as-process that by its very nature provides this stability. This "curiously alive and lonely body" is what loves; it "offers to carry us for nothing"; it "is made of energy compacted and whirling." In a passage that would read more traditionally if we could reverse the poet's usage and put "soul" where he puts "body," Bly says:

> This body longs for itself far out at sea, it floats in the black heavens, it is a brilliant being, locked in the prison of human dullness. . . .

Here we see what is distinctive about Bly's religion: he has made the body equivalent to the Western-Christian-Protestant "soul," an entity of nearly unspeakable longings that has its true abode in the vast beyond and that can realize its essence only in the momentary gestures of escape and ecstasy.

> Friend, this body is made of camphor and gopherwood. So for two days I gathered ecstasies from my own body, I rose up and down, surrounded

only by bare wood and bare air and some gray cloud, and what was inside
me came so close to me, and I lived and died!

Ecstasy now manifests what daily existence hides: the true nature of
the body. The body is both a passage to the bare elements and itself a
congeries of religious and erotic scents; it is its own ark and covenant.

It is difficult to transform—or translate, or convert, or in-
stitutionalize: whatever the metaphor, the difficulty remains—the
ecstasies of one's body into a shareable, communal vision. What I think
Bly's poetry enacts, especially in the strengths and weaknesses of
Camphor, is the persistent desire of American poets simultaneously to
celebrate the body and to incorporate the universal energies, thus
making them available to all. How to domesticate the sublime? Bly's
answer seems to be to deify the *truly* immediate, that is, the data of
consciousness understood not as thought, but as bodily sensation.
Bodily presence and process—the purview of natural history, with its
emphasis on seeing, on turning the given into a specimen by an act of
loving attentiveness to detail and change—thus become equated with
bodily ecstasy—the evidence of religion, with its proffered hope that
the bodies of men and women can become one body, which will
manifest, in a Blakean way, the transforming and divine energies of the
universe.

Interchapter

The Metaphors for the Poem

It would be possible to write a lively and perceptive literary history by tracing the rise, development, and eventual fading of each epoch's central metaphor for the literary "work." One classic study, M. H. Abrams's well-known *The Mirror and the Lamp*, explores these two polar images of art as incarnating either a mimetic or an expressive base for aesthetic objects. Another metaphor, implicit in Cleanth Brooks's title *The Well Wrought Urn*, is the sense of the poem as a construct built of tensions and opposing forces, somehow "fixed" by the artist's use of paradox as the verbal means of resolving these tensions. For the romantic era, Keats's poetry and letters are filled with phrases, as suggestive as Donne's "well wrought urn," that could easily serve such a metaphoric role. Recall, for example, how Keats speculated that the events in a man's life were an allegory and his poems could be seen as the commentary on that allegory; surely much of the Keats criticism in the last forty years has tried to come to terms with this notion in discussing Keats as a literary-biographical subject.

The metaphors for the poem, then, can be various, overlapping, and even centrifugal, catching up notions of psychology and the poet's career as well. But now and again there are shifts in these metaphors that mark undeniably important developments in literary history, though the larger the shift the more difficult it is to trace the exact moment when a new metaphor wins dominance. We might even speculate that after Rimbaud the central focus has fixed on metaphors for the poet, rather than for the poem; and voyager, madman, shaman, aesthete, and so on have suggested themselves as unifying roles, both to locate the poet for his audience and often to insist on his remoteness. Also implicit in the metaphor for either poem or poet is an evaluation, sometimes polemical, of the place poetry has in the epoch, since the metaphor might sharply differentiate between what is available, or necessary, for a poem to do and what a novel or play might achieve. Though it can't be relied upon as an universal key, the prevailing metaphor for the poem might help readers, directing them to the scope, the intent, and even the texture of the poetic act.

The poetry editor for the *Saturday Review*, John Ciardi, once wrote a book that employed the assumptions and standards of the "New Criticism." It was called *How Does a Poem Mean?* and it advanced the notion that a poem was "a machine for making choices." The formalism of the book's title was given a perhaps too-clear thrust in this metaphor of a machine, picking and choosing words as it went along, each choice more and more circumscribed, but when well made, more and more forceful in its "integrity." This aesthetic was a dominant one in the decade of the 1950s, and its sense of the poem as a self-regarding, self-justifying statement was instilled into many readers and would-be writers of poetry in American universities. Because of the role universities played in fostering poetic talent, this aesthetic came to influence the writing of poetry in a special way, as it carried with it a special authority and a built-in defense. The poem became a kind of academic set piece, an object so hemmed round with ironic deprecation, so often reliant on allusion to other poems, and so internally consistent—the poem had always to be well "brought off"—that it demanded explication before experience, analysis before assent. No transcendent values could be directly affirmed, since these might raise questions about the poet's "intentions"—thorny questions that had also been ruled out of bounds by another tenet of formalism, the intentional fallacy. This tenet held that either an artist had realized his intentions in the poem, and so we didn't need an independent account of them, or he hadn't, and in this case we had no way of establishing what those failed intentions were, except through another statement by the poet that could be as equally flawed as the poem. Therefore, all that was left was the poem itself—logically, an unassailable argument, but one that ignored how reading, being made up of anticipated meanings as well as realized ones, actually occurs. Only an assumption that poems were objects, removed totally from use or from any dialectical shifts in meaning caused by history or cultural patterning, could subtend such an abiding faith in formalism.

Gradually, this dominant sense of a poem as an autotelic, self-explaining statement, or "object," began to lose its force. In its place in the late fifties and early sixties came at least three other metaphoric images for the poem: the poem as a force field; the poem as a "leaping," or associatively linked cluster of nondiscursive images; and the poem as commentary on some unspoken myth, what Galway Kinnell has called a "palimpsest." The first of these metaphors was formulated with especial drive by Charles Olson in his "Projective Verse," written in 1950, but not widely known till some years later. The second has as one of its chief proponents Robert Bly, who coined the term *leaping*, but there are many poets who sympathize with its emphasis on nondiscursive elements without necessarily agreeing completely with Bly. The third metaphor, clearly the least well defined of the three, has no one major theoretician, but would include among its practitioners such poets as W. S. Merwin, Mark Strand, and various avant-garde poets like Clayton Eshelman and Robert Kelly. But, perhaps most important, each of the three metaphors is at odds with any sense of the poem as a completed, self-enclosed artifact. Whatever their usefulness for readers, or for poets, and whatever larger cultural forces they might reflect and syncretize, these three metaphors helped put an end to the concept of the poem as a machine or "well wrought urn." Though all the poems written out of these three new metaphoric approaches might not differ radically from previous poems, clearly an aesthetic boundary has been redrawn.

I. Composition by Field

Charles Olson drew much of his metaphoric language in "Projective Verse" from his reading in the philosophy of Alfred North Whitehead and from the developments in theoretical physics near the turn of the century. Olson was never a systematic thinker, of course, and the extent to which he actually mastered either Whitehead or force-field theory is not really relevant. What is relevant, however, is Olson's attempt to get outside the tradition of the Western lyric as it had developed since the Renaissance. "The lyrical interference of the ego"—this was how he termed what he considered the main stumbling block. Olson was after a poetics that cut short any subjective indulgence in emotive states for their own sake; he wanted to restore poetry to its mythical potency, that is, he wanted to use it to investigate and record those activities and cultural habits that men needed words to embody.[1]

Throughout Olson's work, there appear two related drives: to present some transcribed evidence and to cut against the grain of assumptions built up by any kind of social narcosis, since through such narcoses men had used language more as a shield than as a sword. Olson's use of a persona in his *Maximus Poems* has a completely different intent from that of most other contemporary poets; unlike Berryman, say, whose persona was a way to at the same time display and toy with his authorial ego, Olson used his character to achieve a larger base and thus give more resonance, historically and morally, to what he said. This use is in many ways profoundly conservative, and Olson's political vision is in many ways a precapitalist one, as if he had adapted agrarian principles to the fishing village of Gloucester, Massachusetts. "It is hard to be a historian and a poet at the same time," he says at the end of the *Mayan Letters*, and he shows in those letters how he wanted to return poetry to its central, and centralizing, position in the culture. For this centering, poems had to be more than set pieces; they had to reflect and register forces that were at the edges of formulability and give shapely utterance to values that were pervasively dispersed throughout the cultural consciousness. This is why his poems often revert to incidents and even texts from foreign cultures, in order to gain a "perspective by incongruity," and why they often seem (and are) fragmentary, like random jottings or the quick and barely traceable path of a subatomic particle. The poem is like a force field: on and through it occur seemingly random recognitions, but if the poet properly positions himself, in order to increase his attentiveness, he can use the poem to register indefinite but powerful forces that would otherwise pass unnoticed. The poem is neither mirror nor lamp, since the poet neither imitates nor expresses; rather, the poem is a mental construct drawn up to record the underlying structure of phenomena.

Olson says in "Projective Verse" that the poet must follow the "track" that "the poem under hand declares for itself"; furthermore, the poet must be "aware of some several forces just now beginning to be examined." In a sense Olson's poetics is passive, since its main concern is to superinduce in the poet a kind of altered consciousness. Once this pervasive awareness is fostered, the poet turns his focused awareness to the job of recording it. But he must be aware that this new consciousness cannot use the old language, especially the old *patterns* of the language. Instead, he must "step back here to this place of the elements and minims of language" and there "engage speech where it is least careless—and least logical." The sense here that the poet is engaged upon an attempt resembling the exploration of subatomic particles is deliberate, of course, and is Olson's way of dealing with that urge toward primitivism in all modernist thought, but it is also his way of depersonalizing the activity.

That peculiar sense of language as completely free ("least logical") and completely determined ("least careless") supplies Olson with the dialectic that runs throughout his poetry. He wants to posit a completely formed utterance—often a document or historical notation or first version of a tale—and have it be seen in context with the freely generated utterances that it gives rise to (we might almost say gives permission to). The "sweetness of meter and rime" Olson calls a "honey-head," that is, he sees prescriptive meters as the equivalents of social narcoses, taking over and gumming up the production, even the "emission," of syllables. Replace the meter with the syllable, he insists, shift the instruments to a new field. Or to put it differently, "Listening for the syllables must be so constant and so scrupulous. . .that the assurance of the ear is purchased at the highest. . .price." The poet must be able to register all the forces at work in his consciousness, even the protosemantic ones.

Olson's theories are idiosyncratically presented, and—he resembles

Emerson among others in this regard—through selective quotation, he can be made to say almost anything. But I think most critics (even Robert Bly is culpable in this regard) are wrong to present Olson as offering some innovative technical advice, some keylike "breath-line" that can be taken over by all poets for whatever "message" they can adapt it to. Olson's work fundamentally challenged poetry as it was being written in 1950; it did more than simply extend Pound's theories (though Olson's relation to Pound is both obvious and reciprocal) because it took the scientistic metaphors strewn throughout Pound's criticism and used them seriously and consistently. But only if the poet abandons the lyric mode, at least as it is generally practiced, and turns toward narrative or something like a mythical, epical structure will the "technique" of Olson be completely useful. Otherwise, what Olson had to say about the poem—his metaphor for the poetic act—is no more (and no less) than what Pound and Eliot had said, that the "emotional slither" of etiolated Victorianism had to be replaced with the concision, the affective exactitude of such diverse poets as Villon, Donne, and Baudelaire.

William Carlos Williams, for one, saw that Olson was after more than technique, and he reprinted a large portion of "Projective Verse" in his *Autobiography*. In doing so, Williams acknowledged that he and Olson were engaged in a common task: to present "the reconstruction of the poem as one of the major occupations of the intelligence in our day." Williams understood Olson's sense of "field," and the chapter in which he reprints "Projective Verse" is to my mind the subtlest and in some senses the most complete of Williams's aesthetic formulations. Williams devotes the remainder of the chapter to an account of his friend the painter Charles Sheeler and of the "adaptations" Sheeler has made of Shaker furniture, his Russian wife's past, and the environment of his Hudson River valley farm. Sheeler's house, or rather the field of forces that he is conscious of, working in and through his house, becomes Williams's metaphor for the reconstruction of the poem. "To transfer values into a new context, to make a poem again" is how Williams put it, restating his lifelong concern to "make it new" and invent aesthetic order at the same time. But, like Olson, Williams is concerned with a new sensory and evaluative interaction, not for the sake of newness, not simply to provide grist for some technical innovation, but because the old ways of expressing awareness, of showing the mind to itself, aren't effective. The mind occludes itself when it relies on a previously shaped language or on a language imported from some other location, some other "field." "Nothing can grow unless it taps into the soil," Williams says at the end of the chapter. But the organization of the poem proceeds both from and toward another organization:

> It is ourselves we organize in this way not against the past or for the future
> or even for survival but for the integrity of understanding to insure
> persistence, to give the mind its stay.

Integrity of understanding describes quite accurately what field theory
tries to provide physicists, since such theories rely heavily on a statisti-
cal or phenomenological model that interweaves data from several
sources into an integrated whole. For Williams and for Olson the
evidence they were after was simply not obtainable, or at least not
capable of being accurately registered, with the traditional "object" of
verse. What Williams and Olson sought is what is always "at hand,"
this is what makes them inventors; but what is at hand can often only
be revealed by a discharge into our consciousness of some remote
historical energy, and this is what makes them conservers. Some of the
poets who place themselves in the Williams–Olson "line" (poets such
as Levertov, Creeley, and Snyder) are aware they don't have the same
mythical concerns as the two older poets, but they also realize that the
metaphor of the poem as a "field of forces" satisfies the modernist
demands for accuracy of perception and complexity of apperception.
After the example of Olson, many contemporary poets proceeded with
much more care for the recording instruments, knowing that the way
they drew up the evidence was as important as the audience they
addressed.

II. Associative Poetry

We see in Robert Bly's theories, though of course in different terms
and with different emphases, many of the same polemical aims that
animated Charles Olson. Bly wants the poem to record more than a
preestablished emotional truth, some previously mediated value
statement that the poet offers to his audience to reassure them all is
well. Bly, like Olson, wants most deeply the word behind the words,
some statement that will be both a befuddlement and a challenge to our
daily chatter. Also like Olson, Bly develops a way of proceeding toward this statement, a kind of moral discipline in the form of a poetics,
but unlike Olson, Bly does not want to talk about "technique." This
avoidance, one might almost call it a fear, of technical skill comes from
Bly's belief that to plot an arrival, to plan an intuition, is inherently
self-defeating. One must proceed differently if what is desired is what
has been missing. All of Bly's theory revolves around this key sense:
something is missing, a knowledge, an awareness was once available
to us, and a conspiracy of rationality and order keeps it from us.
Evidence must be gathered, but if we trust the ordinary evidentiary

schemes we are foredoomed to arrive at the same conclusions. Unlike Olson, Bly is willing to admit personal, subjective testimony as valid (in fact he insists on it), but at the same time such subjective speaking must not insist on ownership or self-regard. Bly's experience of two years of enforced solitude and silence in a snowbound Minnesota cabin convinced him that only after such an experience did he truly know what he wanted to say. In other words, Bly's type of discipline must lead through the self, beyond the self. This is what produces in Bly's poetry that otherwise curious mix of pastoral quietism and moral harangue. The image—the truth leaped toward, beyond the connectiveness of rational discourse—will say it all, but it must be strictly attended to. Any attempt to transliterate the image, to use one's "technique" to make it presentable, will not only betray its accuracy, but will also involve us in a disauthenticating ego game.

Bly has edited an anthology of short poems, statements that ask for no involved justification, cries of joy or insight that rest their case on the belief that what is missing is so large and has been hidden for so long that the most we can manage, the most we can bear, are quick glimpses.[2] For Bly the poem as leap becomes a way back to a different order of understanding, for the missing truth has left its traces, its broken and frayed connections that can spark into conductivity once again. Bly challenges the lyric poem to resume one of its aboriginal functions, to rectify a mode of awareness that is prerational. In this sense, both Bly and Olson are indebted to books like Bruno Snell's *The Discovery of the Mind* or Eric Havelock's *Preface to Plato*, with their investigation of how mythological modes of thought precede rational ones, though it is through the poets' theories that this temporal priority can be equated with moral authority.

Bly's metaphor for the poem, then, is deeply polemical, and he stresses just those elements in poetry that are absent from prose, fictional and nonfictional: articulation of parts, discursiveness of procedure, and a penchant to "see around" the problems and seek comprehensiveness rather than instantaneity of expression. Bly's poetics gets much of its tension, however, from seeing the poem simultaneously as image and as leap, as a mythically authoritative presence and as a self-saving gesture. In fact, over the last decade or so (from the theoretical pieces in his magazine, *The Sixties*, to his contribution to the anthology *Naked Poetry*, called "Looking for Dragon Smoke," and on to the first number of *The Seventies*) we can sense Bly's concerns shifting from an image-centered poetry, where the danger was in producing a kind of endless series of sensory fragments, to a more energized *movement*, where the poem pointed a direction rather than simply presented a picture. It is almost as if Bly sensed that his body-centered mysticism needed another dimension, that to rely too exclusively on the images was to produce another version of contemplative poetry that included all the dangers of egoism and "plots" that he had so energetically avoided. The "image" might be mistaken for an object, but the same danger could not apply to "leaping."

III. The Poem as Myth

Part of what shapes the theories of Bly and Olson is a feeling that the lyric poem ought to assume a larger role in the shaping of culture, that it is only when poets settle on poems as "set pieces" that they abandon what was a traditionally important function of poetic language, namely to contain and rectify the crucially operative values in any society. This sense also animates those poets who write a poetry heavily indebted to a study of myth and the modes of mythical consciousness. Since Yeats's *A Vision*, however, it has become increasingly difficult for any poet to enunciate a mythical "system" that might justify or elucidate individual lyric poems. After Yeats, poets knew that one crucial element in a *mythos* was its social purpose, that is, a myth operated with fullest potency only when it formed the belief system of many individuals, all of whom drew their value terms from its reservoir of assumptions and exemplary acts. In the fifties, following in part the misleading example of Eliot's *Waste Land*, many poets began to use mythical material, often from a Greek or Roman source, as individualized psychological paradigms for the lyric poem. This practice still goes on, of course, and its main limitation is clear: it tends to melodramatize the poet's mundane concerns, and at the same time it may trivialize the myth. Also aware of this limitation, many contemporary poets use myth ironically, to suggest or measure the gap between an archaic but heroic culture and our more self-conscious, but commonplace, egocentricity. At one of its more brittle extremes, this use of myth can degenerate into manipulating motifs in purely decorative ways; at another extreme, it results in a simple retelling of the ancient story in modern terms, with the poet acting as a noninstitutionalized teacher, conveying cultural riches from the past. It would be extremely unusual to find, say, a Yale Younger Poet or a National Book Award winner between 1950 and 1965 whose book didn't include at least one poem named after a Greek or Roman deity and whose structure didn't illustrate these two extremes.

As the use of myth by poets became more self-conscious over the last two decades, the understanding of myth and of its various social and cultural functions also developed in almost exponential ways. Mythography seemed to generate a kind of cultural warehouse of mythical motifs, and the revolution marked by Frazer's *The Golden*

Bough appeared commonplace. *The Golden Bough* was subject to interpretations from at least two qualitatively different perspectives: it
could demonstrate the economy of the mythical imagination, which,
though capable of producing myriad variations, always used a limited
number of basic structures, or it could foster a thorough-going cultural
relativism. In either case, the poet's awareness might be compromised,
since he was free to use mythical material without having to vindicate it
specifically in terms of his own experience. Myth threatened to assume
the status of rhetoric in Renaissance poetics, that is, it answered several
formal questions without raising troublesome notions of sincerity, all
the while allowing the poet to achieve a "public" (even "universal")
resonance. Some poets were aware of these shortcomings and took
several measures to avoid them; others felt the difficulties, but stayed
with a more or less traditional use of myth. Examples of the former
would include many avant-garde poets, such as Armand Schwerner,
whose *Tablets* is an extended work based on the notion that he is
translating certain fragmentary codices; Michael McClure, whose tan-
tras featured animal noises and protosemantic sounds; and Ed Dorn,
whose *Gunslinger* took over certain myths about the American West,
but used them to deal with philosophical questions in a half-comic
vein. McClure also wrote plays that featured a mythologized version of
such people as Billy the Kid and Jean Harlow, while Dorn's *North
Atlantic Turbine* was a brilliant attempt to break open the myths of
Anglo-American imperialism. In other words, there are several poets
who use myth for personal or satiric or merely lyric ends, or for all three
purposes and more. For some of these poets, mythmaking becomes
intertwined with personal fantasy and can arise out of a need to deal
with social issues in a nonpropagandistic way; for example, Diane
Wakoski's *George Washington Poems* are simultaneously a debunking of
the public-school myths about our first president, an extended meditation on rolemaking and the masculine "mystique," and a surreal autobiography.[3]

In these new uses of myth, contemporary poets often strove for a
transpersonal scope by adapting a body of historical materials to their
purposes, or, as in the case of Robert Duncan's "Passages" and *Structure of Rime*, to a more or less traditional notion or structure that then
allowed the poets maximum inclusiveness. Often the larger works that
resulted from such procedures were purposely kept fragmentary, "in
process," since myth had come to be seen as a dialectic, often involving
a growth and development of stories or motifs through many versions,
the "total" truth being a construct that spanned and included but also
went beyond the single versions. In many such poetic "sequences" a
kind of "projective verse" was employed, though in weaker cases this

simply meant breaking up of any typographical consistency in the poem. Part of this aesthetic developed, of course, from the example of such poets as Yeats and Stevens, and others such as Blake before them, who invited the reader to consider all a poet's separate lyrics as parts of a unified statement; Stevens, for example, had considered calling his collected poems "The Whole of Harmonium." The poet's myth in this case becomes the transrational "vision" articulated by all his or her poems, not locatable in any specific poem or passage, but animating and pervasive throughout them all. But with many contemporary poets, unlike Stevens and Yeats, the "system" is something self-consciously chosen; it doesn't slowly arise out of several decades of poetic practice and it isn't later pieced together by critics and scholars.

Another way myth is used by contemporary poets can be seen at the level of diction. To strip one's words of most particularity and specific detail yet still write a highly charged syntax, so that instead of vague emotive drift one creates a portentous but abstract narrative tension; to use a certain group of nouns like door, stone, ring, or feather that vaguely resemble the key objects in a primitive ritual: all of this comes together (with a different "mix" for certain poets, to be sure) to form a poetic language with a definite "mythical" feel. Many of the poets who write in this mode are also translators; from working with the demands of that discipline they seem to have developed what we might call a "secondary" language, that is, a flat syntax and bland diction that resemble what is often used in translations. This language also must avoid slang, colloquial idioms, and any overly specific noun that would place or date the work. Clearly this language often produces parables, where archetypal actions and significant detail suggest a mythical consciousness at work. Here is an example, the first several lines of a poem by W. S. Merwin:

> Fear
> there is
> fear in fear the name the blue and green walls
> falling of and numbers fear the veins that
> when they were opened fear flowed from and
> these forms it took a ring a ring a ring
> a bit of grass green swan's down gliding on
> fear into fear and the hatred and something
> in everything and it is my death's
> disciple leg and fear no he would not
> have back those lives again and their fear as
> he feared he would say but he feared more he
> did not fear more he did fear more
> in everything it is there a long time

as I was and it is within those
blue and green walls . . .

Merwin's poems often use this language, and certain devices occur fairly frequently in his and others' poetry to create a sense of anonymity and at the same time to suggest a very strong ego at work in the language (this particular poem ends: "there is fear in everything and it is/me and always was in everything it/is me"). There is often a vague "other" in the poem; often a use of certain mythological topics, such as an etiologic or apocalyptic terminus for the action, and often a stylized repetition or ambiguity to suggest ritual structure.[4] In a sense this particular example can be read as a stream-of-consciousness lyric about a child's first experience of fear, but the elaborate structure and the riddling intertwining of phrases make for considerable complexity. (Often this complexity can mask a fairly banal content, as the last three lines of the poem might indicate.) Often we sense in Merwin's poetry a conflict between a need to use mythical material and the impulse to shape individual lyrics on a "self-bound" scale; this conflict some readers see as Merwin's main asset, while others find it produces poems that read like well-dressed truisms. In any case, his poems are more like hierophantic testaments than songs, as if he had created a litany in search of a redeeming mystery, hoping that after the half-gods of melody departed, the gods of rapture would arrive.

No one of these three metaphors for the poem now dominates contemporary poetry; in fact, their overlapping and mutual interaction often account for the strength of individual poets, and they certainly add to the pluralism of styles available today. This pluralism is both cause and effect of a mushrooming of theoretical speculation about poetry and how best to "achieve" it. I say "achieve" it, rather than write it, because what such metaphors often do is provide individual poets with a way to anchor their practice, to promote and justify a way of entering into their own poetry. As more and more isolation threatens the writer, as more and more the interview takes the place of the creative utterance, and as more and more the figure of the poet or the sense of the "poetic" outstrips the importance of individual poems, these metaphors may increase in importance. But while they are more than the trappings of artistic speculation, the metaphors might be called upon to do too much of the work of generating poetic meaning and excellence. Ours is an age when linguistic philosophy—words about words—seems at times to usurp the entire domain of philosophy. So far, poets have not settled for making only poems about poetry, but it is a temptation that needs stout resistance.

8

"The Burned Essential Oil"
The Gestures of Philip Levine

In the bleak paintings of Edward Hopper, emptied of saving human contact, or in certain Hemingway stories, like "A Clean Well-Lighted Place," we enter a world built out of almost unremarkable personal survivals. These survivals occur not when people are making out, but when they are barely making do: "I'm getting by," as the saying has it, and we can hear the swish of a heavy blade or see a minefield already half-detonated, but still hiding a hundred triggers. Out of such unpromising prospects Philip Levine makes his poems, poems of singing victims at once rootless and condemned to limited living space. Despite this world of harsh consequences and fierce limitations, Levine's poetry seldom displays scenes of agony. Seldom does anyone die on stage, there is nothing obscene in the root sense of the word, but throughout every poem we sense that someone, no matter how blear-eyed the dawn has left him, is looking hard at hard facts. In an elegy for his cousin, who was killed while fighting in the Spanish civil war, an old peasant woman stripping the bodies of the dead finds the cousin's knife, shoes, and socks worth keeping.

> She blessed your feet, still pink,
> with hard yellow shields of skin
> at heel and toe, and she laughed
> scampering across the road, into
> the goat field, and up the long hill,
> the boots bundled in her skirts,
> and the gray hunting socks, and the knife.

Human flesh, either pinkly innocent or yellowed with fatigue, or both at once, lives on in sorrow and in the fatigue of others. "She thought you understood," the poet says, excusing the old woman, who gives away the socks and shoes to her nephew. All that's left thirty years after the war, and ten years after the woman's death, when this gripping elegy is composed, is

> The knife. . .still used, the black handle
> almost white, the blade
> worn thin since there is meat to cut.

The wearing away of edges and the bleaching of color signal use and

150

purpose, but they also reveal how useless war can render the young and brave. The elegy ends:

> . . .there is no one to look for you
> among the wild jonquils, the curling
> grasses at the road side,
> and the blood red poppies, no one
> to look on the farthest tip
> of wind breathing down from the mountains
> and shaking the stunted pines you hid among.

No more peasant woman, no more volunteer, only the worn knife and the vegetation, wild, curling, blood red, and stunted.

The first book by Philip Levine to receive wide attention was *Not This Pig* (1968), and its subject matter and tone set it apart from almost all the other books published in the late sixties. Levine's aesthetic sources were easy enough to identify; his hard edges and urban imagery recalled a strain from William Carlos Williams, as did his repeated return to the victims of modern blight as central antagonists. This latter element, of course, linked him to a pure American strain that ran from David Ignatow back through Williams, Kenneth Patchen, and Weldon Kees, and at least as far back as Edwin Arlington Robinson.[1] Though such family resemblances are obvious when we read Levine, we can also detect a development in his work that carries far beyond this tradition into a mythically resonant, less detailed, but not less urgent singing, where we are likely to hear more threnodies than complaints and, finally, more invocations than laments. In *They Feed They Lion* (1972) and *1933* (1974), this mythical resonance increases markedly until it begins to dominate in the later book. Akin to the work of Robert Bly and W. S. Merwin, Levine's most recent poetry remains distinctive, however, as if the almost mystical brooding of his stay in Barcelona has merged with the abrasive gratings of his Detroit childhood. Both cities are built on the backs of sullen, exploited workers, and the faded revolution in one smolders like the blunting, racist fear in the other. No wonder, now he is settled in Fresno, California, that Levine sees the scar tissue of his past with a modicum of distance, though, as we shall see, much of the hurt is portable.

In *Not This Pig* the common structure for most of the poems rests on a narrative foundation. As often occurs in the case of lyric poems with a narrative component, we get what resembles the final act of a sequence presented with such force that it retains the texture and weight of the entire sequence. What we see, this final gesture, often cries out against a remembered and irremovable past, and what we often look toward is an unremitting future. Here is a typical poem from *Not This Pig*:

Blasting from Heaven

   The little girl won't eat her sandwich;
she lifts the bun and looks in, but the grey beef
   coated with relish is always there.
   Her mother says, "Do it for Mother."
Milk and relish and a hard bun that comes off
   like a hat—a kid's life is a cinch.

And a mother's life? "What can you do
With a man like that?" she asks the sleeping cook
   and then the old Negro that won't sit.
   "He's been out all night trying to get it.
I hope he gets it. What did he ever do
   but get it?" The Negro doesn't look,

   though he looks like he's been out all night
trying. Everyone's been out all night trying.
   Why else would we be drinking beer
   at attention? If she were younger,
or if I were Prince Valiant, I would say that fate
   brought me here to quiet the crying,

   to sweeten the sandwich of the child,
to waken the cook, to stop the Negro from
   bearing witness to the world. The dawn
   still hasn't come, and now we hear
the 8 o'clock whistles blasting from heaven,
   and with no morning the day is sold.

What remains interesting about this poem after several readings is the
slippery tone, or tones I should say, since the poem never fixes on
satire or sentimentality as its controlling mode. The narrator might be
characterized as "tough guy with tongue in cheek," as the line that
ends the second stanza half-grimaces, half-jokes its way into the third
stanza, where the second line could be read as if it were the punch line
for a comedian telling blue jokes or the unflinching, near-
melodramatic despair of a fellow sufferer. The third stanza is a wonder
in several ways, of course, as its rhetorical question simultaneously
reveals and conceals the narrator and the following subjunctive sentence muddles degraded, lowbrow, escapist art with genuine,
humane, almost grandly heroic sympathy. (In fact, this poem, and
others in this volume as well, reminds me of the strange world of mixed
realms we find in Flannery O'Connor.) In Levine's poetry people are a
long way from accepting their failures, but certainly those failures
don't come as a surprise to them.

   Occasionally the narrating voice can rise to something like a taunt
("You think you life is over?/It's just begun"), but more often than not

there lingers a suspicion of all forms of speech, especially of firm, unequivocal conclusions. "I learned by these words I hid my thought," Levine complains at one point. He often implies that he, or at least the people of and for whom he speaks, considers words a form of mystification; as is often the case with laborers and other people whose lives are filled with pressured actions, there is a mistrust of too-glib talk, of a speech that doesn't know when to shut up or to say the simple thing that will leave everyone alone with their own feelings. This accounts as well for the near-dominance of the narrative mode in Levine's work, for most of his narratives point simply to observed and irreducible events. I was there, they seem to say, and this is what happened: you can ignore it but you can't deny it. But laconic temperaments can be burdensome to the poet. One way Levine avoids this is by stretching out to a larger audience, even if that audience is itself the dispossessed in search of the inarticulate.

> Come with us tonight,
> drifters in the drifting crowd,
>   we shall arrive, late
> and tired, beyond the false lights
>   of Pasadena
> where the living are silent
>   in America.

This wider, more comprehending, though often less communicable vision will become one of the sources of his later mythical interests.

One other important observation about *Not This Pig*: it is a volume with many strong poems but very few striking lines. Levine's strength involves us in a colloquial, a spoken rather than a polished or well-shaped language. His poems often end with an anagogic leap that depends on a rather tangential, elliptical angle of vision; these poems need to be enacted rather than pondered. Paradoxically for poetry whose frequent subject is often a form of disarticulation, Levine's work needs a very keen "speaking" sensibility to register fully its complete texture. (As one might guess, Levine is an excellent reader of his own poetry: his voice grows slowly louder and more insistent as it moves through the poem and ends with a wavering that is part bitter execration, part triumphant challenge.) The climactic poem of *Not This Pig* offers a good example of this; spoken from the viewpoint of a pig being driven to the slaughterhouse, the poem is filled with manic images of broken language and corrupted systems of communication:

> The boy
> who drives me along believes
>
> that any moment I'll fall

> on my side and drum my toes
> like a typewriter or squeal
> and shit like a new housewife,
>
> discovering television,
> or that I'll turn like a beast
> cleverly to hook his teeth
> with my teeth. No. Not this pig.

Seldom has the inarticulate been more precisely shown, seldom has denial seemed so eloquently victorious.

With *They Feed They Lion* Levine's poetry deepens its entire range of emotion. Its opening poem, "Renaming the Kings," evokes a singular afternoon in order to occasion a new version of an old myth: a river god is rechristened, or rather the river takes up a new name for itself after the poet leans over the stone banks to drink "the first darkness flowing/from the river bottom":

> I named the stone John
> after my mysterious second born.
>
> High in its banks, slashed with silver,
> riding the jagged blade of heaven
> down to earth, the river shouts its name.

The anagogic leap is more surely made, the narrative occasion more deliberately regenerative as Levine moves into a more interior awareness, using his imagination to project a new order as well as to empathize with a weary, fallen one. But of course he continues to use his interest in articulation and survival to full account. Many of the poems in *They Feed They Lion* are discontinuous, with three or more sections, each having several brief narrative frames linked together affectively (here the similarity with Robert Bly is apparent), as if Levine now knew more surely his deepest emotional concerns, was indeed seeing them everywhere, but was still respecting the struggle of discursive language at odds with the contingencies of experience. He speaks, in "To a Fish Head Found on the Beach Near Malaga," of "an iron yawn/out over the waves, the one poem born/of the eternal and always going back." Like Elizabeth Bishop in her poem "The Fish," the speaker here ends with a surrender, but this fish has both more corruption and less pliancy than Bishop's:

> I throw the fish head to the sea.
> Let it be fish once more.
>   I sniff my fingers
> and catch the burned essential oil
> seeping out of death. Out of beginning,
> I hear, under the sea roar, the bone words

> of teeth tearing earth and sea,
> anointing the tongues with stone and sand,
> water eating fish, fish water,
> head eating head to let us be.

Another key link between this book and the ones that precede and follow it is forged by Levine's use of angels. They occur first in *Not This Pig* as, variously, a lover whose voice is like a "raiment of victory"; a fallen brother who, when carried, leaves the speaker's "chest and arms smeared with dust/and tipped with bloodless feathers"; and a young costumed child who collects money for the poor and hungry and who, the speaker tells us, "gave me back my life." Levine's angelology at times seems distinctly Hebraic, for, while he never directly wrestles with them, their messages challenge his equilibrium or settle his despair. In *They Feed They Lion*, a rather Christian angel appears, protective and domesticated:

> I wore angels.
> They saved me in the streets
> where the towers hung above
> suspended on breath, they
> saved me from the pale woman
> who smoothed the breasts
> of chicken or the red-armed
> one who sold bread in
> the shop of knives.

But the most memorable angels, of course, are his Rilkean ones, those manifestations of the not quite destroyed spirit persisting in the waste and spoilage of the mundane world.

> Don't matter what rare breath
> puddles in fire on
> the founding floor. The toilets
> overflow, the rats dance, the maggots
> have it, the worms of money
> crack like whips, and
> among the angels
> we lie down.

For Levine the angel seems a mythical figure able, in part at least, to make his own history, one who won't simply be the victim of destiny or of an exploitative economic system disguising itself as destiny. But in the sequence "The Angels of Detroit" the history often has to settle for being a history of defiant, futile gestures:

> In a toilet on Joy Rd
> long Eddie on alto.

The yellow of his eyes
brown on pot, the brown centers
burned like washed gold.

Never knew the tune. 16
years old, drummer
had to prod him to music.
So much sorrow in hatred,
so much tenderness
he could taste coming up
from the rich earth.

Little clown. Caught all alone,
arm in a mail-box.
Never did nothing right,
except tell the cops to suck
and wave them off like flies.

The angels appear on commemorative, celebratory occasions, but they
are also clearly harbingers of alienation; though they are far from
demonic, their presence and their identity testify to a world insistently
fallen, despite its defiance.

Nowhere does the insistent fallenness of the world in Levine's
poetry present a more unyieldingly rapacious spirit than in the title
poem of *They Feed They Lion*. Here the confrontation of urban, industrial, mass man with his own fouled and rotting systems reaches a
terrifying pitch. An early poem of Levine's is called "Animals are
Passing from Our Lives," and it laments the loss of feral energy. But
"They Feed They Lion" offers a bestial totem—the exploitative spirit as
a universally hungry animal anthropomorphized by a blind greed only
humans could recognize. The poem begins slowly, like a litany:

Out of burlap sacks, out of bearing butter,
Out of black bean and wet slate bread,
Out of acids of rage, the candor of tar,
Out of creosote, gasoline, drive-shafts, wooden dollies,
They Lion Grow.

And grow it does. There are few other thirty-line poems that manage to
say as much about America as this one; if there were a dark counterpart
to the figure of the poet laureate hymning his country's grandeur,
Levine by this poem alone would earn the right to be considered for the
title. Beginning as it does with images of the grime-coated detritus of
America, the poem recalls Ginsberg's "Sunflower Sutra," but what
sprouts from this soil is something utterly different from Ginsberg's
ecstasy-inducing flower.

From pig balls,

> From the ferocity of pig driven to holiness,
> From the furred ear and the full jowl come
> The repose of the hung belly, from the purpose
> They Lion grow.

The purpose may remain dark, but the shape and sound of the beast get clearer and clearer. I said earlier that none of Levine's poems was obscene, and despite the social obscenity this poem depicts, I would leave that statement unaltered, for somehow—by poetry, by magic, by the expressiveness of the inarticulate—this poem *comes clean*. By the time we reach the concluding stanza we are in a realm of discourse mythically remote and yet oppressively mundane, at once chthonic and crass:

> Come they Lion from the reeds of shovels,
> The grained arm that pulls the hands,
> They Lion grow.
>   From my five arms and all my hands,
> From my white sins forgiven, they feed,
> From my car passing under the stars,
> They Lion, from my children inherit,
> From the oak turned to a wall, they Lion,
> From they sack and they belly opened
> And all that was hidden burning on the oil-stained earth
> They feed they Lion and he comes.

Ignoring the slight possibility of a sexual pun on the last word, we have an image of ravening hunger faintly counterpointed by the ambiguity that the Lion is also *theirs*, of their creation, in their lineage. (The identity of the first-person speaker in the poem is also ambiguous, since he speaks with the authority of an earth god and the dialect of an oppressed worker. Also, because of the ambiguity of the dialect, "Lion" could be the subject, the object, or the predicate nominative of "grow.") In any case, this is one of Levine's most memorable poems; in it his empathy with the wretched of the earth, his fascination with the rich possibilities of the barely articulable, his pained awareness of social destiny, and his mythical consciousness come together with perfect and awesome force.

In *1933*, Levine has flattened his narrative texture even further. He spends more energy developing the lineaments of interiority, exploring recesses of his own personal history as well as widening his access to archetypal depths. His poems still frequently exhibit an unresolved ending:

> In a white dress
> my little girl goes to the window.
> She is unborn

> she is the thin flame
> of a candle,
> she is her mother
> singing a song.
> Her words frost
> the mirror of the night,
> a huge wind waits
> at the back of her breath.

If *Not This Pig* is his "Book of the Exploited" and *They Feed They Lion* his "Book of the Indomitable," then *1933* is Levine's "Book of Originals." It begins with a poem about his grandfather, and its title poem commemorates, if that is the word, the year his father died. There are also poems about his sister during the war ("she dreams her husband/is home, his fists burned red"), his mother ("Nothing is lost/she says to the darkness, nothing"), and his grandmother:

> someone's beautiful Polish daughter
> with a worn basket of spotted eggs,
>
> an elbow of cabbage, carrots, leaves,
> chicken claws scratching the air,
>
> she comes up the cracked walk to the stairway
> of shadows and lost dolls and lost breath.

All these poems, while beautiful as celebrations of others, are concerned with Levine's search for the origins of his own consciousness, that exploration of original images and emotional force fields that Freud made virtually inevitable for all of us. But the urgency of the search, for Levine, springs from his concern to discover who we are, in terms of how we came to be that way, what we have done to evolve, and to be willing to accept this set of failures we call our life. This is his major theme, present in all his poems: failure turned not into triumph, but at least into survival, by the revelation of origins. Only someone actually conscious of where he came from—the city, the era, the family, the values that gave him shape and disposition—could be so obsessed with saying his say in his own words, in his own moments. As he tells us in his poem for his uncle:

> In the basement on Grand
> he showed me
> his radio,
> Manila, Atlantis,
> the cities of the burning plains,
> the coupons
> in comic books, the ads of the air.

Cities of all the world, the embattled and the lost, spring out of a shortwave radio band in a house on Grand Avenue in Detroit—where else would they seem so mysterious, who but an uncle could be so wise, so strong as to bring them within range? He goes on to describe the uncle:

> Prophet of burned cars
> and broken fans, he taught
> the toilet the eternal,
> argued the Talmud
> under his nails. The long boats
> with names of winds
> set sail
> in the sea of his blind eye.

In the year 1933, when the poet was only five years old, his father "entered the kingdom of roots," Levine tells us, and now "the world is different in many places." But again and again in the title poem and throughout the whole of *1933* the poet tries to fix the unknowably human with a telling gesture. In a sense we reveal ourselves at every moment—in a room of friends we can tell who sneezes by the sound alone, we recognize people by their stoop, their smell, the way they point—and the revelatory gesture is like the signature of destiny. The family, for all its shortcomings, will allow us to know a few people so intimately that no human can ever be a total stranger.

> he drove the car all the way to the river
>   where the ships burned
> he rang with keys and coins
> he knew the animals and their names
>   touched the nose of the horse
>   and kicked the German dog away . . .
>
> my father opens the telegram under the moon
>   Cousin Philip is dead
> my father stands on the porch in his last summer
> he holds back his tears
> he holds back my tears

Our most fundamental and unshakable notions of what is possible and what is proper originate in such moments. Somehow identity survives in these gestures, and during them we transmit something like humanity. I "thought of you one by one/and tried to hold your faces/in my eyes," Levine says in "Letters for the Dead," his longest, most threnodic poem. The world changes in many places, but the roots persist and give us just enough evidence to enable us to classify and to praise:

I carved the old scar
again and again
my signature cut
almost to bone
even the brown silky hairs
and the mottlings from birth
will never hide it

Let the scars shine

The pain and suffering, in either enveloping myth or linear narrative, give the authenticating touch, the node of intensity from which all progress or decay will be measured.

For Levine, the change in style from harsh particularity to a richer, mythological idiom was clearly not abrupt. Because *They Feed They Lion* includes both these stylistic possibilities in its orbit of various occasions and concerns, it remains for me the richest of Levine's books. However, there are poems in *They Feed They Lion*, such as "The Children's Crusade" and the long sequence "Thistles," that strike me as flawed by an inconsistency between the colloquial and mythical voices, poems unhappily out of phase in a work that otherwise presents a fruitful and engaging growth in the poet's powers. In *1933*, though, Levine has achieved an enviable harmony of voice and concern that will surely lead many sensitive readers to rank it highest among Levine's books and very high indeed among the recent work of all American poets. One of the things it demonstrates conclusively is the thoroughly American character of Levine's poetry. From the vantage point of this book we can look back over the bedeviling culture America presents its poets; almost totally nonsupportive, it often splits them into multiple selves or sends them looking for whatever personal belief system they can fitfully restore—family, or fame, or power. It teaches them to curse the excesses that are so obvious few people see them. All the while it makes them hunger for a healing, inclusive language that will be strong enough to become instructive, yet humble enough to remain honest. For poets as serious about their calling as Levine is, America presents an endless vocation.

In "The Poem Circling Hamtramck, Michigan All Night in Search of You," one of the best poems in *1933*, Levine presents a scene of survival set in a barroom, late at night, involving a lonely old woman who has "seen them before/with hard, knotted bellies,/with the bare white breasts of boys," and a man abandoned by his wife, "gone home, mad,/with the baby on one arm." The old woman and the man don't speak to one another, and the poem's transcendence is, somewhat like that in "Blasting from Heaven," by turns subjunctive, negative, and numinous. Here it is not so much the tone that is slippery and hard to fix as the frames of reference, for at the end the world of laborers and the imagery of apotheosis are mysteriously joined.

> If someone would enter now
> and take these lovers—for they
> are lovers—in his arms
> and rock them together
> like a mother with a child
> in each arm, this man
> with so much desire, this woman
> with none, then it would not be
> Hamtramck, it would not be
> this night. They know it
> and wait, he staring
> into the light, she into
> the empty glass. In the darkness
> of this world men
> pull on heavy canvas gloves,
> dip into rubber coats
> and into the fires. The rats
> frozen under the conveyors
> turn to let their eyes
> fill with dawn. A strange star
> is born one more time.

"They know it/and wait"—it is the slogan of all survivors, in a way. The line and the whole poem have the tonelessness that characterizes many contemporary lyrics, brief poems that intimate a larger mythical consciousness. We have replaced the tones of colloquialism and dialect with a bland, almost reportorial voice, as if the pained, personal speaker has become suddenly distant or vatic. At the same time this poem, with its anagogic leap from the world of mundane objects and events, clearly owes much to Levine's early work, but instead of saying "I was there," it implies that we have all been here once before, though then the world was different.

What began, then, as an incisive gift for capturing the terminal moment, the final gesture, in *Not This Pig* has developed into a capacity for finding the sustaining originals, the freshening sources. In the process, Levine has sometimes used more varied stanzaic forms, a more neutral diction, a less singularizing imagery. But as the success of *1933* makes plain, he can still reach back to a redolent personal past and project it into a healing inclusiveness, with no loss of vigor and no weakening of urgency or authority in a voice at once gritty, dark, and expansive. We can finish with a gesture of his, one that itself originates with a gentle survivor:

In May, like this May, long ago
my tiny Russian Grandpa—the bottle king—
cupped a stained hand under my chin
and ran his comb through my golden hair.

Sweat, black shag, horse turds on the wind,
the last wooden cart rattling down
the alleys, the clop of his great gray mare,
green glass flashing in December sun. . .

I am the eye filled with salt,
his child climbing the rain, we are
all the moon, the one planet, the hand
of five stars flung on the night river.

"This Leaving-Out Business"

The Poetry of John Ashbery

The first few books by John Ashbery contained a large proportion of a poetry of inconsequence. Borrowing freely from the traditions of French surrealism, and from his friends Frank O'Hara and Kenneth Koch, Ashbery tried out a fairly narrow range of voices and subjects. Subject matter, or rather the absence of it, helped form the core of his aesthetic, an aesthetic that refused to maintain a consistent attitude toward any fixed phenomena. The poems tumbled out of a whimsical, detached amusement that mixed with a quizzical melancholy. This aesthetic reached an extreme with *The Tennis Court Oath* (1962), a book in which no poem makes even the slightest attempt to marshal a rational context or an identifiable argument. Line follows line without the sheerest hint of order or apparent plan; this studied inconsequence delighted some readers at the time. But this is not a book to reread; seeing it outside the context of rebellion against the too-conscious aesthetic then fostered by academic poetry, it is difficult to understand why the book was published. (Wesleyan seems an especially unlikely publisher, except that its program was committed to innovation, and with this one title it seemed to fulfill that aim once and for all.) With the exception of *The Tennis Court Oath*, Ashbery's first four commercially published books (the others are *Some Trees* [1956], *Rivers and Mountains* [1966], and *The Double Dream of Spring* [1970]) included some poems with interpretable meanings and recognizable structures. But reading the first four books together, one is struck by how precious are those poems that do make poetic sense, surrounded as they are by the incessant chatter of the poems of inconsequence. Slowly, however, it appears as if Ashbery was gaining confidence for his true project, and, as his work unfolds, an indulgent reader can see how it needed those aggressively banal "experiments" in nonsense to protect its frailty. Ashbery's later poetry often uses the traditions of prose discourse, but instead of a poetry of "statement" he has evolved a most tenuous, unassertive language. The first four books, one feels, would have turned out insufferably banal, or perhaps would have remained altogether unwritten, if Ashbery had faced his subject directly or made too various or rigorous demands on his limited language.

Some Trees was selected by W. H. Auden as a winner in the Yale

Younger Poet competition, and one might guess Auden enjoyed the
campy joke such a selection appeared to be. Ashbery disliked Auden's
introduction intensely, and when Corinth Books republished the volume in 1970, they excluded it. In the midfifties there was little like
Ashbery's poetry to be found, except of course for the poems of Frank
O'Hara. But Ashbery's work at this time, despite its being the rival of
O'Hara's for preciosity and surreal wit, felt more "literary" than that of
his friend. This feeling is hard to locate, but it grew stronger with
Ashbery's career and in some way accounts for the partisanship some
academic critics have recently shown for his work.[1] In some of the
poems in this book, we see a straightforward whimsy such as that often
used by Kenneth Koch. The humor remains deadpan, the juxtapositions being between the high-minded expectations of "art" and the
flat, unheroic irony of the disaffected speaker. For example, "The
Instruction Manual" and "The Painter" are like comically neuter pro-
test poems in which alienation is turned into a commonplace, and what
might be the "howl" of the outsider sounds instead like the whimper of
a repressed clerk. (The masterpiece of this sort of thing is Koch's "The
Pleasures of Peace.") Ashbery also includes a few examples of a favorite exercise of the so-called New York school of poets—the formula
poem in which a simple grammatical structure is repeated over and
over with bizarre language. This method of generating whimsy may
well owe its origin to the surreal concern with *objectif hasard*, where the
consciously selected "format" is juxtaposed to whatever chance as-
sociations the writer can release. Here is part of "He":

> He knows that his neck is frozen.
> He snorts in the vale of dim wolves.
> He writes to say, "If ever you visit this island,
> He'll grow you back to your childhood.
>
> "He is the liar behind the hedge
> He grew one morning out of candor.
> He is his own consolation prize.
> He has had his eye on you from the beginning."
>
> He hears the weak cut down with a smile.
> He waltzes tragically on the spitting housetops.
> He is never near. What you need
> He cancels with the air of one making a salad.

The poem unveils twelve such quatrains, and each line begins with
"He" followed by a verb. "The vale of dim wolves" and the tragic waltz
on "the spitting housetops" typify the imagery of Ashbery's early
poetry: arbitrary, coy, disaffected, "smart." Moreover, the arbitrary
continuation of the poem lies at the center of Ashbery's aesthetic,

which seems a flirtation with nihilism, the fag end of an autotelic art that apotheosizes symbolism's elevation of style over content. The stochastic movement of the poem reminds one of the music of John Cage; the levelling of values suggests the painting of Andy Warhol.

We can place alongside the above passage from *Some Trees* two other passages. The first is from *Rivers and Mountains:*

> The sedate one is this month's skittish one
> Confirming the property that,
> A timeless value, has changed hands.
> And you could have a new automobile
> Ping pong set and garage, but the thief
> Stole everything like a miracle.

The second is from *The Double Dream of Spring:*

> The mountain stopped shaking; its body
> Arched into its own contradiction, its enjoyment
> As far from us lights were put out, memories of boys and girls
> Who walked here before the great change,
>
> Before the air mirrored us,
> Taking the opposite shape of our effort,
> Its inseparable comment and corollary
> But casting us further and further out.

These lines show how Ashbery's poetry sidles up to and slips away from meaning, as each line clearly links to the one before and after it, but the overall context remains vague and elliptical. Increasingly Ashbery resorts to the contextual devices of prose: pronominals, appositive and subordinate clauses, logical coordinates, and so forth. But at the same time certain "poetic" devices come to the fore, for example, startling similes, metaphoric verbs, ambiguous suspensions of predicates, and highly figurative language—what Ashbery calls "the great 'as though.' " Often the element of play in his poetics causes Ashbery to drift into a boring "castles in the air" approach, as if he were testing the limits of significance; likewise, he can become ponderous when his poetry takes on a pseudophilosophical cast where irony ought to be operating but a sodden rumination drains off the flow of wit. Ashbery himself describes the perfect balance, when his language becomes most distinctive and most rewarding; this is from "Clepsydra," in *Rivers and Mountains:*

> Each moment
> Of utterance is the true one; likewise none are true,
> Only is the bounding from air to air, a serpentine
> Gesture which hides the truth behind a congruent
> Message, the way air hides the sky. . .

Havelock Ellis once characterized decadence as a style that subordinates the whole to the part, and we can glimpse something analogous here in the way in which each moment of the poem seems true (and in the further implication that *only* in its moments is the poem true, as any larger significance is illusory). Also, the paradox that no moment is true (because its truth must immediately be displaced by that of the next moment) suggests a sort of polymorphous perversity of contextuality. Add to this Ashbery's equivocating suspension between a referential and an emotive sense of meaning (air doesn't really hide the sky, it *is* the sky, so meaning and utterance are perfectly equal; however, the utterance must be a serpentine gesture, something other than merely "factual"), and you begin to understand why his poems seldom resort to traditional lyric modes of expression. Straightforward narrative; direct, spontaneous outcries; or deeply urgent shows of authenticity: none of these will be readily available to Ashbery's readers. Each decadent style, as Ellis also suggests, must be seen against a classical style from which it has "fallen down," and throughout Ashbery's work we catch the dying echoes of English romanticism, especially of those poets most haunted by the past, Wordsworth and Shelley. These echoes are spawned by Ashbery's relation to language and meaning, a relation that is both tenuous and diffident, because his feelings are evanescent, and offhanded, and condescending, because his utterance is derivative.

In many ways, *Rivers and Mountains* is Ashbery's most frustrating book, for it avoids the total meaninglessness of *The Tennis Court Oath* yet lacks the richness of *The Double Dream of Spring*. The book, full-size as poetry books go, has only twelve poems in its sixty-three pages. But an average of five pages per poem would be deceptive, for one poem takes up almost thirty pages; this poem, "The Skaters," is in many ways the quintessential Ashbery poem, the epitome of his career. Mixing bland, straightforwardly prosaic passages with the most inane, jumbled poetry of inconsequence, "The Skaters" is a nervous tour de force, a paean to solipsism and an anguished cry against its imprisonments. Few of the other poems in this book are especially distinctive, though "Into the Dusk-Charged Air" offers a special instance of the tenacity of Ashbery's aesthetic reaping unusual, inexplicable rewards:

> Mountains hem in the Colorado
> And the Oder is very deep, almost
> As deep as the Congo is wide.
> The plain banks of the Neva are
> Gray. The dark Saône flows silently.
> And the Volga is long and wide
> As it flows across the brownish land. The Ebro

Is blue and slow. The Shannon flows
Swiftly between its banks.

So it goes for over 150 lines, as if some catatonic were suddenly afflicted
with logorrhea in the presence of an atlas. The last images are of frozen
rivers, and the poem has a curious, baffled, antitranscendent structure
that seems somehow just right. The other feature of the book is the
poet's tendency to break up the flow of surreal images with occasional
axioms, though these sometime take the form of bemused rhetorical
questions or half-resuscitated clichés. This contributes to the "literary"
feel of Ashbery's antiliterary attack on meaningful structure and uni-
versalizing particulars.

But obviously it is "The Skaters" that this volume features, and the
poem itself introduces clearly one of Ashbery's most insistent self-
questionings: what should he put in, and what leave out? "This
poem. . .is in the form of falling snow," he ingenuously announces,
and as the meanings float and melt, the overridingly reflective mood
casts the poem into melancholy, which in turn throws up images of
self-defense and self-abasement. Here is one entire stanza:

But this is an important aspect of the question
Which I am not ready to discuss, am not at all ready to,
This leaving-out business. On it hinges the very importance
    of what's novel
Or autocratic, or dense or silly. It is as well to call
    attention
To it by exaggeration, perhaps. But calling attention
Isn't the same thing as explaining, and as I said I am not
    ready
To line phrases with the costly stuff of explanation, and
    shall not,
Will not do so for the moment. Except to say that the
    carnivorous
Way of these lines is to devour their own nature, leaving
Nothing but a bitter impression of absence, which as we
    know involves presence, but still,
Nevertheless these are fundamental absences, struggling to
    get up and be off themselves.

I think this passage says more about Ashbery's poetics than all that has
been written about him, especially since some critics have forgotten
that "calling attention/Isn't the same thing as explaining." But most
evident here is Ashbery's fear of the banal, the "dense or silly," as well
as his craving for the truly fresh, the "novel or autocratic," and more
importantly his sense that it has become increasingly difficult to distinguish between them. The resort to surrealism can be seen as a response

to this fear, for surrealism's levelling of values mixes the mysterious and the mundane, and so seeks to solve the problem by embracing it. At the same time, the impulse toward inconsequence can be seen as an elaborate flight, a defensive reaction against this fear of meaningless-ness; thus the poet celebrates his own "carnivorous" quest for the meaning he knows will always elude him—unless he abandons his search and accepts reality as it is. The problem, however, remains one of locating the truly "fundamental" absences. Five or six pages later we find this entire stanza:

> Uh. . .stupid song. . .that weather bonnet
> Is all gone now. But the apothecary biscuits dwindled.
> Where a little spectral
> Cliffs, teeming over into irony's
> Gotten silently inflicted on the passages
> Morning undermines, the daughter is.

The worst part of it is that the absences here are apparently less than fundamental, and seeking connections in such a text is like playing cat's cradle with a rubber band. In "The Skaters" we confront a stiffer problem yet, as the poetry of inconsequence mixes indiscriminately with some of the poet's more pellucid and lyric efforts, and this rather decreases the overall meaning that's available to most readers. (I sus-pect, however, that for the "we" in the phrase "which as we know involves presence" this mixing is the stamp of excellence, the proof of Ashbery's suspension between the burden of traditional meaning and the bathos of playful absurdity.)

Other hallmarks of Ashbery's style show up in "The Skaters" and throughout *Rivers and Mountains*: most noticeably, a fear of social reality and a dire, overwrought emotionalism. These are central to the problem of putting in and leaving out, for apparently Ashbery is far from thoroughly comfortable in the role of aesthete or plangent late romantic. The very ambitiousness of "The Skaters" indicates he wants to address a wide spectrum of reality, even if large hunks of modern-day reality are simply not assimilable to his style and he must resort to rhetorical questioning, as in this passage:

> But another, more urgent question imposes itself—
>   that of poverty.
> How to excuse it to oneself? The wetness and coldness?
>   Dirt and grime?
> Uncomfortable, unsuitable lodgings, with a depressing view?
> The peeled geranium flowering in a rusted tomato can,
> Framed in a sickly ray of sunlight, a tragic chromo?

Only by aestheticizing the harsh reality, by turning the moment into a genre scene, can the poet imagine the other world and excuse it, to himself, notice. Later we are told (after a long, aggressive solipsistic fantasy about being stranded on an island):

> In reality of course the middle-class apartment I live in is
>   nothing like a desert island.
> Cozy and warm it is, with a good library and record collection.
> Yet I feel cut off from the life in the streets.

He describes himself at one point as a "professional exile," and like all such exiles he must make a song of himself, a song that makes the universe and its secret meanings available to him, but only through the mediacy of strong feeling:

> The west wind grazes my cheek, the droplets come pattering
>   down;
> What matter now whether I wake or sleep?
> The west wind grazes my cheek, the droplets come pattering
>   down;
> A vast design shows in the meadow's parched and trampled
>   grasses.
> Actually a game of "fox and cheese" has been played there,
>   but the real reality,
> Beyond truer imaginings, is that it is a mystical design
>   full of a certain significance,
> Burning, sealing its way into my consciousness.

Here the obvious echoes of poems by Shelley and Keats are undercut by the fey diction ("pattering down"), and the mystical meaning is simultaneously exposed as putative (hence false) and esoteric (hence really real). But just as we can detect the essence of a wounded liberal conscience, however embarrassed, behind the passage on poverty, so we can hear real emotional loss, however ironically distilled, behind the wan textures of such passages.

And so, at roughly the midpoint of his career to date, Ashbery's *Rivers and Mountains* demonstrated that he was in many ways still our most private and our most public poet, an egoist and an exile. But the style was becoming clearer with each book, and the paradoxes, cultural and poetic, were intensifying. Ashbery's poetry had attained the acme of defensive irony, yet it also offered a way beyond what had become such a limiting aesthetic. Even if Ashbery could not decide what to put in and what to leave out, at least he had clearly identified this as the problem; however, as the later books were to show, stating the problem did not always reduce it, let alone dispense with it. "All right. The problem is that there is no new problem," as he says in the opening of the last section of *Three Poems* (1972). What saved Ashbery from the desiccation of defensive irony was not just his hunger for innovation, or his return to romantic themes, but his willingness to come round (and round and round) onto the *sources* of his own feelings, as well as to speak openly about the nonappearance of feeling. We can even speculate that his sense of an audience grew more secure and slightly more public, and he slowly began to abandon his sense of being no more than a coterie poet. But we shouldn't make too much of this; the hermeticism is part of his project, and Ashbery will probably never achieve the freewheeling humor of Kenneth Koch or the feckless self-definition of Frank O'Hara.

Much of the particular feel of Ashbery's poetry comes from the tension between its proselike discursiveness and the random, sometimes elliptical tenuousness of its associative gatherings. The "self" in a typical Ashbery poem will almost stumble over a defensive displacement of what is really affecting him; at the same time, reticence never appears as a real possibility. This self wants your attention, but he is counting on your good taste not to inquire too rigorously or peremptorily. The author–reader contract is a conspiratorial one for Ashbery, as he writes not simply for those "in the know," but for those who can dally at will. Here is "The Chateau Hardware," the shortest poem in *The Double Dream of Spring*, but otherwise typical of Ashbery's rhetorical strategies:

> It was always November there. The farms
> Were a kind of precinct; a certain control
> Had been exercised. The little birds
> Used to collect along the fence.
> It was the great "as though," the how the day went,
> The excursions of the police
> As I pursued my bodily functions, wanting
> Neither fire nor water,
> Vibrating to the distant pinch
> And turning out the way I am, turning out to greet you.

Several phrases contribute to the elliptical structure of the poem; "a kind of," "a certain control," and "used to collect" all rely on an assumed body of shared knowledge or at least prior reference and seem to take for granted an easy mix of comfortably common values and emotions. Note, too, how the fifth line suggests a predication that is never completed. The average reader might well look for a "that" clause, expecting to hear that it was the great "as though" *that*. . . . Instead, the last five and a half lines of the poem are grammatically in apposition to the initial clause that completes the "It was" of line five. The poem, then, instead of gathering to some sort of dramatic resolution, trails off into a series of qualifying clauses governed by participles ("wanting," "vibrating," and "turning"). This structure strengthens the mundane "It was" that opens the poem; in a sense, the entire poem is simply an elaboration of that initial moment. (Note, too, that that "moment" is both past and unchanging.) At the same time, as the elliptical details filter through the poem's meandering syntax they seem to deepen a mystery that is unresolvable. For example, the surreal juxtaposition of the police excursions and the speaker's bodily functions has an apparent logical context based on the adverbial relation ("as"). Yet this juxtaposition is no sooner set up than the bodily functions are further placed in another context, one of total sufficiency. What began as oppressive has suddenly become carefree. The "distant pinch" could metaphorically be something as threatening as death, like the "old catastrophe" of Stevens's "Sunday Morning," or something as reassuring as missing someone who nevertheless soon returns ("turning out to greet you."), or the police making arrests, more simply.

But this combination of the mundane and the mysterious is reinforced by the imagery, which combines "little birds" and "excursions of the police." Likewise, the poem yokes the plain declarative opening sentence with the last sentence in the poem, which combines the declarative with the bracketed "as though" that suggests the whole experience, or at least its experiential essence, takes place in a subjunctive, virtual framework. The farm appearing as a kind of "precinct," together with the exercise of a "certain control" and the mockly picturesque "little bird. . .along the fence" add up to something like an antipastoral. Clearly the speaker is too self-conscious, too urbane in his fey manipulation of pastoral markers to be celebrating the "green world" of literary tradition. Yet the surrounding police metaphors and activities help create the feeling that the poem is about an escape, a momentary temporal haven from the usual "wants," a haven in which a sense of bodily wholeness and fellow feeling is restored. We never see the physical locale in any detail, nor do we clearly hear a celebratory tone. That the season is autumnal contributes to the elegiac mood, which in turn adds to the wan, etiolated sense of diffidence at the core of the poem's affections. Forced to a summary statement of the poem's theme, we might say it argues that the impulse toward the pastoral can itself become imprisoning, yet such escapism allows the affections to reassert themselves with simplified dignity, to convey the feeling that they are fated. The poem obviously leaves out a great deal, and it is rather fastidious and at the same time offhanded about what it puts in.

But something else that makes up the feel of Ashbery's poetry—it is both the cause and effect of its distinctive quality—can best be described as its essentially proselike movement. Ashbery eschews the ordinary lyricism of verse, seldom bothering with rhyme or alliteration or strict meter. At the same time the prosaic run of his sentences is neither Pateresque nor euphuistic. This prose quality goes hand in hand with the flat, affectless tone as well as with the wan, etiolated attitude. The run of his argument, the flow of the poem's display of itself, suggests a ruminative impulse at work. Very seldom do the metaphors result from the pressure of emotion, and we miss the metermaking argument that Emerson asked of poetry. Often the metaphors and similes seem illustrative rather than functional, supplied to the reader as a courtesy, lest the sinuosities of the ego's search for a balance between a too-ready order and a hopeless chaos weary him beyond limits. This part of Ashbery's aesthetic is clearly pushed to extremes in his *Three Poems*, where the dense Jamesian prose is studded with clichés. Obviously Ashbery felt the ordinary reader's demands, for fresh images and authentic if not desperate emotions, could be utterly denied. No reviewer of this work had the temerity to suggest it was a good-natured hoax, a jeu d'esprit in which the confessional impulses of contemporary poetry were so gluttonously satisfied that they were simultaneously scorned. Ashbery stuffed his "poems" with so much mandarin prose, masking such banal content, or at least cultivating such stultifying surface banality, that the modesty of the book's title can be read as either a deadpan joke or a high-handed taunt. The modernists' insistence that no subject matter or language is intrinsically nonpoetic confronts a severe test in this instance.

But *Three Poems* isn't a hoax, despite the self-indulgence of its format and its seeming refusal to mediate its feelings into a language public enough to allow response. The work's main concern is the theme of individuation, the reemergence of a new self out of the old. This theme, central to much contemporary American poetry, is of course an important modernist preoccupation as well. With Ashbery, the temporal aspects of the theme emerge forcefully, and his book becomes a severe meditation on time—the trappings of time as well as the trap of temporality. In fact, the two tutelary deities seem to be Walt Whitman and Marcel Proust. The poem seeks to embrace contradictions by recovering the past; but the recovery, or at least the attempt to recover, throws up such a welter of conflicting and unresolved emotions that the confusions of the self, rather than its individuation, become the dominant focus. Here is a sample of how the pursuit of a subject becomes the subject:

Are you sad about something today? On days like this the old flanking motion almost seems to be possible again. Certainly the whiff of nostalgia in the air is more than a hint, a glaring proof that the old irregular way of doing is not only some piece of furniture of the memory but is ours, if we had the initiative to use it. I have lost mine. It has been replaced by a strange kind of happiness within the limitations. The way is narrow but it is not hard, it seems almost to propel or push one along. One gets the narrowness into one's seeing, which also seems an inducement to moving forward into what one has already caught a glimpse of and which quickly becomes vision, in the visionary sense, except that in place of the panorama that used to be our customary setting and which we never made much use of, a limited but infinitely free space has established itself, useful as everyday life but transfigured so that its signs of wear no longer appear as a reproach but of indications of how beautiful a thing must have been to have been so much prized, and its noble aspect which must have been irksome before has now become interesting, you are fascinated and keep on studying it.

The push of mind here combines an anal retentiveness with an insistent shedding of disguises and contexts. "I thought that if I could put it all down, that would be one way. And next the thought came to me that to leave all out would be another, and truer, way," Ashbery says in the first sentence of the book. His self often takes a passive role ("the thought came to me"), but he also draws on deep sources of meditative energy and is unwilling to surrender the slightest psychological clue, as he tracks down all traces of the self, its transformations and evasions. The mind, like time itself, knows no fixity, but neither can it escape the rigidities of the past and the irrevocable oncoming of the future.

As was often the case with the poems in *The Double Dream of Spring*, Ashbery's language and theme involve him in that mixing of the mysterious and the mundane, that transvaluation of value that is one of the major heritages of surrealism. The old humanistic assurances fail to satisfy the quester: "you will realize that just having a soul was not enough: you must yield it up, vanish into the oblivion prepared for you by your years of waiting that all your practice of stoicism was not enough to seal off." The threat of nihilism energizes the pursuit as thoroughly as would any real hope, for Ashbery plainly agrees with Stevens that "Death is the mother of beauty." But death offers a mundane possibility, too, almost a banal one, for everywhere he looks he sees exempla and simulacra of unexceptional dissolution.

And you know at last the condition of weightlessness and everything it implies: for the future, the present and most of all for the past into which you now slip helplessly, no longer prevented by the grid of everyday language, remaining in suspension in that greenish aquarium light which is your new element, compelled to re-enact the same scene in the old park, with snow on the ground and the waiting look on the faces of the nearest buildings, some distance away. All this in the interests of getting at the truth.

Ashbery's speaker fitfully becomes aware of social reality, reacting with an almost paranoid suspicion of being watched, as in this passage where the buildings' faces hover expectantly over the scene. This social reality also mixes elements of the mysterious and the mundane, as we might expect in a poetry threatened and yet enticed by solipsism.

> And finally and above all the great urban centers with
> Their office buildings and populations, at the center
>   of which
> We live our lives, made up of a great quantity of
>   isolated instants
> So as to be lost at the heart of a multitude of things.

This is from a poem in *Double Dream*, but echoes can be found throughout Ashbery's work of this sort of dissociated fear and paralyis. A passage, too long to quote fully, from *Three Poems* reads,

> but at this time of year the populations emerge again into the arena of life after the death of winter, and one is newly conscious of the multitudes that swarm past one in the street; there is something of death here too in the way they plunge past toward some unknown destination, leaving one a little shaken up on the edge of the sidewalk.

Like Eliot's "I had not thought death had undone so many," this passage shows mass urbanized man as threatening in his complexity, and indeed narcotizing in his lack of purpose. The "plunge" of the masses ironically resembles the quest of the enlarged individual ego for some psychological satiety (or even surcease). The "I" is inescapable and constantly turns into the "not-I"; this paradox is both astonishing and commonplace, and so also is the existence of many such individuals. At one point Ashbery describes mass man as an "imbroglio of defeated desires. . .a sort of Thirty Years' War of the human will." We are clearly worlds away from Whitman's democratic idealism. Yet Ashbery finds the mundane mysterious, just as he occasionally presents the mysterious in mundane colors—echoing Baudelaire's sigh of "I have read all the books."[2]

Despite its circuitous structure, *Three Poems* does have at least a partial climax and resolution, though its third and final part, "The Recital," returns to a questioning and questing mood. It's in the middle section, "The System," that Ashbery adduces a tentative "lesson," for the book does have a moral hunger at its core, obscured though it often is by epistemological complexity and aesthetic play. The poem poses the problem of how to integrate a visionary happiness into the everyday, of how, when the self is so kaleidoscopic in its fears and hopes, to make a transcendent "light" illumine everything we do. Here is part of a passage where the crucial moment of reentry is recounted:

> it is certain you will rise from the bench a new person, . . .and when the light of the street floods over you it will have become real at last, all traces of doubt will have been pulverized by the influx of light slowly mounting to bury those crass seamarks of egocentricity and warped self-esteem you were able to navigate by but which you no longer need.

But this moment seems more optative than real, and twenty pages later we read that "our apathy can always renew itself, drawing energy from the circumstances that fill our lives, but emotional happiness blooms only once, like an annual, leaving not even roots or foliage behind." Part of the drama of the poem comes from the poet's need to choose between two kinds of happiness, what he calls "the frontal and the latent." His characterization of each is difficult and rich; suffice it for the moment to say he longs to choose the latter. It is a happiness that has "spread through us even into our pores like a marvelous antidote to the cup that the next moment has already prepared." The aura of this privileged moment lingers, and he is "able to consider its traces in the memory as a supreme god, as a god come down to earth to instruct us in the ways of the other kingdom."

The middle section of *Three Poems* is Ashbery's grandest attempt to answer the unresolved problems, problems of mind and self and value that are the legacy of English romanticism. In many ways this is Ashbery's most serious writing, where his project is most insistently questioned; but at the same time it is where his defensiveness is most perplexing. We can understand his nervousness, his radical ambiguity, and his polymorphous syntax only if we grant that the book is a grand elliptical commentary on a problem that is never directly stated. As such, this section presents the reader with the central difficulty in reading Ashbery: one senses an enormous uneasiness, but the high level of play and the almost choking egocentricity of the language call into question the author's ultimate seriousness. Should the reader be convinced of the validity, let alone the lucidity, of Ashbery's vision, he still must grapple with how this vision can be mediated into the world of his everyday experience. The complexity, in other words, might argue not so much for a long tradition of meaning, or a shared cultural crisis, as for a unique, idiosyncratic formulation that forbids any social application of whatever solace or transformation it might putatively offer. But Ashbery, ever the anticipator of problems, and of problems within problems, sets out to answer these questions.

Answering the question of what to do with this visionary light leads him to the choice, which turns out *not* to be a choice, of what sort of happiness he truly wants, the frontal that "has already proven itself" or the latent "that could lead to greener pastures." But it isn't a choice because

> it is certain now that these two ways are the same, that we *have* them both, the risk and the security, merely through being human creatures subject to the vicissitudes of time, our earthy lot.

So we move from a Wordsworthian dilemma, from being torn between the sweet past forever lost and the bittersweet compensation of an all too available present, to what seems an existential resolution, where we embrace our temporal sentences because they create the only precincts in which we can continue being human. Joined with this traditional romantic and late romantic nexus of paradox, we find Ashbery's praise of the ordinary.

> But that is the wonder of it: that you have returned not to the supernatural glow of heaven but to the ordinary daylight you knew so well before it passed from your view, and which continues to enrich you as it steeps you and your ageless chattels of mind, imagination, timid first love and quiet acceptance of experience in its revitalizing tide.

Our chattels can be enriched because they are of the mind, and the idealism of Ashbery continues to be his first burden and his final blessing. Consciousness can never dissolve the curse of consciousness, nor can time cure the blot of temporality. "We were surprised once, long ago; and now we can never be surprised again." The book is studded with willed and longed-for consolations, but unremitting dolor is finally its major tone.

Ashbery's *Self-Portrait in a Convex Mirror* (1975) contains a mix of poems and one masterpiece, the title poem. There are even a few lyrics that seem almost "regular," as if they could have been written by any number of other poets; they have more or less expectable metaphoric structures and thematic content, and their language is scarcely surreal. This group includes "Fear of Death," "Mixed Feelings," and "As One Put Drunk into the Packet Boat," and these poems show how far behind are the puerilities of *The Tennis Court Oath*. There is another group of poems that reads like a series of glosses on the complex meditations of *Three Poems*: "Ode to Bill," "Voyage to the Blue," and "Grand Galop." The last of these presents the most succinct expression of Ashbery's concerns and strategies, though it is itself hardly a concise poem. It begins, "All things seem mention of themselves/And the names which stem from them branch out to other referents," and it pursues that special kind of abstract thought that Ashbery excels in. Ashbery once said that his poems were about the experience of experience. . .and the particular experience is of lesser interest to me than the way it filters through to me. I believe this is the way it happens with most people, and I'm trying to record a kind of generalized transcript of what's really going on in our minds all day long.

"Grand Galop" exemplifies the approach that is adumbrated here, as it skillfully weaves a set of reflections together with musings on the very act of gathering and sorting and releasing such reflections. The poem clarifies much that was baffling and unproductive in the earlier books. However, there are at least two poems of inconsequence in *Self-Portrait*, "Sand Pail" and "Foreboding," and the dogged nonsense of these two is at least fitfully present in some other poems as well, the "Farm" sequence, for example. So it is too early to announce that Ashbery has abandoned completely the practice of surrealism in its most inconsequential aspects. But Ashbery does seem more intent on circling reality than on arbitrarily dipping into its recesses and surfaces, as if he has realized (and commendably accepted his realization) that the search for patterns is, at the very least, more interesting than the willful neglect of all consequentialness.

With his masterpiece, "Self-Portrait in a Convex Mirror," his circlings become majestic. As the title suggests, this poem is a meditation on solipsism, but it is also a cry against temporality as well as a celebration of the commonplace attempts we make to overcome its ravages. The poem is unusual in several respects, at least for Ashbery. For example, it is a rare instance of his announcing a fixed subject for a poem, in this case the Renaissance painter Parmigianino's masterpiece of "distorted" perspective. Also, Ashbery quotes not only Vasari on Parmigianino's work, but a modern art historian as well, gracefully blending in these "objective" reports with his own thoroughly subjective reading of the painting. The poem is over five hundred lines long, in a blank verse of a relaxed sort, its diction and syntax being remarkably straightforward, again considering Ashbery's previous work. But what provides the masterly dimension of the work is its philosophical seriousness. Ashbery's connoisseur's eye and his deep affection and puzzlement in the face of Parmigianino's art have found ample expression through a poetry that draws on both the "ordinary language" philosophy of the British tradition and the phenomenology of modern French and German thinkers. But the philosophical reflections, questions, and formulations are all lightly cast; the poem never resorts to a technical vocabulary. And the meditation on art serves admirably to focus the poem's energies as they arise out of a grappling with everyday experience and the "classic" problems of epistemology and time.

The poem begins with a meditative description of the portrait that introduces the problem of "putting in and taking out"; but the problem is here presented as one of interpreting the gesture of the painting's subject and intention, what Ashbery calls the painting's desire "to protect/What it advertises":

> The time of the day or the density of the light
> Adhering to the face keeps it
> Lively and intact in a recurring wave
> Of arrival. The soul establishes itself.
> But how far can it swim out through the eyes
> And still return safely to its nest?

What can the artist reveal, what can the ego, looking to sound its own depths, find as ground or containment to insure its own continuity: this is the meditator's problem. Seen from a different angle, this problem threatens to be resolved by the discovery that nothing can be put into the soul because everything has been left out:

> The secret is too plain. The pity of it smarts,
> Makes hot tears spurt: that the soul is not a soul,
> Has no secret, is small, and it fits
> Its hollow perfectly: its room, our moment of attention.
> That is the tune but there are no words.

Clearly Ashbery is here confronting a fundamental absence, and we can see the threat as something like Berkleyan idealism, for only when we are attending moment by moment to our selves can we be said to have a principle of existence. Pursued logically this would mean there is no meaningful past; our self would be like the self in Hume's philosophy, without causality or connectivity, remade at every moment, like "a ping pong ball/Secure on its jet of water." Yet art is one way we do establish a usable past, for the fixity of art, whatever it may distort, assures us that we had ego functions—memory, desire, intention—at some other time.

> But it is certain that
> What is beautiful seems so only in relation to a specific
> Life, experienced or not, channeled into some form
> Steeped in the nostalgia of a collective past.

"Experienced or not" shows us that Ashbery believes in the empathetic powers of art, and of art viewing; and "collective past" indicates he might be willing to embrace some form of social reality, if only an elite and historically conscious one. But the solipsism isn't that easily cured, and the poem's many twistings and unfoldings indicate that a grappling with such problems can't be "logically" concluded.

But what art offers, especially an art redeemed from temporal dissolution, is a radical form of "otherness," an evidence of another human will and consciousness, much like ourselves perhaps, but insistently other, hence again mundane and mysterious. This otherness spreads out from the "enigmatic finish" of art to our common activities:

> Is there anything
> To be serious about beyond this otherness
> That gets included in the most ordinary
> Forms of daily activity, changing everything
> Slightly and profoundly, and tearing the matter
> Of creation, any creation, not just artistic creation
> Out of our hands, to install it on some monstrous, near
> Peak, too close to ignore, too far
> For one to intervene? This otherness, this
> "Not-being-us" is all there is to look at
> In the mirror, though no one can say
> How it came to be this way.

This is the poem's central insight, its highest truth, and its most reassuring consolation, suspended as the poem is between slight and profound changes, near and remote distances. "The ordinary forms of daily activity" have attracted Ashbery all along, as if the aesthete in him needed just this ballast to steady him in the swells of self-exploration. James Schuyler's "Hymn to Life" also makes this kind of affirmation, and it should be read along with "Self-Portrait" as the most brilliant extension of the poetic mode of the New York school since the death of Frank O'Hara.

"Self-Portrait" ends, as does *Three Poems*, with a coda that mutes any excessive feeling of "triumph," and the note of dolor, of autumnal falling, sounds in the closing lines:

> The hand holds no chalk
> And each part of the whole falls off
> And cannot know it knew, except
> Here and there, in cold pockets
> Of remembrance, whispers out of time.

The absence of sustaining warmth and integrating knowledge will always be Ashbery's true subject, his lasting concern; for him nothing is more fundamental. The surfaces of mundane reality *are* reality, yet only our much more than superficial reflections can make us realize that, and Ashbery's poetry will probably always be suspended between this admission of defeat and a calm claim of victory. He addresses Parmigianino, or rather his sustained surface in the self-portrait, with these words:

> And just as there are no words for the surface, that is,

No words to say what it really is, that it is not
Superficial but a visible core, then there is
No way out of the problem of pathos vs. experience.
You will stay on, restive, serene in
Your gesture which is neither embrace nor warning
But which holds something of both in pure
Affirmation that doesn't affirm anything.

Ashbery here clearly addresses himself, and his poetry as well.

But this leaves us with the problem, if that is what it is, of Ashbery's
recent fame, for how has this difficult, often abstruse poet found an
audience? After Frank O'Hara's death in 1966, it appeared as if the
New York school would slowly disintegrate. The coterie of poets
around St. Mark's Church on the lower east side of New York had
developed a second generation, informally led by Ted Berrigan.
Ashbery himself made few public appearances, though his work still
attracted fervent supporters. In addition, the art scene, which had long
served as the nexus of much of O'Hara and Ashbery's work, went
through several transformations, from abstract expressionism to
color-field painting to pop art, picking up more public acceptance with
each new phase. It was clearly becoming more difficult for the avant-
garde to sustain anything like an adversary relation to the mainstream
cultural forces. In fact, the original sense of the military term *avant-
garde* was beginning to be once again appropriate, for the advance
guard was meant to bring back news to the central command and thus
support and facilitate its strategies. Ashbery has not commented pub-
licly on his own development in the late sixties and early seventies, so
we can't know if he tired of the poetry of inconsequence, or if he felt
drawn to the traditional postromantic set of themes and problems after
an intensive reading of, say, Wallace Stevens, or if he simply developed a calm philosophic mind to replace his wearied surreal eye.
But we do know that *Self-Portrait in a Convex Mirror* was given the
Pulitzer Prize, the National Book Award, and the National Book Critics
Award, an unprecedented sweep for a poet. And an inexpensive
Penguin edition of this book went quickly into a second printing, aided
no doubt by the prizes and their publicity, but also, I suspect, because
not only was the poetry more "available" in its feelings and meanings,
but also there were many academic critics willing to push Ashbery as
the major poet of the seventies.[3] After the cultural confusion of the
sixties, we probably shouldn't be surprised that a putatively major poet
has produced six commercial books of poetry that include one volume
that is totally meaningless and another written in prose! But clearly
Ashbery's ascension, though partly the result of a unique talent, re-

flects larger cultural forces and energies, not least among which is the
assimilation of the experimental impulses of modernism into the standard, though pluralistic, framework of contemporary poetry.

What stands behind Ashbery's rather sudden succèss d'estime is the
triumph of a poetic mode. A mode demands less aesthetic energy than
a truly individual style but usually offers more gratification than the
average school or "movement." Ashbery's mode has what most
modes have, a distinctive blend of sensibility, verbal texture, and
thematic concerns. In each of these categories, or elements, a mode
must not become too rigid; its sensibility cannot turn into a set of static
attitudes, its verbal texture cannot be reducible to simple matters of
vocabulary and verse forms, and its thematic concerns must allow for a
range of subjects. Successful modes, then, thrive on their distinctiveness, their ability to be set off against a larger, more public set of
expectations. But the moment this distinctiveness becomes too rigid,
the mode slips into self-parody, consciously or unconsciously. Just
when and how a mode calcifies (or what is less likely, fails to achieve a
distinctive feel) is hard for literary historians to measure precisely,
especially in contemporary literature. But ample evidence for the existence of Ashbery's mode can be found in one of the first issues of
Partisan Review for which he acted as poetry editor. Here are the
openings of four poems from volume 43:4:

> First of all I'm naked
> while I'm typing this,
> only my rash is airbrushed,
> the rest is visceral energy
> for my poetry, in this case
> depicted objects of tough minded
> harsh light that emphasizes
> the previous generation of
> dismayed bridegrooms at the
> altar of the cosmic alienation.

● ● ●

> It's nice to sit down in the evening
> With the rain out of doors
> And the dog lapping water from the toilet bowl
> To a dinner given in your honor

● ● ●

> From my doorstep, at twenty,
> Swinging in and out of the pastoral setting;
> My father gone, my mother waiting idly
> Beside the buzz of a hazy world—

Perceive it—at twenty—surrounded
By weak prospects and thin possibilities. . .

• • •

Of postures taken
Little indication was given
We were to spend hours watching slender
Black lines erratically divide fields
Of primary color. Clouds pursued me
With insinuations of previous neglect
Like a dried wash rag limply hanging
From a towel rack.

The sensibility here might roughly be described as that of the mock confessional joined to the surrealistically coy; the verbal texture relies on a mix of the familiarly colloquial with the etiolated irony of self-conscious diction; and the themes all arise out of a search for privileged moments of awareness, furtively snatched from a world where the madcap pluralism of values (and value systems) is the almost disconcerting norm.

These selections, written by four different poets, demonstrate a recognizable mode whose chief immediate influence is, of course, the work of Frank O'Hara. But Ashbery's own contributions to the mode are significant, though one senses he has done more to keep the mode alive than to widen its possibilities. This brings us back to the problem of the limits of a mode. Does Ashbery's sudden reputation reflect the adoption of his mode by other poets, or vice versa? Has the mode finally achieved respectability, or has its perfection, its final self-definition simply made it more immediately available to other poets? Certainly the panels who praise Ashbery's "originality," his "breathtaking freshness and adventures in which dazzling orchestrations of language open up whole areas of consciousness no other American poet has even begun to explore" (to quote a typical jacket blurb), must be made up of readers who simply don't follow contemporary poetry. Ashbery's relation to the mode in which he works seems little more adventurous than the relation of several other poets to their modes. Is it, then, the mode itself that impresses the judges as intrinsically more adventurous than the other modes currently being developed and practiced? This seems the most charitable explanation, though the obvious point must be made: the mode has been available since 1950 or so, jostling and sometimes obscurely mixing with other modes. Ashbery's domination of this mode is fully achieved, and in those terms his reputation is warranted. But his success may well have something to do with the cultural moment and with a weariness with moral and political fervor in poetry now that the 1960s are past.

Ashbery's peculiar dissociation of feeling, his syntactical bracketing or suspension of affect, produces a poetry that simultaneously submerges itself in emotion and moves beyond it. "But the fantasy makes it ours, a kind of fence-sitting/Raised to the level of an aesthetic ideal."

Interchapter

Magazines and Magazine Verse

If the mediocre are truly the enemy of the good, then the merely talented may become the enemy of the visionary. Since the examples of Pound and Eliot, contemporary poets in America have been almost embarrassingly talented. It has seemed that no poet wants to appear ill prepared now that the equation between technique and moral earnestness has been established (no verse is ever free for the man who wants to do it right, said Pound). But this emphasis on technical proficiency has produced some unexpected results, especially in what has come to be known as "magazine verse." Verse instead of poetry, regularity of expectation instead of the rigors of ecstasy: the choice was not presented only to American postwar poetry. But given the terms of the choice, the very format of either the "little mags" or the polished "journals" tilted the outcome in favor of predictability. Early in the modern age, E. E. Cummings could satirically pose the delusive trap:

> "let's start a magazine
> to hell with literature
> we want something redblooded
>
> lousy with pure
> reeking with stark
> and fearlessly obscene
>
> but really clean
> get what I mean
> let's not spoil it
> let's make it serious
>
> something authentic and delirious
> you know something genuine like a mark
> in a toilet
>
> graced with guts and gutted
> with grace"
> squeeze your nuts and open your face

Now that the war against gentility has been won, some of the satirical gibes here have lost their point. But a grim truth remains: "lousy with pure/reeking with stark" is just right in the way it captures the triumphant elevation of attitude over content. Many magazines delete substance, as Cummings here deleted his substantives, as long as they can catch the right combination of qualities. The magazine, because of its publicness and its often ephemeral status, becomes the perfect medium for testing and developing style.

So many magazines either originate from or calcify into this combination of elements: singularity of style and uniformity of technique. Magazines that choose this fate may often do so for polemical purposes. The neosurrealist poetry in *Paris Review* when Tom Clark was the poetry editor there was uniformly of a certain aesthetic disposition, and the charitable understanding of that situation was that Clark knew what he wanted and knew what was best. Perhaps beyond a certain date, when Clark's steadfastness was apparent, other poets not of his disposition stopped submitting poems to the *Paris Review*. Most magazines that operate within as narrow a range as Tom Clark chose for himself do not pretend to accept manuscripts from "just anyone"; the stand of the magazine, if not an actual editorial statement in the front of each issue, makes that clear. Some editors, however, have a piously liberal sense that they should always keep their pages open to new talent. But consciously or unconsciously, these editors are infected with hypocrisy, and the dream of the young poet to crack the barrier of the *New Yorker*, say, is thoroughly vain. Howard Moss, poetry editor of the *New Yorker*, often prints his own poetry there, and occasionally that of his staff assistants, and he repeats regularly the dozen or so "names" he feels he has discovered. But how could anyone discriminate intelligently among the tens of thousands of poems that arrive at the *New Yorker* each year? Yet the lure of well-known magazines like the *Paris Review* and the *New Yorker* continues to make the "self-addressed, stamped envelope" a part of every poet's initiation.

Of course the *Paris Review* may be even less polemical than the *New Yorker*; it is hard to measure intention in such cases. Maybe editors simply exercise their not-to-be-disputed tastes, and, if the magazine is solidly enough established, that taste persists, even if it doesn't prevail. But some magazines are quite clearly polemical: Cid Corman's *Origin* and Clayton Eshelman's *Caterpillar* were aggressively antiestablishment and generated enthusiasm and loyalty among their followers. Such ventures almost invariably have a limited life span, as the dedicated editor exhausts his funds, or, more happily, as his poets go on to further successes in other places, as was the case with most of the contributors to *Origin*. These polemical, programmatic magazines stake out their portion of the aesthetic spectrum and seldom budge or evolve. Other magazines seek balance, and contemporary poetry is so diverse and (sometimes) partisan that the seemingly dull virtue of evenhandedness can be polemical. But whether narrow or catholic in their bias, magazines all too often suffer from a kind of institutional arteriosclerosis. As Cummings says, "graced with guts and gutted/ with grace," and we hear in this neat turn of phrase a turn of mind that will eventually be turning in on itself.

Reflecting the pluralism of American society, poetry magazines present a consensus that evolves out of localized extremes. From the second-generation New York school outlet of Anne Waldman's *World* to the deep-image stringencies of George Hitchcock's *Kayak*, contemporary poets apparently need excessive clannishness in order to clarify their purposes. Several causes contribute to this balance of manifold extremes. Obviously the plurality of standards is one, and the absence of a truly "official" taste has increased the number of new magazines founded since 1950 or so. W. H. Auden argued a few decades ago that with avant-garde poetry all that one can finally say is that he likes a poem because a friend of his wrote it. This personalist aesthetic (satirized and yet advocated by Frank O'Hara in his "Personalist Manifesto") was not limited to the underground poets. Dangers of paranoia notwithstanding, many poets see at the very least a conspiracy of shared tastes at work in virtually every poetry editor's selections. The solution is simply to start one's own editorship. Also contributing to the proliferation of magazines is the relative physical ease with which they can be produced. If clannishness determines much of the originating energy, the most difficult part of publication, namely distribution, presents no real problem, as copies are mailed free to friends or just dropped off in a few metropolitan or campus bookstores. Poetry thrives with the aid of a network, if not a community (Robert Bly discussed this distinction in *American Poetry Review*), so that, even if not geographically close, many poets find common ground and share intimate concerns through correspondence—and the magazine is often just an eleborate form of correspondence, a sort of postal salon.

There is at least one more reason for the abundance and variety of magazines: they embody the very texture of *promise*. Anyone who follows some magazines with care and interest (it would be virtually impossible to follow them all with absolute regularity) knows that despite the trap of predictability, each individual magazine or issue suggests the possibility of a startling discovery. Some people hate to leave a party for fear the most interesting guest will arrive shortly thereafter; likewise with little magazines. The stunning success of certain magazines, like *Criterion* or the *Dial* or the early *Partisan Review*, has created this important, sustaining myth.

Despite the proliferation of magazines that publish poetry, there are two distinct types. The first, at least in terms of visibility, consists of those general literary magazines that range from the *Sewanee Review* to the *American Review*. Some of these are frankly conservative in their tastes, and the selection of poems is generally restricted to those of published poets: here the major names are the *Sewanee, Southern, Virginia Quarterly*, and *Yale* reviews. This group rarely if ever published "projective verse" poets, for example, and it generally avoids all experimental voices until they have become more or less accepted; Anne Sexton and other confessional poets appeared there often, but only after confessionalism had become routinized. Another group, made up of such magazines as *American Review, Partisan Review*, and *Hudson Review*, is more likely to publish innovative poems, but one often gets the impression that these magazines limit their commitment to poetry, that they use poems, as the cynical quip has it, to keep the edges of stories and essays from running together. In any case, the general literary magazines and quarterlies have little appreciable effect on the shaping of contemporary poetry, for they remain content to reflect trends rather than initiate them.

The second distinct type of magazine includes those whose primary commitment is to poetry. Only occasionally do they run a short story or an essay on a general cultural topic; they are more likely to fill up the nonpoetry space with reviews or theoretical discussions of "poetics." This group is far larger in numbers than the group consisting of general literary journals and is almost too diverse to classify in any but superficial ways. Some of these magazines are connected to universities that might or might not have established writing programs: *Iowa Review, Ohio Review*, and *Chicago Review*. Others can be loosely grouped because they have been inspired and guided by a single individual, such as *Kayak* (George Hitchcock); *The Sixties*, later *The Seventies* (Robert Bly); *Chelsea* (David Ignatow); *Choice* (John Logan); and so forth. Still others are programmatically avant-garde, such as *Hanging Loose* (in which all the pages are unbound and sold in an envelope), *Ant's Forefoot* (vertically elongated in its format), *Angel Hair* (expensively printed and restricted to the New York school and its descendants), and *Second Coming* (a San Francisco magazine that devoted a special number to Charles Bukowski). But the landscape here is always shifting, subject to sudden faults and eruptions.

One distinctive example of a magazine with a fierce commitment to poetry was *The Sixties*, edited by Robert Bly. Born as *The Fifties*, and extending its life somewhat as *The Seventies*, this journal featured many poems in translation and essays by Bly himself, often written under the pen name of Crunk. The magazine discovered no major indigenous North American poet, and one could almost sense that Bly wanted to do away with the notion of major poet altogether. What he wanted instead was a community of poets committed to a mystical sense of poetry, a poetry that presented a radical challenge to ideals of "rational intelligence." How he proposed to do this was never spelled out in a single manifesto, but rather exemplified by the dozen or so issues of the journal that appeared sporadically over the decades. The "typical" issue would include parodies of poems by "establishment" poets (Nemerov, Lowell); an extended essay on one of Bly's contemporaries (Levertov, Wright, Dickey); an assortment of translations, usually short poems, and usually grouped by nationality or heavily weighted with surrealists. There were seldom reviews of single books of poems; never any essays built around a close reading or an extended intellectual exposition. The magazine was feisty, but never querulous; its negative strictures were always energetically expressed, and if its desires or program were somewhat less than clear, it wasn't through lack of self-confidence.

But rereading issues of this journal today, one is most struck by Bly's balanced criticism. At the time the issues appeared, no one would have thought to use a word like *balance* to characterize Bly's argumentative style. Most readers of the journal probably recall Bly's strong support of James Wright, and his equally strong denunciation of James Dickey. But a backward glance reveals a different story. In number 8 (Spring 1966), Bly's essay on Wright pointed to many of the faults in Wright's poetry, faults such as a repetitive grammar, a "sense of a vague and shifting ego," and an evasion of practical problems. These faults stayed with Wright, I feel, and they seriously mar his latest work. But few other critics at the time were able to assess Wright's abilities and failures with any sort of balance; in fact, for many, Wright's poetry was an occasion for polemicizing about the issues of free form, sincerity, the death of academic verse, and so forth. Likewise with Dickey's work: for almost all the reviewers, Dickey's career was controversial, something used to illustrate either a general decline in American poetry or the arrival of a new era of mystery and strength. But Bly was capable of praising Dickey—in number 7 (Winter 1964)—for his concern with spiritual transformations and the way in which his war poetry was distinctive and capable of nourishing the imagination. It is true, to be sure, that in a later issue Bly severely castigated Dickey's *Buckdancer's Choice*, and did so in language especially direct and abusive. But in both cases (and with Levertov's poetry as well, in number 9) Bly wrote thoughtful, searching criticism.

He was not, however, always able to make his sense of any particular poet clear. His characteristic weakness as a critic was that his exposition of the poet's ideas or themes was never tellingly illustrated by his excerpts from the poetry. Often his remarks on the poet's prosody or metrical effects were unconvincing. But there was always the sense that poetry mattered, and mattered beyond the concerns of "craft" or "talking shop." Bly's audience in his best critical writing is always *both* the poet he's discussing *and* the larger body of informed readers who come to literature for a moral and spiritual nourishment. Though he was often led into moral harangues, and though his own dogmatism seemed to make him unable to recognize that other people's dogmatism was often more a mask for insecurity than an actual refusal of other positions, he nonetheless engaged other poets' work as one concerned person addressing another, rather than as a theoretician out to unleash his scornful purity.

At the same time, many of the poems by Americans that appeared in the magazine were rather weak. In some cases, such as Kinnell's "The Bear," Bly obviously chose well. But in some others, one senses that his need to push one kind of poetry against another led him to pick poems that are now noticeable for what they *don't* do and offer very little in the way of sustaining vision or verbal energy. Here's an example:

> Hoot!
>
> 1. Something lights my way
>   In the soft country of the future—
>   Like one hundred sixty acres
>   Of buried
>   Owls.
>
> 2. I'm journeying, in darkness journeying. . .
>   And for my light
>   Only a sackful
>   Of imperfect (sleepy)
>   Owls.
>
> 3. Sometimes I really see—
>   Like an owl here
>   An owl
>   There.

This is excruciatingly bad, and one is tempted to call it a parody, whether conscious or unconscious. In fact, Bly has a sense of humor and even printed a parody of himself in one issue. But this poem is printed with the other "straight" poems. You can see what might have attracted Bly to this poem: it loves its own nonrational "darkness"; it refuses to expound its intellectual assumptions; it seems deliberately "underdeveloped," as if any prosodic or rhetorical shaping were death to poetry. But of course the break between lines four and five, the poeticized inversion at the start of the second stanza, the bathetic parenthesis, and the mixture of the concrete and the abstract in the second line (which seems a direct assault on Pound's negative dictum and even echoes his example of a bad line, "The dim lands of peace") all stand out against the poem. It would be unfair to judge Bly's taste by this one poem, yet there are others like it in the complete run of the journal, and, perhaps more importantly, one can see why and how Bly would have been led to see this as a good poem, even a "courageous" one, when now it sounds slack and hackneyed. But perhaps the just assessment of Bly as an editor and polemicist will have to wait on a longer historical perspective. Still, one can say that *The Sixties* made a difference as few other magazines did in this period and that its own balance was more considerable than is usually claimed. One can also say that the journal was able to grow and extend its theories and its taste for a substantial period of time.

As a general rule, the longer the life of a magazine the less narrow its tenets. But even short-lived titles have special energies, and one could almost create a grouping out of those whose brevity has made them memorable, if not altogether legendary. This group would include *Locus Solus*, *Big Table*, and *Yugen*. Still another rubric might be created to include magazines that began with promise but eventually staled completely, so that the contents of the magazine tended to be far below the level of its word-of-mouth reputation. Here some obvious choices are *Beloit Poetry Journal*, *Poetry Northwest*, and *Carleton Miscellany*. All told, the staggering diversity of contemporary poetry is clearly related to the diversity of these outlets. But the "scene" is more than an indiscriminate jumble, even if reducing it to a clear order would take several volumes of careful analysis. The life of contemporary poetry, in the sense of its emerging sensibilities, its linguistic innovations, and its lines of force and growth, is importantly nourished by these magazines. They are like the greenhouses where the usual conditions of literary life are purposely unbalanced in order to foster certain phenomena and diminish others. As such, their diversity must be taken as a sign of health. But most people read poems either in anthologies, where presumably much pruning has already been done, or in volumes of individual poets, where the single plot can reveal order more clearly. Still, there are some things to be "read" out of the magazines, however random and subjective the interpretive procedures might be.

For example, in the late fifties and sixties the standard way for a poet to advance his public career was to garner two dozen or so magazine acceptances and then approach a publisher with a book-length manuscript based on the published poems, with the list of "acknowledgments" acting as an unofficial "imprimatur." After a while, a careful reader could tell what to expect in the volume itself with only a quick glance at the list of magazines that had accepted the poet's work. Now, where a poet has been published is less important; for one thing, even high quality magazine acceptances no longer guarantee an entrée to a major publisher. Some publishers are likely to take on a new poet because of a strong recommendation by one of their own "established" poets. Also, there was a short period when some major publishers would take a poet completely on speculation (but with the economic recession this practice stopped quickly.) Editors who deal with poetry at major publishers often know very little about contemporary poetry, so little that they dare not trust their own taste, let alone rely on their own judgment. So they simply defer to the poets they feel they can trust, that is, the ones they're already committed to, or they cut back their commitment and take on only two or three new titles a year. Convinced ahead of time that poetry will lose money, they repeat the adage that its only value is what prestige it can lend their list. (After all, poets still occasionally win awards, even the Nobel Prize.) So one major and useful function of the poetry magazine has been obviated. Publishers and editors *could*, however, read through the poetry magazines to "keep up," but it seems unlikely that they will choose to do so.

But magazine acceptances still give sustenance and even shape to a poet's career and talents. Seeing one's own work alongside that of contemporaries, and even that of older, more established writers, constitutes a sort of testing that is uniquely valuable. Over the long haul, a poet gains part of his self-identification from the magazines he chooses to submit to and from those he thinks of as his "audience." Many poets also pace their careers in part through acceptances, knowing that a certain amount of exposure in magazines is necessary between volumes. As the commercial publishing houses slowly but steadily cut back on their poetry offerings, it falls to small presses and the more dedicated and established magazines to sustain the dailiness that contemporary writing needs to survive. Most readers of poetry, of course, know the magazines serve this function, even if, as readers, they cannot lend much active support, either through regularly reading or through subscribing to the magazines. So the magazines seem to thrive by a kind of "benign neglect"; they are the objects of focused attention only when a young poet feels it's time to send out several groups of poems, or perhaps when a special issue features essays as well as poems, and so might momentarily widen its readership. Always somewhere in the background floats the hope that *this* magazine, even *this* issue, will contain a poem that one day will be used to measure other poems, that here in the midst of other nearly anonymous poems, in an apparently mundane context, will appear the genuine article.

But it is seldom easy to tell the genuine article, especially when our culture confuses the uses of poetry; indeed, if poetry's paramount use is self-expression, then the very signature of the writer constitutes the fullest demonstration of the poem's worth. Magazines have contributed to this cult of personality, for often they feature the work of established writers as a way to draw attention to themselves. If an editor writes and asks an established poet for a submission, it will be rather hard for the editor then to reject it. Likewise, if a poet is asked for a poem by an editor he doesn't know well, and if the magazine is not especially widely circulated, the poet will be tempted to submit work that is less than top quality. It's hard to be precise about how often this situation occurs, but judging from many poems that appear in not quite established magazines, it seems rather the order of the day. Here, for example, is a poem from a recent issue of the *Ohio Review*, a magazine clearly committed to excellence in poetry, featuring special issues with interviews and essays on the work of well-known poets. But this poem is not part of the featured work—though is it right to call it excellent?

The Fig Tree

Against the south wall of a monastery
where it catches the first sun
a fig tree a shadowy fig tree
stands by the door
all around the flowing trunk
suckers grow
it is against
the law of the church to pull them out
nobody remembers why
tree roots older than the monastery

To paraphrase slightly Dr. Johnson on "Lycidas," could anyone read this poem with pleasure if they didn't know the name of the author? If submitted by an unknown poet, it would strike most editors as very slight, at best the verbal equivalent of a harmless genre painting, with a pseudoprofound ending. The third line seems especially fraught with the "emotional slither" Pound warned against, while the sixth line might well bring a whoop of derision if read with the wrong note of false piety. In fact, the whole poem could easily be taken as a parody of a certain kind of magazine verse based on an etiolated imagism.

From the same issue of this magazine (of course, the whole for which these parts must stand isn't completely wretched, and the *Ohio Review* is fairly typical in terms of quality, catholicity of taste, and so forth), we find this effort:

Two Poems

Trees are human:
they too have to stand
and take it. And see
how beautiful they are
holding their leaves
above the ground
as if to bless.

* * *

The trees are tall gods
commanding a view
of my study. I bow
my head over my typewriter
and start the ceremony
of a prayer.

This is again the work of a nationally recognized writer (recently awarded the Bollingen Prize), one whose work is not usually connected with that of the author of "The Fig Tree."[1] Yet it is striking how similar the poems are in their assumptions and effects: the slightness turned to piety, the hushed religiosity in the face of the mundane, the metaphors strained by the burden of too much seriousness and a lack of invention. It is hard to resist the guess that these were tossed-off scraps, notes perhaps for a larger, more sustained effort, or else the sort of workaday effort that most poets nevertheless save, knowing the real touch is lacking.

But what these two examples tell us is how formulaic are the expectations of the editor. We live in an age where any scrap of an artist's life record is invested with extraordinary significance. Isolated like this, these poems hover on the edge of banality; brought into the context of a collected edition, they might earn their space. But their fragility, their very offhandedness, presumably invests them with some value. If the reader is in the know about the journal and is familiar with the large body of accomplished work these two poets have produced, then he will recognize here the signature of personality. He is not expected to look for larger significance; the editor offers the poems only as a way of keeping in touch with the writing of two poets who are, in a way, beyond criticism by the editor. But surely many young poets will look at these poems and say, without vanity or error, that they can do as well. Thus the very availability of such workaday poetry contributes further to the assumption that poetry is easy, that if anyone can squeeze his nuts his face will open.

Of course an editor would be hard pressed to apply to each and every poem he selects the same unyielding standard. Though an editor might select each poem after considering only its own merits, by the time his dozen or more selections have been made, the effect of all the poems together will quite likely be surprising to him. The lyric poem relies on distinctiveness of pace, expression, and development to capture the right touch of the authentic. But too many authenticities cannot coexist. Soon the editor is looking for some sort of balance, lifting his eye however slightly from the individual lyric, and thus falling back on some general sense of aesthetic rightness. Here of course taste or polemics enter the picture—indeed, they've been there all along, but only now do they get called on directly. Imagine the quandary of an ideal reader, one who could respond with perfect freshness and complete empathy to each poem in a magazine. Such a person would be an emotional vacuum, or sponge, with no clear identity of his own. Surely, since such a reader doesn't exist there is no reason for the average editor to tailor his choices with such a figment in mind. The editor, after all, must operate with some selective sense of audience, as do the poets themselves. Once one allows that the absolutist goal of a perfect reader can never be achieved, or isn't even worth pondering, then the rationale for selection is almost bound to become various and arbitrary.

Still, something like a "committee poem" can be found in many magazines, and "The Fig Tree" and "Two Poems" are examples of it. Some poets write a great many poems like this, consequently their names are found with great frequency in a wide variety of magazines. Such poets—Susan Fromberg Schaeffer and Charles Simic are prominent examples—often produce disappointing volumes of poetry. The family characteristics of the "committee poem" are easy to list (its structure usually resembles a parable, it's imagistically self-conscious, it usually ends with an ironic twist suggesting profound disaffection or disaffected profundity), and it gathers together what can be seen as the lowest common denominators of various stylistic impulses. But magazine editors want and need this predictable sort of statement. The "committee poem" deserves the damning with faint praise that it often receives. In its own way it lengthens the life of editors by doing some of their work for them.

Many might argue that all this is unfair, that just because two poets sent some not quite excellent poems to an otherwise acceptable magazine, this doesn't prove that most magazines foster a certain kind of bad writing. Furthermore, they might say that every age produces its genre paintings, its more or less academic set pieces, and that, as set pieces go, these poems are probably more interesting and more technically accomplished than analogous efforts from earlier decades. In addition, they might claim that a magazine is just what the original meaning of the word suggests, a storage place, a spot for collecting odds and ends that might later be strategically important, though now they seem only miscellaneous. All these counterarguments have weight, and when the field of inquiry is as diverse as are the little magazines,[2] then no one can keep opinion and bias out of his final estimation. Additionally, the level of little magazines cannot be raised by an act of will; because of their free-floating, spontaneous, and often ephemeral mission they more than most art formats must reflect the low as well as the high, the merely talented as well as the visionary. No poet I know in America doesn't make use of the good and available offices of some magazine or another, and if few writers would defend the merits of all of them, no one would wish away the phenomena or the diversity they symbolize.

Reflections in Place of a Conclusion

Since 1945 the major change in American poetry has been the gradual but certain lessening of a reliance on defensive irony. In many separate ways, poets have adopted a strategy of immersion in their experience, rather than suspension above it. One might possibly imagine something like the Bollingen controversy occurring again, but one feels that now the argument would be sharper, the sides more evenly divided (in the 1949 controversy, of all the judges only Karl Shapiro was a dissenting voice). Even so apparently "evasive" a poet as John Ashbery can be thought of as going beyond irony, since his work has a drive to reveal its innermost insecurities, though it often requires a good deal of involution to do so. Confessional poetry started in large part as a kind of immersion in experience, though its assumptions rather quickly became commonplace, and then its brashness lost much of its innovative force. But by absorbing some of these assumptions, poetry at large tended to forgo the specially focused kind of exacerbated sensibility that characterized the work of Plath and Sexton. What resulted was that "period style" often found in what I have called "surrealist parables," a poetry of escapism and quietism, where the rabid inventiveness of the figurative language searched out every corner of the interior life. What resulted in turn from this was a poetry immersed in the self, where the major tensions were those that operated between an almost clarifying allegory and an almost deliberate mystification. Gone were the ultimately rational tensions and ambiguities praised by the New Criticism.

The consequence of the lessening of defensive irony has often been felt in the area of form. Many poems of the 1970s feel slack and indulgent, as if all could be redeemed by absolute sincerity. Since Emerson urged the discovery of a "meter-making argument," American poetry has often been bedeviled by attempts to justify its forms. One extreme example of this bedevilment is Williams's "variable foot" as a prosodic unit; as some wag remarked, this makes about as much sense as an elastic inch. In the surrealist parable, the measure of sincerity became the very bizarre imagery; the more irrational the pictures, the deeper the source, the truer the feeling. Still, we sense in Williams's often unconvincing essays on measure and form, and in the polemics of Robert Bly, something more than the modernist play with formal possibilities. Instead, we catch the urgent moral sense of what seem simply the poet's technical concerns.

This fusion of the aesthetic and the ethical—some would say the confusion—has itself been a mark of the modernist sensibility. The strong emphasis in the post-Poundian era on technical proficiency was shaped by several forces: these included a need to both separate and entangle the "levels" of ambiguity, and a moral sense that the poem ought to open out onto more and more possibilities, since all forms of fanaticism—that is, all narrowings of meaning and consciousness—were evil. So the richly ambiguous poem was presumably the most honest. Often, however, that ambiguity resulted from a kind of intellectual dalliance, a suspension of all apparent moral enthusiasm that was justified by the claim that the realm of art was free from moral imperatives to action. When the surrealist parable came along, it too had a hidden moral claim in its formal demands. Irony and controlled ambiguity were devices to protect the poet, who used the rational notion of form to aestheticize psychological tensions. Only by releasing these tensions, by getting in touch with their deepest sources, the new surrealists argued, could the poet finally address the demons of his or her own psyche. It was to be the logic of the dream, not the skill of form, that would provide the most trustworthy access to the deepest truths.

In a recent essay in the *New York Times Book Review* (3 December 1978), Denis Donoghue asked, "Does America Have a Major Poet?" He replied:

> Few recent poems insist that their nature is to be an object, remote, keeping its secrets, beyond interrogation; they are content to be treated as statements, counterstatements, actions, without claiming to be occult in any of these capacities; and partly because secrecy of form has been rendered innocuous by recourse to the diversity of voice. Anything is formally acceptable if it is maintained by the continuity of a single voice or even by a concert of voices. In the current mood, poets have made a pact with their readers to observe the continuity and decency of discourse: Poetry will not appeal its case to a higher court, a secret discipline, or justify its formal character by pointing to sculpture, painting and music, arts that signify without speaking.

Donoghue here has recourse to ethical terms in discussing what are primarily questions of form: the "decency of discourse," "appeal its case," and so forth. Of course, in part Donoghue is making a fairly simple but important point, that all aesthetic compacts are supported by social and ethical networks of one kind or another. But I think he has also caught a spirit here in a revealing way, a spirit of laissez-faire

("Anything is. . .acceptable") that nonetheless contains a firmly held, though often unacknowledged and negatively framed, governing condition ("will not appeal to a higher court"). I think this spirit is pervasive in the current cultural mood, in the feeling that certain aesthetic assumptions are no longer valid, though as yet no firm axioms are available for replacement. The aesthetic compact might not seem especially demanding in an age of many diverse styles, but there are still limiting conditions, not the least of which is a need to define oneself against the preceding generation. If irony was once indispensable, it now seems superfluous.

Another way to express Donoghue's argument is to say that the spirit of symbolist poetry is on the wane, if it has not altogether fled. No more elitist "secrecy of form," no more overly aestheticized analogues for the form of the poem, no more defensive irony. Donoghue goes on to encapsulate what he sees as a major shift, the change from "Form to Discourse." For him, this shift removes the stress on the desire to be "major," or to put it more positively, the current mood "enhances the notion of poetry as a collective act rather than an individual assertion." If true, this might well be a healthy change in the working conditions of American poets, freeing them from the competitive pressures and distended egos that so often accompany literary life in America. But Donoghue is not offering a pollyanna version of the artistic vocation, for he also says the "constituents of experience are deemed to be social, at best communal, even though they are privately enacted and suffered." So the ego of the individual sufferer may well remain central to our poetry, and if it does, it is easy to imagine that questions about authenticity will continue to be interwoven with questions about form.

But then there is a darker view of the situation Donoghue has described. This view regards the absence of questions about "secrecy of form" as the result of a breakdown in any shared aesthetic assumptions, a realization that poetry now occurs only among isolated groups, each with its own content, its own accepted shibboleths. At least with an elitist aesthetic the secret codings were meant *eventually* to be treasured and opened, if only by the Stendhalian "happy few." But today some aesthetic programs, if that isn't too rigid a word to use for them, seem to exist on a take-it-or-leave-it basis. Certain poets are currently willing to have their poetry used in the service of an ideology, such as feminism or black nationalism, and to let such refined questions about "secrecy of form" sort themselves out later. But we shouldn't be too quick to think of this as a "darker" view. If the symbolist assumptions about the religion of art are dead or dying, then poetry might again become what it has often been in the past, a

handmaiden of experience, thought, and value rather than the culmination or substitute of these things.

The problem, however, may be a critical rather than a poetic one.
What is the critic to do with "programmatic" poetry, a poetry of
"statements, counterstatements, actions," especially when the critic
was raised on autotelic art? What, for example, can a male critic say
about this poem by Adrienne Rich:

August

Two horses in yellow light
eating windfall apples under a tree

as summer tears apart milkweeds stagger
and grasses grow more ragged

They say there are ions in the sun
neutralizing magnetic fields on earth

Some way to explain
what this week has been, and the one before it!

If I am flesh sunning on rock
If I am brain burning in fluorescent light

if I am dream like a wire with fire
throbbing along it

if I am death to man
I have to know it

His mind is too simple, I cannot go on
sharing his nightmares

My own are becoming clearer, they open
into prehistory

which looks like a village lit with blood
where all the fathers are crying: *My son is mine!*

The male critic could take refuge behind the observation that the poem
isn't aesthetically integrated, that what begins as some sort of natural
description turns into an ideological argument; that the poem doesn't
play fair, not with the "other side of the story" or with its own
premises, which are a jumble of symbolist allegory (the ragged grasses), an extended metaphor for emotional awakening (the magnetic
fields and the change of the last two weeks), and a declarative claim
that is not qualified, but rather "proven" by recourse to a coded
mythical vision. But surely the only way to hear the poem's last line
correctly is to read the poem as a straightforward statement of a

feminist claim, namely, that the paternalism on which European history and culture are founded is the result of a nightmarishly self-
destructive murderousness on the part of the male half of the species in
a desperate, but ultimately vain, attempt to protect its "blood rights"
and social supremacy. Whatever vacillation the poem exhibits on the
level of Form, it more than compensates for on the level of Discourse.

We could cite another poem, utterly different from Rich's in many
ways, yet sharing the same sureness of Discourse, though this time
with what we might call an anti-ideology. This is Gary Snyder's "All
through the Rains":

> That mare stood in the field—
> A big pine tree and a shed,
> But she stayed in the open
> Ass to the wind, splash wet.
> I tried to catch her April
> For a bareback ride,
> She kicked and bolted
> Later grazing fresh shoots
> In the shade of the down
> Eucalyptus on the hill.

Whatever we might identify as the poem's theme, a Lawrentian celebration of the primitive over man's ego-centered longings, is less
important than the offhanded texture of detail, the willingness of the
speaker to leave his utterance unpolished, and the simple trust in the
spontaneous closure of anecdote. The poem, to use Donoghue's terms,
is willing to be taken as an action, if not as a statement, and avoids any
"secrecy of form." It seems to gain its confidence as Discourse by never
raising any questions about Form.

But is either of these poems "formally acceptable" because of some
continuity of voice? As Donoghue says in his essay, "The problematics
of voice may turn out to be just as difficult as the often unanswerable
question of form." But the question of form, even in esoteric poems like
the *Cantos* and *The Waste Land*, was eventually answered, answered in
part by a community of readers, not extensive in numbers perhaps, but
extensive in time, as the commentary eventually grew toward clarifica-
tion. But what of these two poems by Rich and Snyder, and other quite
different poems, like those of Imamu Baraka that espouse racist hatred
and vengeance? Such poems have a communal audience and may be
widely read, but I think they are seldom *discussed*. Snyder, Rich, and
Baraka seldom receive thoughtful reviews (I am speaking of the latest
work of these poets),[1] and the easy explanation for this is that reviewers know such poetry cannot be responded to in the usual critical terms
without the reviewer being reduced to irrelevancy. The glib response is

that such poets are merely "preaching to the converted." But once poetry no longer appeals to a "higher court" of pure aesthetic standards, then won't it necessarily have to rely for its truth—or its truths—on the pressing issues of the day, with all the attendant dangers of ideological confusion, emotional overcompensation, and historical guilt?

These are obviously difficult issues, and I offer no solutions to them. In fact much of the difficulty comes from the availability of a sophisticated aesthetic tradition—that of Pound, Eliot, and the other "modern masters"—that was developed to express an ideology that remained largely hidden or unrecognized as such, but that is now used in the service of ideological arguments that simply won't accept the usual disclaimers about distance, detachment, and disinterestedness. In certain ways, these same questions were raised by Robert Bly's poetry in the early sixties, when he aggressively committed his every effort to ending the war in Vietnam. But as that war became increasingly and more obviously destructive, foolish, and morally reprehensible, Bly's polemics were absorbed, as it were, and the difficult aesthetic issues they raised were pushed aside for more pressing discussions. Bly's poetry since then has returned to what may be its fundamental interest, a longing to rescue the larger religious energies that have been occluded by commodity consumption. Now that a politics of quietism has returned to large portions of American life in the 1970s, ideological poetry may quickly appear irrelevant.

But the larger historical, or at least literary-historical point seems to remain. The theories of autotelic art, of an art committed to the maximum in ambiguity and the minimum in direct moral urging, no longer command general acceptance. And there seems no generally acceptable replacement for them, unless it is the sort of negative consensus that Donoghue describes. One response to this situation has been the development, and subsequent dilution, of a characteristic tone that Robert Pinsky has described as "raffish and hierarchic." This poetry, with its dominant concern for the interior life, its use of what I have called the surrealist parable, mediates between the persistent feeling of alienation and social displacement in American life and the equally strong feeling that no response is effective save that of a poised escapism into the world of fantasy and myth. As Pinsky acutely observes,[2] the theme of much of this poetry is the presence of the imagination in a world totally uncongenial to it, a theme explored at length, though in a different idiom, by Wallace Stevens. (One could also see this poetry as "raffishly" or even a bit embarrassedly rejecting and yet clinging to the "hieratic" codes of symbolism.) This poetry salvages some of the distance of autotelic art yet tries to magnetize the reader's affective response and drive it beyond mere reflectiveness. It is a poetry that wants to chill the reader and thus win him over, to use its dream-induced imagery and narrative juxtapositions to earn a kind of sympathy and identification that Prufrock, not to mention his author, would have found unacceptable.

But theory always lags behind, trying to homogenize the particularity of aesthetic experiences. In that famous essay "Tradition and the Individual Talent," it is both painful and comic to see Eliot resort to an unworkable distinction between emotion and feeling in order to make his notions consistent:

> The effect of a work of art upon the person who enjoys it is an experience different in kind from any experience not of art. It may be formed out of one emotion, or may be a combination of several; and various feelings, inhering for the writer in particular words or phrases or images, may be added to compose the final result. Or great poetry may be made without the direct use of any emotion whatever.

These truisms tricked out as axioms, these "or" clauses that try to make key distinctions (earlier in the essay Eliot insists on two categories, emotions and feelings, without saying what distinguishes them) but in fact simply multiply possibilities without order, and the concluding absolute claim—"any emotion *whatever*"—which is patently overstated: all of these rhetorical devices show the argument is under great strain to keep up the appearance of consistency and is trying desperately to hide what it really wants to say (that "only those who have personality and emotions know what it means to want to escape these things.") But few things seem as factitious as the preceding generation's aesthetic theories. Still, a veritable cottage industry developed in the wake of Eliot's essays, which now so often seem pragmatic and arbitrary despite their mandarin tones, and such industry was obviously produced by a larger cultural need to address and contain certain facts and to defuse others. Thus, any theory that looks to explain how poetry might become more directly ideological and yet remain "poetic" will also be subject to rhetorical contortions.

Some might see in this an argument for abandoning theory altogether, for turning poetry directly over to readers, or at least to reviewers without any theoretical axes to grind. But it is increasingly difficult to imagine poetry without criticism, if only because today all communication is cursed with the burden of interpretation. In the welter of codes faced by postindustrial society, people constantly have to screen and unpack and perform the various other semantic "operations" the linguists are busy exploring. Even if the "decoding" takes some other form than "simple" literary criticism or theorizing, it takes place nonetheless. Adrienne Rich's readers see her poems through a complex set of other texts,[3] not the least of which is her book on the experience of motherhood, *Of Woman Born*. One reviewer remarked of Rich's *The Will to Change*, "It has the urgency of a prisoner's journal." But what may have been intended as a reviewer's illustrative metaphor might be read by a feminist as a nearly literal description.

In other words, we have a criticism whether we like it or not, so we had best make it clear and answerable. I would argue that criticism has a responsibility to be a public discourse in a way that poetry doesn't. Poetry, especially lyric poetry, has an autonomous status, or ought to have the protection reserved for autonomous activities, as long as it is being written. But once written and freely offered to the public, it must suffer the fate of being critically judged. But criticism is not autonomous in the same way, not only because it owes its being to poetry, but also because it owes a debt to other values of public discourse, such as clarity, judiciousness, amenability to evidence, and so forth, from which debt poetry is generally free. I am aware this split between poetry and criticism might end up sounding as tortuous as Eliot's distinction between emotion and feeling. But the more we ask from poetry, the more we demand from the realm of the aesthetic, then the more we need a criticism that attempts to integrate as much as possible the skills of interpretation, literary history, and aesthetic theory.

Of course the relationship I posit between poetry and criticism can easily degenerate into one step forward with poetry and two steps backward with criticism. In some sense this already happens, as the "new" poetries are inevitably explicated and domesticated by criticism. But I am suggesting something further, namely, that criticism must be willing to engage in Discourse as well as to elucidate Form. Too often poetry is greeted with benign neglect, or facile enthusiasm,[4] or polemical maneuverings. For contemporary poetry some of this is profitable and even necessary, if only as a precritical activity, a way of preparing what are often the stringencies of truly innovative poetry for a larger audience.[5] But criticism of a more considered kind, operating with the advantage of at least limited hindsight, must be willing to discuss the content, the argument, the philosophical assumptions and implications of contemporary poetry. To take one example removed from the contemporary: the question of Pound's politics and economics. Many people have written on Pound, and many have argued for his status as a major poet, one of the great shapers of the language in this century, and so forth. But how many of these same critics have made a clear and thorough assessment of Pound's economic theories and of his use of them in his critique of modern society? Instead, most critics are content to paraphrase a bit of Major

Douglas and shake their heads at Pound's inflammatory eagerness to take up sweeping theories.

The dangers that adherents of autotelic theories are always warning against still remain, of course: people will be tempted to argue politics or economics exclusively and forget about the poetry. Or worse, they will distort and misquote the poetry, or try to use its authority to advance their partisan positions.[6] But I don't think such dangers should outweigh the larger, more pressing need to read our poetry as fully, as straightforwardly as it is written. The sudden outpouring of poetry exulting in black nationalist or feminist feelings and arguments may already have peaked,[7] or it may be entering a new phase. But the point is not what course is followed by any single ideology or political program (though such courses need to be studied and analyzed), but rather the willingness of criticism to deal more comprehensively, and more pointedly, with such issues in the future.

I hope to be clear on several points: that I am not calling for a "politicized" poetry (such a call would either be futile or supererogatory), nor am I advocating a politicized criticism, nor am I saying all autotelic art or strictly formalist criticism is useless. I think, I hope, it is possible to use the insights of people with largely or exclusively formalist preoccupations to illumine areas of thought, expression, and action that are concerned not only with form. I also think purely formalist concerns are only part of the aesthetic experience, and critics must not neglect the larger cultural life that sustains such experience. To put it (perhaps too) simply: when all one's ethical and political and social concerns and values are sublimated or displaced into questions of aesthetic form, the realms of both the social and the artistic grow thinner and thinner. That large mass of forces that acted as the preconditions for the rise of autotelic art—rapid industrial growth, urbanization, secularization, and so forth—in the middle of the nineteenth century has not, of course, been dissipated, however much it has altered in the last hundred years or so. And so autotelic art, and criticism answering in the same key, will go on being written. But though criticism alone will not save us, will not heal the breach between the artistic and social realms, at least it can face more squarely the terms and consequences of the theories it elucidates and implicitly condones. Contemporary American poetry has, I think, often suffered from this breach between the social and the artistic, and since Whitman our poetry can be read as desiring a fuller, more direct way to confront its experience and enrich its saying. It is because our poetry has been willing to risk its securities, to immerse its longing for form in the unsettled waters of desire and judgment, that we should expect a similar risk from our criticism.

Notes

Chapter 1
Audience and Form

1. Allen Tate, in "Ezra Pound and the Bollingen Prize," included in *Ezra Pound: Perspectives*, ed. Noel Stock (Chicago, 1965), pp. 86–89, makes a tortuous argument that reads as if he voted against Pound, when in fact he did the opposite and defended himself in the ensuing controversy published in the *Partisan Review*. Tate argues that "Pound's *Cantos* lack a sense of history" and that they are "about nothing at all"; but as "a result of observing Pound's use of language in the past thirty years," Tate has become convinced that Pound "had done more than any other man to regenerate the language, if not the imaginative forms, of English verse." Tate has to face the "disagreeable fact that he had done this in passages of verse in which the opinions expressed ranged from the childish to the detestable." Despite the inconsistencies in this argument—if they are about nothing at all, how can their opinions be detestable? can someone regenerate the language of verse without regenerating the imaginative forms?—Tate goes on to say that the "assumption of many persons that a vote for the *Pisan Cantos* was a vote for 'formalism' and a vote against 'vitality' in poetry makes no sense at all." Yet praise for a poetry about "nothing at all" must in some sense be a vote for formalism.

2. In an interview reprinted in *Writers at Work: The Paris Review Interviews*, 2d series (New York, 1963), pp. 337–68, Lowell argues: "But it seems to me we've gotten into a sort of Alexandrian age. Poets of my generation and particularly younger ones have gotten terribly proficient at these forms. They write a very musical, difficult poem with tremendous skill, perhaps there's never been such skill. Yet the writing seems divorced from culture somehow. It's become too much something specialized that can't handle much experience. It's become a craft, purely a craft, and there must be some breakthrough back into life." This separation of poetry from the culture is discussed in Chapter 10.

3. See Walter Ong, "The Genie in the Well Wrought Urn," in *The Barbarian Within, and Other Fugitive Essays and Studies* (New York, 1962), pp. 1–33. For the remark on Olson near the end of the paragraph, see "Poetry, Raw or Cooked?," in *A Time of Harvest: American Literature, 1910–1960*, ed. Robert E. Spiller (New York, 1962), p. 159.

4. In this regard, see Ralph J. Mills, Jr., *Cry of the Human: Essays on Contemporary Poetry* (Urbana, Ill., 1975), especially chapter 1.

5. See Paul Goodman, *Speaking and Language: A Defence of Poetry* (New York, 1971). Goodman is especially valuable for showing the limits and the uses of linguistics in literary criticism.

6. Elizabeth Bishop's poem is in *The Complete Poems* (New York, 1969), p. 34. Karl Shapiro's "Auto Wreck" is in *Selected Poems* (New York, 1968), p. 17. Ginsberg's "Sunflower Sutra" appeared first in *Howl and Other Poems* (San Francisco, 1956), p. 28, and is often anthologized. "The Day Lady Died" is in *The Complete Poems of Frank O'Hara*, ed. Donald Allen (New York, 1971), p. 325.

7. Charles Altieri, "From Transcendence to Immanence: Post-Modern Poetics in Contemporary American Poetry," *Boundary 2* 1:3 (Spring 1973):605–41. This is the best discussion of the philosophical basis of contemporary poetics.

8. Richard Howard's essay is in *Alone with America: The Art of Poetry in the United States since 1950* (New York, 1969), pp. 316–412.

9. For an especially acute treatment of the use of sensory "lifting" in modern American poetry, see Hugh Kenner, *A Homemade World: The American Modernist Writers* (New York, 1975), chapters 4 and 5, pp. 91–157.

Chapter 2
Theodore Roethke

1. In the essay "Theodore Roethke: The Poetic Shape of Death," in *Theodore Roethke: Essays on the Poetry* (Urbana, Ill., 1965), p. 96.
2. Ralph J. Mills, Jr., *Cry of the Human: Essays on Contemporary Poetry* (Urbana, Ill., 1975). In the chapter on Roethke's last poems, Mills discusses how "the poet exceeds the limits of previous development and sets forth on an arduous but successful quest for mystical illumination." Also see *The Contemporary Poet as Artist and Critic*, ed. Anthony Ostroff (New York, 1964), pp. 49–53, where Roethke comments on several readings of "In a Dark Time": the speaker of the poem does not merely "make his peace with God. . .he transcends God: he becomes the Godhead itself, not only the veritable creator of the universe but the creator of the revealed God." Needless to say, the lyric voice can hardly claim more, and such self-deification may be seen as a result of Roethke's putting all his belief into poetry, fulfilling with implausible bravado Matthew Arnold's prediction that poetry would perform all the functions of religion.

Chapter 3
Robert Lowell and Allen Ginsberg

1. The back cover of the City Lights edition of *The Fall of America* (San Francisco, 1974) conveys the pessimistic flavor of Ginsberg's views in this period.
2. In his *Robert Lowell: The First Twenty Years* (London, 1962), Hugh Staples traces the publication history of the poem (pp. 90–91). It once bore the title "The Capitalist's Meditation by the Civil War Monument," and its satire was much more bitter and direct. For a discussion of Lowell's mixture of Catholic symbology and political concerns, see Alan Williamson, *Pity the Monsters: The Political Vision of Robert Lowell* (New Haven and London, 1974). Marjorie Perloff, in *The Poetic Art of Robert Lowell* (Ithaca and London, 1974), p. 48, finds the poet's sensibility "basically elegiac" and says the apocalyptic voice "in some of his early poems sounds shrill and hollow."
3. Volume 22:10 (12 June 1975):27.
4. Lowell's last book is discussed in considerable detail by Helen Vendler in *Parnassus* (Spring/Summer 1978):75–97. I also discuss the book in more detail than I do here in *Salmagundi* 44 (Spring 1979).

Chapter 4
Confessional Poetry

1. In a class at Queens College, in the spring 1969 term.
2. "An Interview with John Berryman," *Harvard Advocate* 103:1(Spring 1969):9.
3. *Harvard Advocate* 103:1(Spring 1969):11.
4. See Judith Kroll, *Chapters in a Mythology* (New York, 1977), for a discussion of Plath as a mythmaking poet.
5. See Robert Pinsky, *The Situation of Poetry* (Princeton, 1976), pp. 116–18, for a discussion of how certain contemporary poems are cramped by conventions similar to those I mention here. Pinsky's book reveals much about the language of contemporary poetry, its assumptions and its limitations.

Interchapter

1. In *American Poetry since 1960: Some Critical Perspectives*, ed. Robert Shaw (Cheshire, Eng., 1973), Alan Williamson has an essay, "Language against Itself: The Middle Gener-

ation of Contemporary Poets," pp. 55–67, that separates poets who were around forty years old in 1973—Snyder, Wright, Kinnell, Merwin, and Bly—from their predecessors and says they share a common preoccupation with the insufficiencies of language.

2. For Robert Duncan's reaction to the Allen anthology, see *Allen Verbatim: Lectures on Poetry, Politics, Consciousness*, ed. Gordon Ball (New York, 1974), p. 131.

3. See also James Dickey, *Babel to Byzantium: Poets & Poetry Now* (New York, 1973), pp. 5–6, where Dickey discusses the Allen anthology in utterly dismissive terms.

4. For Allen Ginsberg's relation with three of his contemporaries, Olson, Jack Spicer, and Frank O'Hara, see *Allen Verbatim*, pp. 135–36. Ginsberg speaks of how Olson became *his* poet, "a poet like I had not seen in all my life." He also talks about how O'Hara rejected his reading of an O'Hara poem as a "pouring out of the soul," presumably because O'Hara couldn't accept the directly expressionistic, nonironic mode that Ginsberg was implicitly praising. For his part, O'Hara was extremely involved with an ongoing assessment of his contemporaries, as the next chapter will argue, and as is clear from the writings collected in Frank O'Hara, *Standing Still and Walking in New York* (Bolinas, Calif., 1975).

Chapter 5
Frank O'Hara

1. See the *Collected Poems of Frank O'Hara*, ed. Donald Allen (New York, 1971), and the full-length study by Marjorie Perloff, *Frank O'Hara: Poet among Painters* (Berkeley, Calif., 1977).

2. In the *New Yorker*, 20 August 1973, pp. 73–74.

3. In *One-Dimensional Man* (Boston, 1964), p. 68.

Chapter 6
Galway Kinnell

1. See Richard Howard's essay in *Alone with America: The Art of Poetry in the United States since 1950* (New York, 1969), pp. 258–71, where Kinnell's use of fire imagery is discussed.

2. The essay was originally presented as a lecture at Colorado State University in 1969.

3. In *Naked Poetry*, ed. Stephen Berg and Robert Mezey (Indianapolis, 1969), p. 441.

4. In *Field* 4 (Spring 1971):56–75. See also the interview with Kinnell in *Ohio Review* (Fall 1972):25–36.

Chapter 7
Robert Bly

1. In *Tennessee Poetry Journal* 2:2(Winter 1979):14. This issue contains several assessments of Bly's work, some sharply negative.

2. In an excellent essay on James Wright in *Ironwood* 10, pp. 74–76, Robert Hass discusses Bly's attack on American society, with its prizing of outer as opposed to inner reality. Hass is perceptive and eloquent in formulating the limits of this polemic, and the anti-intellectual, eventually antihuman, positions it can lead to.

Interchapter

1. The best single essay on Olson is by Martin Pops, "Melville: To Him, Olson," in *Contemporary Poetry in America: Essays and Interviews*, ed. Robert Boyers (New York, 1973),

pp. 189–220. But several full-length studies have recently appeared: *Charles Olson: The Scholar's Art*, by Robert von Hallberg (Cambridge, Mass., 1978); *Charles Olson: Call Him Ishmael*, by Paul Christensen (Austin, Tex., 1978); and *Olson's Push*, by Sherman Paul (Baton Rouge, La., 1978).

2. *The Sea and the Honeycomb: A Book of Poems* (Madison, Minn., 1966).

3. See Wakoski's pamphlet "Creating a Personal Mythology" (Los Angeles, 1975), published as *Sparrow 31* by Black Sparrow Press.

4. See the essay by James Atlas, "Diminishing Returns: The Poetry of W. S. Merwin," in *American Poetry since 1960: Some Critical Perspectives*, ed. Robert Shaw (Cheshire, Eng., 1973).

Chapter 8
Philip Levine

1. See Ralph J. Mills, *Cry of the Human: Essays on Contemporary Poetry* (Urbana, Ill., 1975), for a discussion of Levine's work. And Stephen Yenser, "Bringing It Home," *Parnassus* (Fall/Winter 1977):101–17, has a useful assessment of *The Names of the Lost* (1976), Levine's book that appeared after 1933. An interview with Levine in *Parnassus* (Spring/Summer 1978):40–54, deals with the poet's political vision.

Chapter 9
John Ashbery

1. For example, "John Ashbery: The Charity of the Hard Moments," by Harold Bloom, in *Contemporary Poetry in America: Essays and Interviews*, ed. Robert Boyers (New York, 1973), pp. 110–38.

2. Almost as if to show contempt for the theme of lost visionary power, Ashbery says in the *Double Dream*: "Finally he decided to take a turn past the old grade school he'd attended as a kid. . . .Time farted."

3. See the first chapter by Laurence Lieberman, in *Unassigned Frequencies* (Urbana, Ill., 1978), pp. 1–63, where some very prolix and extravagant claims are made. A much more searching and useful essay is Charles Altieri, "Motives in Metaphor: John Ashbery and the Modernist Long Poem," *Genre* 9(Winter 1978):653–87. This is the best exposition of Ashbery's poetics.

Interchapter

1. "The Fig Tree" is by W. S. Merwin; "Two Poems" by David Ignatow.

2. See the especially compendious gathering of material in *The Little Magazine in America: A Modern Documentary History*, *TriQuarterly* 43(Fall 1978), edited by Elliot Anderson and Mary Kinzie.

Chapter 10
Reflections

1. The issue of Baraka's racism is at least raised in Karl Malkoff, *Crowell's Handbook of Contemporary American Poetry* (New York, 1973), pp. 53–57, though Malkoff can hardly be faulted for not resolving it. He says at one point, "For Baraka, the writing of poetry is a political act. And this adds to the complexities of literary judgement the complexities of political judgement. Probably the best we can do while we are attempting to unravel the

tangle is accept the poems on their own terms." But I don't think this means we should accept the political judgments in the poems, nor condone the political feelings. Malkoff takes something other than a formalist stand when he discusses the relation of political reality to New Criticism, in the same book, pp. 35–39.

2. In *The Situation of Poetry* (Princeton, 1977), p. 85. This was the first book to make serious negative judgments about contemporary poetry.

3. An excerpt from Rich's speech rejecting the 1974 National Book Award as an individual, but accepting it in the name of all oppressed women, is in *Adrienne Rich's Poetry*, ed. Barbara Charlesworth Gelpi and Albert Gelpi (New York, 1975), p. 204.

4. Robert Bly, in "Where Have All the Critics Gone?," *Nation*, 22 April 1978, p. 456, issues a call for a "healthy pugnacity" in criticism and suggests that the low level of poetry reviewing results in part from people being unwilling to write negatively. "We have an odd situation: although more bad poetry is being published now than ever before in American history, most of the reviews are positive."

5. See *Understanding the New Black Poetry: Black Speech and Black Music as Poetic References*, ed. Stephen Henderson (New York, 1973). Academic criticism of black poetry is virtually nonexistent.

6. Lowell says this of the Bollingen controversy: "But the consequences of not giving the best book of the year a prize for extraneous reasons, even terrible ones in a sense—I think that's the death of art. Then you have Pasternack suppressed and everything becomes stifling." (In *Writers at Work: The Paris Review Interviews*, 2d series [New York, 1963], p. 354). He goes on to argue of Pound's beliefs, "They made him more human and more to do with life, more to do with the times. . .he'd be a very Parnassan poet without them." He then adds, "He had no political effect whatsoever," and was "quite eccentric and unpractical." Here Lowell seems as contradictory as Allen Tate (see Chapter 1, note 1). It is a common error to connect *without any qualification* the suppressions in a totalitarian state like Russia, with the censure, or even the withholding of prizes, from literature that advocates anti-Semitic attitudes. It is also especially disturbing to have as a clear implication of the argument here that being anti-Semitic and pro-Fascist made Pound more human.

7. For one of the most egregious examples of Baraka's racist poetry, see, in *Black Magic Sabotage Target Study: Black Art: Collected Poetry, 1961–1967* (Indianapolis and New York, 1969), a poem called "Black Art," p. 116. Baraka has since embraced Marxist-Leninism, and so has presumably abandoned his racism, which would be incompatible with a true communist ideology.

Index

Italicized page numbers indicate where a poet or topic is discussed at length. Individual poems are listed by title under the name of the author.

Permissions

Chapter 1 first appeared as " 'We Have Come This Far': Audience and Form in Contemporary Poetry," in *Soundings* 59:2 (Summer 1976):204–26.

Chapter 2 first appeared as "Songs of a Happy Man: The Poetry of Theodore Roethke," in *John Berryman Studies* 2:3 (Summer 1976):32–53.

Chapter 3 first appeared as "Republican Objects and Utopian Moments: The Poetry of Robert Lowell and Allen Ginsberg," in *American Poetry Review* 6:5 (September/October 1977):35–39.

Chapter 4 first appeared as " 'With Your Own Face On': Confessional Poetry in America," in *Twentieth-Century Literature* 20:2 (May 1976):163–78.

Chapter 5 first appeared as "The Clear Architecture of the Nerves: The Poetry of Frank O'Hara," in *Iowa Review* 6:3–4 (Summer-Fall 1975):61–74.

Chapter 6 first appeared as "The Rank Flavor of Blood: Galway Kinnell and American Poetry in the 1960's," in *Western Humanities Review* 27:3 (Summer 1973):225–39.

Chapter 7 first appeared as "Thrashing in the Depths: The Poetry of Robert Bly," in *Rocky Mountain Review* 29:3–4 (Autumn 1975):95–117.

Chapter 8 first appeared as "The Burned Essential Oil: The Poetry of Philip Levine," in *Hollins Critic* 12:5 (December 1975):1–15.

Chapter 9 first appeared as " 'This Leaving out Business': The Poetry of John Ashbery," in *Salmagundi* 38–39 (Summer-Fall 1977):20–41.

The second Interchapter first appeared as "The Metaphor of the Poem: Poetics in Contemporary Poetry," in *Georgia Review* 32:2 (Summer 1978):319–31.